Reproductive Ju

This book takes an intersectional, interdisciplinary, and transnational approach, presenting work that will provide the reader with a nuanced and in-depth understanding of the role of globalization in the sexual and reproductive lives of gendered bodies in the 21st century. *Reproductive Justice and Sexual Rights: Transnational Perspectives* draws on reproductive justice and transnational feminism as frameworks to explore and make sense of the reproductive and sexual experiences of various groups of women and marginalized people around the world. Interactions between globalization, feminism, reproductive justice, and sexual rights are explored within human rights and transnational feminist paradigms. This book includes case studies from Mexico, Ireland, Uganda, Colombia, Taiwan, and the United States. The edited collection presented here is intended to provide academics and students with a challenging and thought-provoking look into sexual and reproductive health matters from across the globe. In this way, the work presented in this volume will help the reader understand their own reproductive and sexual experiences in a more nuanced and contextualized way that links individuals and communities to each other in a quest for justice and liberation.

Tanya Saroj Bakhru holds a PhD in Women's Studies from University College Dublin, Ireland. She is currently an Associate Professor of Women, Gender, and Sexuality Studies in the Department of Sociology and Interdisciplinary Social Sciences at San José State University. Her research areas include feminist critiques of globalization, reproductive justice, and transnational feminism.

Reproductive Justice and Sexual Rights

Transnational Perspectives

Edited by Tanya Saroj Bakhru

Routledge
Taylor & Francis Group

NEW YORK AND LONDON

First published 2019
by Routledge
52 Vanderbilt Avenue, New York, NY 10017

and by Routledge
2 Park Square, Milton Park, Abingdon, Oxon, OX14 4RN

Routledge is an imprint of the Taylor & Francis Group, an informa business

Library of Congress Cataloging-in-Publication Data
Names: Bakhru, Tanya Saroj, editor.
Title: Reproductive justice and sexual rights : transnational perspectives / edited by Tanya Saroj Bakhru.
Description: New York, NY : Routledge, 2019. | Includes bibliographical references and index.
Identifiers: LCCN 2019000113| ISBN 9781138297234 (hardcover) | ISBN 9781138297241 (pbk.)
Subjects: LCSH: Reproductive rights. | Sexual rights.
Classification: LCC HQ766 .R44474 2019 | DDC 306.7–dc23
LC record available at https://lccn.loc.gov/2019000113

ISBN: 978-1-138-29723-4 (hbk)
ISBN: 978-1-138-29724-1 (pbk)
ISBN: 978-1-315-09940-8 (ebk)

Typeset in Caslon
by Wearset Ltd, Boldon, Tyne and Wear

CONTENTS

CONTRIBUTORS

Editor

Tanya Saroj Bakhru holds a PhD in Women's Studies. She is currently an Associate Professor of Women, Gender, and Sexuality Studies in the Department of Sociology and Interdisciplinary Social Sciences at San José State University. Her areas of interest include feminist critiques of globalization, reproductive health and justice, and transnational women's health.

Contributors

Kate Antosik-Parsons is an art historian and a visual artist whose research and artwork is concerned with gender, sexuality, embodiment, and memory. She is a Research Associate of the University College Dublin Humanities Institute. She holds a BA in Art (St Mary's College), MA in Women's Studies (University College Dublin), and PhD in Art History (University College Dublin).

Krista L. Benson is an Assistant Professor of Liberal Studies at Grand Valley State University and holds a PhD from the Ohio State University in Women's, Gender, and Sexuality Studies. Their research interests include identity formation and cohesion among polyamorous people, the use of radicalized and gendered threats of sexual assault as normalizing devices for juvenile detention in popular culture, and indigenous reproductive justice.

Soma de Bourbon received her PhD from the History of Consciousness Department at the University of California at Santa Cruz. She received her BA from the Ethnic Studies Department at the University of California at Berkeley. Her research interests include the state's continued control over Indigenous women's reproductive rights, particularly through transracial adoption and foster care. Her current research is in the narratives of trans children and the medicalization of their lives and bodies.

Rayah Feldman is a researcher and activist on migrants' rights, especially the health of migrant women. She is currently a staff member of Maternity Action, a non-governmental organization in the UK. Her background is in Sociology and Development Studies and she formerly taught at East Anglia and London South Bank Universities.

Erin M. Heinz is a PhD student in the School of Sociology at the University of Arizona. Inspired by research in reproductive justice conducted by her advisor, Dr. Louise Roth, of the University of Arizona, she is researching how women negotiate access to reproductive resources in areas of deprivation. Her research interests include economic sociology, human rights, and gender.

Szu-Ying Ho is a PhD candidate in Sociology at Graduate Center, City University of New York. Her research and publications focus on queer studies, assisted reproductive technologies, welfare state theory, and the relationship between flexicurity policies and gender inequality. She is also an LGBTQ rights activist and a founding member of Taiwan LGBT Family Rights Advocacy.

Johanna Kostenzer works as lecturer and research assistant in the department of International Health and Social Management at Management Center Innsbruck, Austria. She has a background in International Health Care Management, with a specialization in International Community Health. She studied in Innsbruck, Oslo, and Charleston, was a visiting PhD researcher at Karolinska Institutet in Stockholm, Sweden and at De Montfort University in Leicester, UK, and is an active board member of the United Nations Women National Committee Austria.

Morgan Melendres Mentz holds an MA in Ethnic Studies from San Francisco State University and a BA in Religious Studies from the University of California at Berkeley. She has worked for various San Francisco Bay Area non-profit organizations and afterschool programs teaching and empowering middle and high school youth. Her research interests include critical mixed race studies, Asian American studies, Xicana/o studies, and visual culture.

Jennifer Nelson, Professor of Women, Gender, and Sexuality Studies at University of Redlands, specializes in U.S. women's history, the history of feminism in the United States, and medical histories associated with social justice movements. She has published widely in these fields, including two books, *Women of Color and the Reproductive Rights Movement* (2003) and *More Than Medicine: A History of the Feminist Women's Health Movement* (2015).

Louise Marie Roth in an Associate Professor of Sociology at the University of Arizona. Her areas of expertise include gender, organizations, law, and the family. Her book, *Selling Women Short: Gender and Money on Wall Street*, was published in 2006. She is currently conducting research on how physician compensation systems affect gender inequality in medicine.

David A. Rubin is an Assistant Professor in the Department of Women's and Gender Studies at the University of South Florida. He is the author of *Intersex Matters: Biomedical Embodiment, Gender Regulation, and Transnational Activism* (2017), and co-editor of *Queer Feminist Science Studies: A Reader* (2017). His research and teaching interests include critical intersex studies; transgender studies; transnational feminisms; feminist theory; queer theory; history of science; history of gender, race, and sexuality; masculinity studies; and disability studies.

Alisa Sánchez is faculty in the Writing Program at the University of Southern California. She obtained her PhD in Rhetoric with a Designated Emphasis in Women, Gender, and Sexuality at the University of California, Berkeley. She has served as facilitator for the Bay Area Reproductive Justice Working Group and is interested in how transnational networks and relations of power have shaped concepts and strategies for achieving reproductive justice.

ACKNOWLEDGMENTS

Working on this book has been both challenging and energizing. First, I must thank Dean Birkenkamp for his enthusiasm for this project and support in getting it published. I would like to thank each of the contributors for their hard work and commitment to social transformation through scholar-activism. Many thanks go to Robin Rogers for her attention to detail, integrity, and friendship. This project would not have been completed without her assistance. I also must acknowledge Michelle Pidgeon, Yvonne Kwan, and Diane Nititham-Tunney for their support, advice, feedback, and for holding me accountable.

On a personal note, I would like to express my genuine appreciation to Daisaku and Kaneko Ikeda and the members of the SGI-USA; in particular my local group, Alameda West. The members of this peace organization taught me, through their thoughts, words, and deeds, that "Sincerity is the key to transforming distrust into trust, hostility into understanding, and hatred into compassion. Friendship and trust are indispensable to true peace, and they cannot be cultivated strategically" (Daisaku Ikeda).

Last, but certainly not least, I must express my most deep thanks to my entire family. I would have liked to have known my grandmothers and my own mother more, but each of them died early in my life. Nonetheless, through the telling and retelling of stories and the passing down of traditions, I maintain a connection to their spirit. Finally, I want to acknowledge and express love and gratitude for my spouse, Kristina McCauley. Her compassion and endless behind the scenes support made this book possible along with our son, Finn, who reminds me to live each moment to the fullest. I am forever thankful to have them in my life.

INTRODUCTION

Thinking Transnationally

Reproductive Justice in a Globalized Era
Tanya Saroj Bakhru

My reasons for thinking transnationally about women's lives are both deeply personal and political. My paternal grandmother, who I called Amma, was born in 1916 in the city of Rohri located in the Indian state of Sindh. Rohri is now in present-day Pakistan but had been a part of the British imperial project for 200 years. Amma was named Nirmala Ahuja by her parents. However, when she was married at the age of 14, she became Heer Bakhru. Pursuant to custom, my grandfather's family changed both her first and last name, signaling a key shift: separate from her birth family, her obligation now belonged to her husband's family. A year later, Amma's first child was born but died in infancy. My father, Keshoolal, was born shortly thereafter, when she was 17.

At the time of the Partition of India in 1947, my grandparents and their four children lived in the city of Quetta. As my dad tells it, one night there was a riot in their town. Unrest between Muslim and Hindu groups had escalated as the end of British occupation drew near. My grandparents, my dad, his brothers, and sister hid anxiously in the bathroom while fighting and rioting continued outside their home. The next morning, the British Army occupied the city, promising residents they would provide safe passage out of town so long as they left all their belongings behind. That night was the beginning of my family's yearlong journey as refugees—moving from Mumbai (Bombay) to Nagpur and eventually settling in Varanasi (Banaras). Once settled, Amma had two more children. Eventually in 1960 my father immigrated to the United States and sponsored, one by one, each of his family members to join him.

I often reflect on my grandmother's experiences, her role in our family, and the gendered limitations to which she was subjected: To what extent did she have a choice in the number and spacing of her children? What, if any, was her escape from intimate partner violence? How did she manage the constraints she faced while raising children within a deeply patriarchal society—especially against the backdrop of British colonization? What would reproductive justice have looked like for her? I had so many unanswered questions, since she passed away when I was a teenager. I have spent years trying to excavate her story through interviews with my dad, aunt, and uncles.

Amma's lived experience and mine, a queer woman and new parent, born and living in the United States, are temporally and spatially discrete. However, we are connected through bloodlines and legacies of not only violence but also resilience and resistance. Furthermore, we are linked by common themes of the struggle for bodily autonomy, the residual impacts of colonization and intergenerational trauma, family violence, and a desire for reproductive freedom. Recognizing these connections, across time and space, national boundaries, and various identity categories are vital to building the solidarities necessary to create a more equitable world. How can we understand the lived reproductive and sexual experiences of marginalized peoples, especially women, in seemingly contrasting social and geographic places and build alliances between individuals and communities? This question drives the formation of this book.

Why is a book of this kind needed? In the present moment, the need for justice, and reproductive justice in particular, feels critically urgent. We have reached an apex of neoliberalism "marked by market-based governance practices on the one hand (the privatization, commodification, and proliferation of difference) and authoritarian, national-security driven penal state practices on the other" (Mohanty, 2013, p. 970). While these trends have emerged around the world, no other event embodies the full realization of such ideologies than the election of Donald Trump in 2016 to President of the United States.

The election of Donald Trump is but one specific event and there has been much rumination about the causes of his ascension to political power. One idea put forth argues that Trump is a symbol of hyper-capitalism and its reliance on racist and sexist ideology to enact and prop up oppressive structures around the world. As Naomi Klein (2017) articulates in her book, *No Is Not Enough: Resisting Trump's Shock Politics and Winning the World We Need*, for Trump "the presidency is in fact the crowning extension of the Trump brand" (p. 5) and the completion of decades-long effort by proponents of neoliberalism to destroy the public sphere and create a fully corporate state. She further explains that among the main pillars of Trump's political and economic project are the deconstruction of the regulatory state; a full-bore attack on the welfare state and social services (rationalized in part through bellicose racial fear mongering and attacks on women for exercising their rights); the unleashing of a domestic fossil fuel frenzy (which requires the sweeping aside of climate science and the gagging of large parts of the government bureaucracy); and a civilizational war against immigrants and "radical Islamic terrorism" (with ever-expanding domestic and foreign theatres).

(p. 5)

Klein's book was published in mid-2017, in the early days of the Trump presidency. As time progresses and Trump remains in office, however, we can see these concepts further materialize through the implementation of a stream of severe policies and practices. There are many examples, but in the context of the work presented in this book, three stand out in particular. This first includes the reinstatement and expansion of the Global Gag Rule/Mexico City Policy, entitled the Policy Protecting Life in Global Health Assistance. This policy restricts "using US foreign aid for abortion-related activities, [and] requires foreign nongovernmental organizations receiving US global health assistance to certify that they do not use their own non-US funds to provide abortion services" (Human Rights Watch, February 14, 2018). The Policy Protecting Life in Global Health Assistance extends the Global Gag Rule/ Mexico City Policy restrictions to billions of dollars in U.S. global health assistance, such as maternal and child health programs, prevention and treatment of tuberculosis, malaria, infectious diseases, neglected tropical diseases, and water, sanitation, and hygiene programs.

Second, sweeping tax cuts made to corporations have resulted in increases in taxes for low- and moderate-income families and increases in the national deficit by over a trillion dollars. This increase in national debt is then used to justify cuts to social welfare services as a 'remedy' to the aforementioned budget deficit. Proposed cuts include, for example, funding for the Supplemental Nutrition Assistance Program (SNAP) upon which many low-income women and children rely (National Women's Law Center, 2018).

President Trump's third draconian policy and practice includes the forced separation of children from their parents who have entered the United States without documentation, frequently seeking asylum, and having been detained as a result. What makes this act particularly harsh is that it was conceived as a means to deter 'illegal immigration' across the U.S. border. As Attorney General Jeff Sessions stated in May 2018, "If you don't want your child to be separated, then don't bring them across the border illegally. It's not our fault that somebody does that." Children who are removed from their parents are placed in the custody of the Office of Refugee Resettlement in shelters and facilities around the country (Burnett, 2018). It has been documented that, "Detention and family separation, even for short periods of time, have serious adverse consequences for mental well-being, particularly for those who have already suffered trauma" (Human Rights Watch, February 28, 2018). Many women who migrate, and especially those who are seeking asylum, are fleeing violence, economic crises, and conflict that are often by-products of the economic restructuring that is a hallmark of globalization (Baran & Hafiz, 2017).

The Policy Protecting Life in Global Health Assistance, Trump tax cuts, and increased immigrant detention and family separation are only a few examples (the list goes on) of the many practices with racist, xenophobic, and misogynistic ramifications taking place under the Trump Administration. Under such conditions of social and economic crisis, it is women, particularly those who are most marginalized due to their citizenship status, socio-economic class, or race, that become the 'shock absorbers' of such policies and practices and shoulder the heaviest burdens. Although, the Trump Administration is not the only example of trends towards authoritarianism and of patriarchal rule in the current era (as Madeleine Albright (2018) points out, authoritarianism is on the rise in Eastern Europe, North Korea, the Philippines, Turkey, and Russia), the size and scope of the United States in terms of its economic and political influence make its global influence far and wide reaching.

Against the background just described, this book takes an intersectional, interdisciplinary, and transnational approach, to present work that will provide the reader with a nuanced and in depth understanding of the role that forces of globalization have played in sexual and reproductive lives of gendered bodies in the 21st century. *Reproductive Justice and Sexual Rights: Transnational Perspectives* draws on two primary conceptual frameworks to explore and make sense of the reproductive and sexual experiences of various groups of women and marginalized people around the world: reproductive justice and transnational feminism.

Reproductive justice is an intersectional, human rights based framework that

> makes the link between the individual and community, addresses government and corporate responsibility, fights all forms of population control (eugenics), commits to individual/community leadership development that results in power shifts, and puts marginalized communities at the center of the analysis.
>
> (Ross, Roberts, Derkas, Peoples, & Toure, 2018, p. 19)

While the reproductive justice movement is rooted in the work and lived experiences of African American women, it involves theory, strategy, and practice that applies to everyone and has brought American reproductive politics into rhythm with work already being done by feminist groups around the world.

Reproductive justice offers a holistic model of theory and activism focused on three principles: (1) the right not to have children; (2) the right to have children; and (3) the right to parent children one already has. It points to the sense that "our collective sexual consciousness has been warped by misogyny, slavery, and colonialism" (Ross et al., 2018, p. 175). While reproductive justice centers the experiences of Black women in America, it also brings to light the ways that systems of oppression like white supremacy, sexism, and capitalism work together in determining the worth, utility, and value of certain bodies over others—a framework that is wide reaching and illuminating when understood in a global context.

The epistemological trajectory of reproductive justice intersects with transnational feminism as both paradigms locate an interrogation of current day globalization and neoliberal economic ideology at the center of analysis. Because globalization and neoliberal economic ideology aim to undermine the public sphere, social welfare networks "naturalize capitalist values as if they are inevitable" (Ross et al., 2018, p. 21). Thus, it is critical that any exploration of the reproductive experiences of marginalized individuals interrogate and complicate notions of "choice" to advocate for justice.

As Andrea Smith (2005) has so succinctly articulated, when we rely on choice as our main framework for understanding women's reproductive and sexual experiences, reproductive health matters become configured from a commodity perspective. Consequently, the processes and circumstances that inform how individuals and communities perceive and negotiate their sexual and reproductive freedoms are obscured. When reproductive rights are embedded in notions of 'free' choice, all the social, political, and economic factors that surround how choices are made become hidden. In addition, when approaching reproductive health from a commodity perspective, the notion that women and marginalized groups have inherent rights is lost. What remains is the idea that choices should only be made if one can afford them or if one is deemed a legitimate choice-maker (Smith, 2005). Examples of this ideology play out time and again in varying historical and geographic contexts and are highlighted in the chapters of this book. Against a global backdrop of legacies of colonialism, exploitation, and economic, social, and political disenfranchisement that carry on through generations, we need more than choices. We need justice.

This quest for justice compels many feminist scholars and activists to frame their work within a transnational context. Transnational feminist frameworks include a commitment to addressing the asymmetries of globalization/capitalist re-colonization as well as the implementation of an intersectional set of understandings, tools, and practices such as paying attention to the raced, classed, and gendered ways that globalization and capitalist patriarchies (re)structure colonial and neo-colonial relations of domination and subordination. As I have discussed in previous work (Bakhru, 2008) transnational feminist scholarship acknowledges the simultaneously constituting relationships between the local and global, employs tools of constant contextualization and historicization, and challenges hegemonic views of global capitalism (Mies, 2007; Bhavnani, 2007; Kim, 2007). Transnational feminism also grapples with the complex and contradictory ways that individual and collective agencies are shaped by and in turn shape processes of globalization. It juxtaposes women and marginalized people in similar contexts, in different geographical spaces, rather than as a homogeneous category across the world (Nagar & Swarr, 2010, p. 5). In a transnational feminist framework, contexts, links, and relationships that are material and temporal between the local and global take our focus. "What is emphasized are relations of mutuality, co-responsibility, and common interests, anchoring the idea of feminist solidarity" (Mohanty, 2003, p. 242). It is through such conceptual reconfigurations of pressing issues that we can create and sustain movements for justice and social transformation.

Over the past several decades, a visible transnational women's health movement has emerged and gathered momentum. Responding to the negative impacts of globalization, the rise of antifeminist and fundamentalist political and religious forces, and the HIV/AIDS pandemic, transnational coalitions formed and leadership emerged from the Global South (Petchesky, 2003, p. 1). United Nations (UN) conferences such as the International Conference on Population and Development (ICPD) in 1994 and the World Conference on Women in 1995 along with the non-governmental organizations associated with those conferences recognized sexual and reproductive health as crucial and complex concepts, including control and decision-making over one's body, and the full realization of gender equality. These conferences strengthened connections between gender equality, justice, education for women, and girls' empowerment and reproductive health. The ICPD in particular "emphasized the ineluctable relationship between poverty, underdevelopment, and women's reproduction" (Ross et al., 2018, p. 43). In fact, some of the founders of the reproductive justice movement in the United States participated in the 1994 ICPD Conference and found solidarity with women from the Global South who were already implementing a human rights framework to push back against the forces of globalization and the use of women's fertility as a means to neoliberal economic ends (Ross et al., 2018, p. 44).

In the finding of feminist solidarity, transnational women's health movements have, in recent years, moved in the direction of being able to see the interconnections between communities of women and look at the "broader pattern and structures of domination and exploitation" (Mohanty, 2013, p. 967) that circumscribe the experiences outlined in this book. If scholars, activists, or policymakers fail to see the points of connection between various groups of people, we run the risk of interpreting sexual and reproductive health decisions and actions as only occurring at the individual level or as private matters. In the work presented here, by using reproductive justice and transnational feminism as theoretical lenses, my hope is to show a history of reproductive and sexual lived experiences that connect across time and place.

The book is organized into four thematic parts: the continuing impacts of colonization on gendered and racialized bodies in terms of sexual and reproductive health; interactions between the State, the law, and sexual and reproductive experiences; the ways in which migration shapes sexual and reproductive health experiences; and feminist engagement with transnational politics. Within these themes, case studies and specific reproductive and sexual health issues are highlighted. These include sex-selective abortion and son preference, the mental and physical health needs of migrant women, indigenous rights, population control and family planning policies, and the criminalization of abortion. Contributors include activists working on the ground as well as scholars and researchers.

The first part, Colonial Legacies and Post-Colonial Conditions, serves as a frame for subsequent chapters by exploring the historical impact of colonial practices and their continuing effect in the present day. Soma de Bourbon's chapter examines the state sanctioned repression of Native women's reproductive freedom as an investment in white Americans dating back to the earliest formations of the United States. The chapter looks at how racial hierarchies formulated in the 1500s continue to be relevant when looking at Native children in the contemporary child welfare system. Kate Antosik-Parsons' chapter uses contemporary Irish art to highlight the body politics of women's sexual and reproductive freedom in Ireland. Set against a backdrop of hundreds of years of British colonization and eventual Irish independence in the early 20th century, the Irish movement for reproductive justice invokes gendered histories as it asserts resistance to current day reproductive oppression. Alisa Sánchez's chapter discusses how neo-colonial relationships influence women's sexual and reproductive rights within the law by examining the debate around abortion in Colombia in the mid-20th century as the Colombian government moved to create a national family planning policy as part of its efforts to 'develop' and modernize.

The second part, The State, the Law, and Sexual and Reproductive Justice, investigates the potentialities and limitations in the relationship between the State, the law, and reproductive justice. Krista L. Benson's chapter uses the U.S. Supreme Court case, *Adoptive Couple v. Baby Girl* (2013) to argue the importance of adoption as a reproductive justice issue for Indigenous communities. Benson's work links together the U.S. legal system, the erosion of Native sovereignty, and the ability of Native families to parent Native children. Szu-Ying Ho sheds light on the processes by which lesbians negotiate and traverse legal restrictions on the use of assisted reproductive technologies by same sex couples in Taiwan. Jennifer Nelson explores the ways in which feminist activists in Mexico employed the discourse of human rights in order to advocate for the legalization of abortion by pushing the State to comply with the programs of action from the 1994 UN conference on Population and Development in Cairo and the 1995 World Conference on Women in Beijing, bringing Mexico into measure with global trends in the use of human rights language.

The third part of the book, Migration and Access to Care, focuses specifically on the reproductive health experiences of women as they are forced to engage with economic displacement due to globalization. Over the past several decades increasing numbers of women have become economic migrants. It is estimated that over half of the world's migrants are now women. As resource poor regions of the world continue to grapple with the lasting effects of colonization, the implementation of neoliberal economic policy in the form of development, structural adjustment, or austerity programs, already existing crises and conflicts have been exacerbated. Economic disparities continue to grow causing increasing numbers of people to migrate. While Rayah Feldman's chapter concentrates on access to maternity care for undocumented migrant women in Europe, Morgan Melendres Mentz highlights the health needs of migrant women in San Francisco Bay Area. Although each author's work is located in geographically distinct places, common themes emerge regarding the obstacles that limit access to care. These include barriers based on immigration and citizenship status, vulnerability to abuse, and exploitation, xenophobia, and stigmatization.

The last part of the book, Globalization, Reproduction, and Transnational Politics, features a series of chapters that demonstrate how international discourses and transnational politics shape sexual and reproductive decision-making in the context of globalization. Erin M. Heinz and Louise Marie Roth illuminate the ways in which women in Uganda negotiate their fertility and family size while balancing economic arguments for small families with traditional norms that encourage high fertility. Through their experience, the ways in which forces of globalization compete with local norms in terms of women's fertility ideals come to the fore. Similarly, Johanna Kostenzer looks at the issue of gender-biased prenatal sex selection and son preference within the context of globalization. Kostenzer focuses on the social, cultural, and economic circumstances that circumscribe the perceived need for sex-selective abortions and the 'demand for sons.' The concluding chapter examines how debates about intersex individuals are shaped by the politics of difference in a transnational and neoliberal context. David A. Rubin's work examines the attempt by the Intersex Society of North America to lobby for the inclusion of intersex in the U.S. federal ban on "female genital mutilation" and the geopolitical, colonial, and consumer citizenship discourses underpinning their work. He also asks, how can transnational feminist perspectives contribute to a rethinking of the local and global trajectories of the intersex movement?

In sum, this book's included chapters focus on sexual and reproductive health experiences around the globe and explore various themes and issues that impact the sexual and reproductive lives of gendered bodies across space and time; both between and within regions of the world. Interactions between globalization, feminism, and reproductive justice are explored within human rights and transnational feminist paradigms. This edited collection is intended to provide academics and students with a challenging and thought provoking look into sexual and reproductive health matters from a transnational perspective. Like my own search to understand myself in my grandmother's story, my hope is that the work presented in this volume will help the reader understand their own reproductive and sexual experiences in a more nuanced and contextualized way that links us to each other in a quest for justice and liberation.

Bibliography

Adoptive Couple v. Baby Girl, 133 S. Ct. 2552 (2013).

Albright, M. (2018). *Fascism: A Warning.* New York: Harper Press.

Bakhru, T. (2008). Negotiating and Navigating the Rough Terrain of Transnational Feminist Research. *Journal of International Women's Studies, 10*(2), 198–216.

Baran, A., & Hafiz, S. (2017). Trump's First 100 Days: Immigrant Women and Families on the Frontlines. Retrieved from https://webelongtogether.org/sites/default/files/WBT 100days_report.pdf.

Bhavnani, K. (2007). Interconnections and Configurations: Toward a Global Feminist Ethnography. In Hese-Biber, S. (Ed.). *Handbook of Feminist Research.* London: Sage.

Burnett, J. (2018, May 30). What Happens When Parents and Children are Separated at the U.S.–Mexico Border. *Npr.org.* Retrieved from www.npr.org/2018/05/30/615585043/what-happens-when-parents-and-children-are-separated-at-the-u-s-mexico-border.

Heltberg, R., Hossain, N., Reva, A., & Turk, C. (2013). Coping and Resilience During the Food and Financial Crises. *Journal of Development Studies, 49*(5), 705–718.

Human Rights Watch. (2018, February 14). Trump's "Mexico City Policy" or "Global Gag Rule": Questions and Answers. *Hrw.org.* Retrieved from www.hrw.org/news/2018/02/14/trumps-mexico-city-policy-or-global-gag-rule.

Human Rights Watch. (2018, February 28). In the Freezer: Abusive Conditions for Women and Children in US Immigration Holding Cells. *Hrw.org.* Retrieved from www.hrw.org/report/2018/02/28/freezer/abusive-conditions-women-and-children-us-immigration-holding-cells.

Kim, H.S. (2007). The Politics of Border Crossings: Black, Postcolonial, and Transnational Feminist Perspectives. In Hese-Biber, S. (Ed.). *Handbook of Feminist Research.* London: Sage.

Klein, N. (2007). *The Shock Doctrine: The Rise of Disaster Capitalism.* New York: Picador.

Klein, N. (2017). *No Is Not Enough: Resisting Trump's Shock Politics and Winning the World We Need.* Chicago: Haymarket Books.

Luibhéid, E. (2004). Childbearing Against the State? Asylum Seeker Women in the Irish Republic. *Women's Studies International Forum, 27,* 335–349.

Mendoza, R. (2009). Aggregate Shocks, Poor Households, and Children: Transmission Channels and Policy Responses. *Global Social Policy, 9,* 55–78.

Mies, M. (2007). A Global Feminist Perspective on Research. In Hese-Biber, S. (Ed.). *Handbook of Feminist Research.* London: Sage.

Mohanty, C.T. (2003). *Feminism Without Borders: Decolonizing Theory, Practicing Solidarity.* Durham, NC: Duke University Press.

Mohanty, C.T. (2013). Transnational Feminist Crossings: On Neoliberalism and Radical Critique. *Signs: Journal of Women in Culture and Society, 36*(4), 967–991.

Nagar, R., & Swarr, A. (2010). *Critical Transnational Feminist Praxis.* New York: Suny Press.

National Women's Law Center. (2018, April). What's in the Tax Cuts and Jobs Act of 2017: Provisions that Impact Women and Families. Retrieved from https://nwlc-ciw49tixgw5lbab.stackpathdns.com/wp-content/uploads/2018/04/Tax-Cuts-and-Job-Act-2017.pdf.

Petchesky, R. (2003). *Global Prescriptions: Gendering Health and Human Rights.* New York: Zed Books.

Ross, L.J., Roberts, L., Derkas, E., Peoples, W., & Toure, P.B. (Eds.). (2018). *Radical Reproductive Justice: Foundations, Theory, Practice, Critique.* New York: Feminist Press.

Smith, A. (2005). Beyond Pro-Choice Versus Pro-Life: Women of Color and Reproductive Justice. *NWSA Journal, 17*(1), 119–140.

I
COLONIAL LEGACIES AND POST-COLONIAL CONDITIONS

1

WHITE PROPERTY INTERESTS IN NATIVE WOMEN'S REPRODUCTIVE FREEDOM

SLAVERY TO TRANSRACIAL ADOPTION
SOMA DE BOURBON

In 2017 at San José State University I, along with students from my classes, hung over 100 red dresses across campus to bring awareness to the missing and murdered Indigenous[1] women in the United States, Canada, and Mexico. The REDress Project was started by Jamie Black to call attention to the more than 1,000 missing and murdered Aboriginal women in Canada. Many Indigenous communities suffer similarly high rates of murder and disappearance. In 2016, the National Congress of American Indians called for a day to acknowledge the missing and murdered Indigenous women in the United States, and, in 2017, United States Senate Resolution 60 was adopted to recognize May 5 as a "National Day of Awareness for Missing and Murdered Native Women and Girls" (United States Senate Resolution 401 (2018)).

The murder and disappearance of American Indian women is not new; it is indicative of a broader system of colonial violence. Unlike most ethnic groups, the majority of crimes committed against Native women and girls are perpetrated by non-Natives, which, as I will argue, can be understood as an outgrowth of white property interests that can be traced back to slavery. The bodily and reproductive violence that Indigenous women face can be understood, in part, as an investment in the state and white American property interest that denies Native American women, parents, and communities of reproductive autonomy. In particular, this chapter will focus on the removal

of Native children from their mothers and communities as an act of reproductive violence linked to slavery.

Native children are the most overrepresented ethnic group in foster care
and state-assisted adoption (Wildeman and Emanuel 2014; DeMeyer 2010;
de Bourbon 2013; Unger 2004), with the highest racial disproportionality
index of any group (Rosay 2016). The removal of 25–35 percent of Native
children from their families is simultaneously a violation of an Indigenous
people's reproductive rights, a group-based harm against the community, and
an investment in whiteness. The state-sanctioned infusion of whiteness with
property interests over Native women's reproductive freedom through the termination of parental rights and divestiture of children is tied to their historical entrapment in state-sanctioned systems of slavery. This chapter
investigates how whiteness has been imbued with property rights vis-à-vis the
control of Native women's reproductive freedom through enslavement, indentured servitude, land dispossession, and the removal of children (for a more
detailed analysis of these issues, see de Bourbon 2013).

The Framework of Whiteness

Although there is a body of literature on whiteness as it is entangled with
property, only a few scholars carefully discuss whiteness and property in relation to Indigenous peoples. Moreton-Robinson's (2015) work looks at several
different aspects of investment in whiteness. In addition to Moreton-
Robinson's work, Harris's (1993) seminal publication uses theories of property interest buttressed by case law to articulate how whites not only have
feelings of entitlement, but actual legal claims over Black and Native peoples,
which she traces back to slavery and conquest, respectively. Other scholars
investigate the way property rights have been and continue to be asserted by
the United States and the general public over Native cultures (Carpenter,
Katyal, and Riley 2009; Moreton-Robinson 2015). It is important to note, as
Moreton-Robinson (2015) does, many scholars address white property interests in Natives, but they do not name it as such (Deer 2010, 2015; Philip
Deloria 1998; Deloria Jr. 1985, 2006; Deloria Jr. and Lytle 1983, 1998;
Deloria Jr. and Wilkins 2011; Forbes 1993; Ramirez 2007; Ross 1998; Tayac
2009).

There are three scholars who specifically address white property rights as
emanating from slavery: Deer (2010), Harris (1993), and Roberts (1997).
Deer articulates the linkage of Native women's reproductive control from
slavery to the sex trade industry, noting that Native women "suffer sexual
violence at the highest rate of any ethnic group within the United States"
(624). Deer argues the disproportionate numbers of Native women in the sex
trade today is not a new phenomenon but rather must be understood in
relation to the history of Indigenous women's enslavement. Deer's work

illustrates the need to continue the effort of relating the sexual exploitation of Native women's reproductive freedom to their historical enslavement; however, her work does not specifically address how this history constituted a white property interest, or how the taking of Native children is part of the larger state-sanctioned investment in white property emanating from slavery. Like Deer, Harris and Roberts address pieces, but not the entirety, of how Native women's reproductive control as a white property interest emanates from slavery.

Slavery: White Property Interests in Native Women's Bodies

Until recently, there was widespread disavowal in historical literature of the existence of Indigenous slavery. The complex history of slavery was and often continues to be flattened into a biracial framework of African American enslavement and white ownership in order to maintain a cohesive narrative of bondage that does not deviate from previous prevailing notions of master/ slave relations. To trouble this biracial dichotomy, a more nuanced scholarship of enslavement is required—one that includes the wholesale enslavement of certain Native groups; the slavery of Chinese women; un-free white labor; American Indian slaveholding (as in the Cherokee slavery of Africans); and the interchanges between Native and Black slaves under colonization, including, but not limited to, intermarriages. A number of scholars have begun to address the historical omissions (Brooks 2002; Carocci and Pratt 2012; Deer 2010, 2015; Ekberg 2007; Forbes 1993; Gallay 2009; Gonzales 2009; Halliburton 1977; Heizer 1993; Ingersoll 2005; Katz 1997; Littlefield 1978; Miles 2005; Miles and Holland 2006; Minges 2004; Naylor 2008; Perdue 2009; Stannard 1992; Sturm 2002; Tayac 2009; Yarbrough 2008).

For example, as Katz (1997) notes: "On both northern and southern American continents, Europeans enslaved Africans and Native Americans and drove both hard to pile up profits in the shortest possible time" (101). Another example shows how the Spanish maximized profits in Native slaves by marking their status as immutable:

> [They] had their chattel status burned into their faces with branding irons that stamped them with the initials of their owners. When sold from one Spaniard to another, a replacement brand was made. Consequently, some slaves' faces were scarred with two or three or four branding mutilations identifying them as transferable pieces of property.
>
> (Stannard 1992, 84)

The branding of Indigenous slaves not only indicated white property interest on the part of the individual "owner," but also inscribed the slave's status as a transferable unit of property. White property interests were literally inscribed on their bodies. This history of brutality is often minimized by arguing that the number of Native slaves was small, yet this assertion is far from the truth. Millions of Indigenous people were captured, tortured, and enslaved: "[b]y 1542 Nicaragua alone had seen the export of as many as half a million of its people for slave labor" (Stannard 1992, 82). While this chapter does not address the whole myriad of slave relations, it does explore how whiteness was and continues to be invested with a property interest in Native women's reproductive freedom: specifically, the right to claim ownership over Indigenous children.

It is important not to conflate the many colonial relationships that existed between Native nations and invading European nations from the sixteenth through the nineteenth centuries; it is also important to recognize—and can be said generally—that no colonizing relationship was "mutually beneficial" as some scholars have claimed (Jones et al. 2014; Anderson 2006). Although the French, English, and Americans entered into treaties and made alliances with Native nations, they did not do so in good faith and simultaneously violated those treaties by enslaving Indigenous women and girls for sexual exploitation (Deer 2010). Deer gives examples of the sexual exploitation of Native women under each colonizer, making it clear these relationships cannot be thought of as "mutually beneficial."

This passage from the *Daily Cleveland Herald* in 1858 regarding frontiersmen "purchasing" Native women throughout the plains illustrates that the United States did not have a "mutually beneficial" relationship with Indigenous nations:

> Almost every white man along this route has an Indian concubine purchased … When a white man gets tired of his slave-wife, he ships her off and gets another. The children of their union are totally neglected by their father and grow up as they may under the care of the mothers.
>
> ("Squaw Slaves" 1858)

This passage underscores the extensive property rights white men exercised over Indigenous women through capture, rape, and ownership of Indigenous women and children. In addition to being able to control Native women's bodies, white men were mandated by law to capture escaped Native and Black slaves throughout the United States and return them to their "owners." Weller (2010) writes about the concept of capture, inquiring who has had, and continues to have, the right (or requirement) to capture, and who was, and is, "capturable." Weller traces minority groups' legal disenfranchisement to their status as "capturable":

the move from legal human objecthood to legal human subjecthood is also a move from captured to captor. A mark of capturable remains on categories of humans who have been in the class of legal object, and removal of this mark is achieved only on an individual basis by those who are both able and willing to capture, able and willing to help police the border between human-person and nonhuman-thing-property, which is always already laced with race-class-gender-sexuality-ability determinations.

(53)

Weller's notion of capture is useful when thinking through the property rights the state enjoined to white citizens over Native women's bodies and children. When theorizing about Native people, it is fruitful to envisage the way the government has framed Native people as lacking subjecthood, as ownable—perpetually positioned as objects, as property of the white state and public—which would encapsulate a wide range of white investiture not only in bodies, but also in reproductive rights, language, culture, religion, land, human remains, and personhood.

Native and Black Entanglements Under Captivity

The idea of being ownable is particularly useful when thinking through Native enslavement in relationship to African slavery. It is important to note how the reproductive control of Native women mirrors and diverges from that of African American women under slavery. Although European enslavement of Indigenous peoples predates entrapment of African peoples on this continent, they should be read together for at least three reasons: (1) colonizers enslaved both diverse groups at the same time, even if initially on different continents, and there was intermixing between these communities while in bondage; (2) Native freedom was often read against Blackness; and (3) Native and Black peoples, although they have very different histories and lived experiences, continue to suffer the highest rates of overrepresentation in state apparatuses of control such as systems of punishment and the child welfare system. This overrepresentation of people of color in state systems of control thus constructs white people as inherently freer, particularly in terms of the right to have and raise their own children.

Confronting Native enslavement requires thinking through how the state thought of and treated Native peoples in relation to African peoples. The reading together of African and Native enslavement began as early as the sixteenth century under the auspices of scholarly debates over the humanity of Indigenous people; the best-known example was a debate between Gines de Sepulveda and Bartolome de Las Casas in 1550 (Mohawk 1992).

The two philosophers placed Native peoples within the existing racial hierarchy (many philosophers at this time thought Indigenous people were a missing link between men and apes).[2] De Sepulveda argued that Natives did not have souls, were made by God to be in servitude, and were therefore "natural slaves." In contrast, de Las Casas argued although Natives were "completely barbaric," they nonetheless had souls and therefore could not be "natural slaves" (Stannard 1992; Robinson 1983). Although some historians laud de Las Casas for "standing up for Indians," his solution was to replace Native slaves with a group both de Sepulveda and de Las Casas agreed were "natural slaves"—Africans—and that is exactly what the Spanish undertook (Robinson 1983). The introduction of African slavery did not obliterate Native slavery; it only meant that Natives and Africans would toil together under the same system of entrapment.

The debate between de Sepulveda and de Las Casas measured Native freedom against African enslavement, not against white freedom, and 200 years later, the framework continued to be argued in court cases in the United States brought by mixed lineage Indigenous slaves in the 1700s. These cases, often called freedom suits, are a site where white investments in capture and enslavement were visible and Native freedom continued to be framed against African enslavement. Many of the slave laws at this time could not account for people who were both Black and Native—a person was either Black *or* Native, but not both. This distinction proved to be precarious, given the complex relationships between Africans and Natives under captivity. Freedom suits can be seen not only as a site of resistance, where interrelations between communities became appreciable, but also as a domain where the state and white citizens calcified racial classifications in order to maintain their property interests by maintaining slavery and a system of white supremacy. These cases were directly linked to Native women's freedom and the freedom of their children, in part because colonizers traced slave status matrilineally: "All and every Negro, Indian, Mulatto, or Mestee shall follow the state and condition of the mother and be esteemed and reputed, taken and adjudged to be a Slave or Slaves to all intents and purposes whatsoever" (Miles 2009, 147). As this passage indicates, whites could accrue wealth through raping their slaves and Indigenous women's children belonged to slave owners, not to their mothers or to Indigenous nations (Hartman 1997; Roberts 1997; Deer 2010, 2015).

Although raping Native or Black women may not have been legal, it was cemented as a de facto acceptable practice. Black and Native standing was usurped in courts, as can be seen in a Maryland statute of 1717:

> No Negro, or Mulatto Slave, Free Negro, or Mulatto born of a white Woman, during his Time of Servitude by Law, or any Indian Slave, or Free Indian Natives of this or the neighboring Provinces, be admitted

and received as good and valid Evidence in Law, in any Matter of Thing whatsoever, depending before any Court of Record, or before any Magistrate within this Province, wherein any Christian white Person is concerned.

(Tayac 2009, 110)

This passage notes two important points: one, freedom did not equal being considered a subject in the legal system, even if you could prove your mother was white; and two, all people of color were subject to harm, including rape, with state impunity. Entire communities' lack of opportunity to testify against a white person became an incredible investment in whiteness and rendered all women of color vulnerable to reproductive control and sexual violence, including Black, Native, Chinese, Filipino, and Latinx women (Deer 2010; Hartman 1997).

Given the freedom invested in white women, who were not enslaved, the majority of freedom suits concerned mixed ethnicity individuals who could prove their mother was white. American Indians and American Indians of African and Indian heritage (referred to as Afro-Indians, Black Indians, African Indians, and Black Natives)[3] also brought freedom cases to court (Ablavsky 2011; Sachs 2012). The landscape of slavery was uneven, as were the rulings on freedom suits and the arguments utilized in them. Native and Black Natives began to argue they were free, not in spite of being Indian, but *because* they were Indian. The case *Robin v. Hardaway* (1772) was a particularly important freedom suit, because the attorney used a similar logic to that of de Las Casas, arguing that Natives had a "natural right" to freedom because they were unlike African slaves, who were "natural" slaves (Ablavsky 2011; Sachs 2012). The attorney won a victory for Robin and 11 other slaves.

Native Codes in California: Retaining Property Interests in Native Women's Reproduction

It may be tempting to think Indigenous people were only enslaved in the South, especially given that the freedom suits are from the South. But even in the 1800s in the North, the entrapment of Native people was ubiquitous. After the 13th Amendment passed, Black Codes were enacted in the South to keep African and Native people in servitude. Similar codes—we could call them "Native Codes"—were already in place for Native people in the North before the passage of the 13th Amendment. Although the ways Indigenous slavery took form in California cannot be conflated with what happened in other areas of the United States where African slavery was pervasive, it is clear from the historical record that California was not a "free" state. Although California is a different site of entrapment, it is important to think through how capture existed well into the mid 1800s when California entered the

Union as a "free" state. The right to capture Native people, particularly women and girls, was extensively asserted as a property right by white men in California in the mid to late 1800s. White men asserted control by employing an 1850 law called the Act for the Government and Protection of Indians, which purported to protect Indigenous people, but more accurately legitimated the already-existing system of entrapment (Johnston-Dodds 2002). The 1850 Act defined "Indian" as having one-half (later expanded to one-fourth) or more of "Indian blood," thereby giving legitimacy to white narrative of "blood quantum" and investing increasing property status in whiteness (Heizer 1993; Tallbear 2009).

The legal boundaries for the enslavement of Natives in 1860 incorporated Natives who were prisoners of war, "vagrants," "beggars," or "immoral":

> Any Indian ... who shall be found loitering and strolling about, or frequenting public places where liquors are sold, begging, or leading an immoral or profligate course of life, shall be liable to be arrested on the complaint of any resident citizen of the county, and brought before any Justice of the Peace ... to hire out such vagrant within twenty-four hours to the best bidder.
>
> (Johnston-Dodds 2002, 11)

Therefore, it took only the word of a white individual saying that an Indigenous person was guilty of vagrancy, begging, going to places where liquor was sold, or being "immoral" to capture and claim ownership over such person. As such, whites were invested with a right to capture and hold Indigenous women captive in sexual servitude similar to chattel status. The *Sacramento Union* noted in 1860: "a large number of Indians are held in domestic servitude in this State, whose condition differs very little from that of absolute slaves" (Heizer 1993, 220–229).

The line between indentured and enslaved Native women was blurred, as California Military correspondence, newspapers, and personal journals make evident. Not all state officials believed the indenturing of Indigenous people was ethical, and the Northern California Superintendent of Indian Affairs in 1861 was one such exception:

> There is a Statute in California providing for the indenturing of Indians to white people for a term of years. Hence under cover of this law (as I think unconstitutional) many persons are engaged in hunting Indians (see my report of this month). Even regular organized companies with their Pres, Sec. and Treas. are now in the mountains and while the troops are engaged in killing the men for alleged offenses, the kidnapers follow in close pursuit, seize the younger Indians and bear them off to

the white settlements in every part of the country filling the orders of those who have applied for them at rates, varying from $50 to $200 a piece, and all this is being done under a plea of "Kindness to the poor Indians."

(Heizer 1993, 230)

As evident from his letter, whites were asserting a property right, attaching a monetary value to Native bodies as exchangeable units of property to be sold both within and outside the boundaries of the United States. Although the enslavement of Native California women and children during this period could be attributed to the demand for cheap labor, it would not account for the dual role of exploitation, both physical and sexual, as an 1856 article from the *San Francisco Bulletin* makes clear:

nearly all of the employees, we are informed, of one of these reservations at least, are daily and nightly engaged in kidnapping the younger portion of the females, for the vilest of purposes. The wives and daughters of the defenseless Diggers are prostituted before the very eyes of their husbands and fathers.

(Reprinted in Heizer 1993, 278)

Statutes and legal assertions of rights provided a framework for white men to exercise a much greater range of freedoms than people of color during this time—they could violate and rape women and girls because of the *de jure* and de facto legal construction of certain bodies as belonging to white men.

Stealing Indigenous Children: Boarding Schools, the Indian Adoption Project, and the Indian Placement Program

In a continuance of the state and white Americans asserting property rights in Native women's reproductive freedom, Indigenous children were taken into guardianship and forcibly removed from their families and placed in punitive, militarized, gendered boarding schools across the United States (Lomawaima 1994; Lomawaima and McCarty 2006; Unger 1977). Boarding schools can be seen as an investment in the state and in whiteness, asserting that white Americans had the right to raise their own children as well as the children of "unfit" Native parents. The forced removal of Native children to boarding schools did not cease until the Indian Reorganization Act (IRA) passed in 1934. Even with the IRA, the forced removal of Native children continued in its morphed form of state-sanctioned foster facilities and homes and adoptive homes. In fact, the removal continued at unprecedented rates, with 25–35 percent of all Native children taken from their families to state care and adoption (Unger 2004; Byler 1974).

After removing large numbers of Native children from their families, the state ran programs to place these children. One of the many projects tasked with permanently separating Native children from their communities was the Indian Adoption Project (1958–67), a partnership between the U.S. government and the Child Welfare League of America aimed at placing the "forgotten" Indian child in permanent white homes (Fanshel 1972). The Indian Adoption Project was responsible for placing 700 Native children in permanent homes. Thousands of other Indian children were taken and adopted through private adoption agencies.

Another program outside the child welfare system aimed at divesting Native people of their children occurred through the Church of Latter-Day Saints (LDS Church, a.k.a. Mormons), called the Indian Placement Program (IPP). According to Unger (2004), the LDS Church was responsible for the placement of 70,000 Indigenous children from at least 62 different Native nations (Riggs 2008) into its IPP from 1947–96. Although the IPP officially ended in 1996, its repercussions continue. For example, in 2016–17, several court cases were filed against the LDS Church claiming that the LDS Church knew of and did nothing about the sexual abuse perpetrated by its members and clergy against several Native children who were enrolled in the IPP (Fonseca 2017). The LDS IPP can be seen, in part, as a continuation of the investment in white men to control Native women's bodies through the removal of their children and rape of Native girls and women with impunity.

Child Welfare: Native and Black Overrepresentation

The capture and removal of Native American children from their families did not stop with the end of the Indian Adoption Project or the LDS IPP. It continues: social workers have become the agents of control. Native American and African American children continue to be the most overrepresented groups in the child welfare system, in part because their trajectories of state control share some similarities, such as enslavement. Dorothy Roberts (1997) insists that Black women's reproductive control, including Black overrepresentation in the child welfare system, is connected to the historical enslavement and control of slave women: "[t]he brutal domination of slave women's procreation laid the foundation for centuries of reproductive regulation that continues today" (23). Roberts argues for a historiography that maintains the linkage from slavery to reproductive control in order that the actions of the state against Black women may be fully understood. Building on the work of Roberts, Harris, and Deer, the lineage from Native entrapment must also be kept in plain sight.

Although the history of reproductive control for Black and Native women is not the same, parallels can be drawn. For example, at the same time that white women were fighting for the right to abortion and contraception, women of color were fighting against coercive sterilization practices and for the right to raise their children (Roberts 1997, 2002). Although both Native and Black women have had to fight, and continue to fight, for the right to care for their children, the investment in white property rights diverges for Native and Black women around the issues of sovereignty and land. Although there were different historical conditions that led to the flooding of the child welfare system with Black and Native children, both Black and Native communities have attested to the group-based nature of the harm caused by the forcible removal of large percentages of their children. The American Indian Movement (AIM) and the National Association of Black Social Workers (NABSW) argued in the 1970s that the transfer of large percentages of Native and Black children, respectively, into the white child welfare system constituted genocide.

The allegation of genocide rings true in that it is a transfer of children from one ethnic group to another, along with abuse, neglect, and violence, from communities of color to the white state, white institutions of "care," and white adoptive homes. In state care and private adoptions, children are not thought of as equal, and the value placed on a child is based on a rigid racial hierarchical structure exemplified by de Las Casas and de Sepulveda. Within this structure, the Black or Native child is assigned a value that is far lower than that of a white child. Harris (1993) underscores the way that whiteness is based on considering white individuals to be superior to other peoples: "as it emerged, the concept of whiteness was premised on white supremacy rather than mere difference. 'White' was defined and constructed in ways that increased its value by reinforcing its exclusivity" (1707–91). The idea that whiteness is a coveted commodity is quite salient in the realm of adoption politics. A white child is requested more by adoptive parents, is easier for an adoption agency to find a home for, and actually holds a higher monetary value in private adoptions, as Simon, Altstein and Melli (1994) note a published fee scale for a private adoption agency in the 1990s:

"White infants	$7,500.00
Biracial infants	$3,800.00
Black infants	$2,200.90"

(11)

The pay scale for adopting infants in the United States is clearly race based, as is the international adoption arena.

Adoptive parents enter into an adoptive system already racially structured to divest value away from communities of color, yet the adoptive system operates as an economic apparatus directly shaped by racist societal attitudes. Banks (1998) emphasizes the connection between adoption preferences and the value placed on Black children:

The severity of the social inequality produced by adoptive parents' preferences is made starkly clear by a fact too often accepted as inevitable, albeit lamentable, rather than as a predictable outcome of our own preference-promoting policies: Black children are simply worth less than white children.

(881)

Banks is referencing the economic underpinning of the child welfare system: a system of supply and demand, which can be understood as linked to monetary values placed on slaves. Satz and Askeland (2006) note a study conducted by the North American Council of Adoptable Children that indicated that African American families were troubled by the monetary adoption system: "due to their deep awareness of the history of slavery, many black adults are very suspicious of adoption fees, which makes the process too much like 'buying' a baby" (55). There is a link between slavery and the current practice of setting fees for children based on the color of their skin. Given that the legacies of slavery remain embedded in a system of adoption fees that reproduce racial hierarchies, it is important to consider the politics of adoption through a framework of whiteness as property.

Adoption, which was run by the adoption preferences of white middle-class families, was infused with racism. As the white child became more and more coveted in the post-World War II United States, with the shortage of adoptable white infants, children of color were still not adopted in great numbers (Roberts 2002). In fact, they were often considered difficult to place or deemed unadoptable, so the government placed them in the "special needs" category with children who were physically and mentally disabled. In some instances, the "special needs" designation increased the monetary incentive to continue to remove high numbers of Black and Native children; states received more money for special needs adoptions than for other adoptions. The foster care system became dependent on "special needs" children for its funding, as William Byler (1977), director of the Association on the American Indian Affairs from 1962 until 1980, stressed in the 1970s:

> The Bureau of Indian Affairs and the Department of Health, Education and Welfare (HEW) bear a part of the responsibility for the current child-welfare crisis. The BIA and HEW both provide substantial funding to state agencies for foster care and thus, in effect, subsidize the taking of Indian children … In some instances, financial considerations contribute to the crisis. For example, agencies established to place children have an incentive to find children to place.

(6)

Because the Bureau of Indian Affairs and the Department of Health, Education, and Welfare paid more for the care of Indigenous children when they were removed and placed under state supervision, states had a financial incentive to remove these children and keep them in foster homes to retain federal monies.

The point Byler makes about state incentives to remove and retain Native children in the foster care system is not just an issue of the distant past. In 2011, National Public Radio (NPR) aired a three-part series on state incentives for removing Indigenous children. One of the highest removal rates for Native children was, and continues to be, in South Dakota, where NPR found that 60 percent of the state-run foster care population was American Indian, while Native children made up less than 15 percent of the overall child population in South Dakota (Sullivan and Walters 2011). These numbers are startling, given the Indian Child Welfare Act (1978) (ICWA) was tasked with halting the disproportionate removal of Native children from their families and communities (Byler 1977; de Bourbon 2013). Prior to the passage of ICWA, in 1976, the Association on American Indian Affairs (AAIA) found that 64 percent of the children in foster care in South Dakota were Indigenous children (AAIA 1976, as cited in Unger, 1977). Adoptions taking place in South Dakota were and are disproportionately adoption of Native children. In 1995, Reed and Zelio (1995) found that 40 percent of all adoptions in South Dakota since 1968 were of Native children.

During this time, South Dakota was receiving 100 million dollars each year from the federal government for its child welfare program, which employed 1,000 workers, funded 700 foster families, and funded group homes receiving millions in subsidies to care for Native children (Sullivan and Walters 2011). Ninety percent of the American Indian children in the child welfare system in South Dakota are in non-Indian care, constituting a transfer of Native children from Native to white care, making clear the 1970s call of genocide by the AIM continues to be relevant. Native children continue to represent a state interest and an investment in white institutions and families through the suppression of Native women's reproductive freedoms—the loss of their children.

"A Dog Shouldn't Live in Some of These Places": Moving Beyond Removal

In addition to genocidal levels of child removal from their communities, Indigenous people suffer the highest rates of poverty, alcohol and drug addiction, unemployment, incarceration, school push out, interracial sexual violence, and murder of any minority group (Sarche and Spicer 2008), which has been used by groups, such as the Christian Alliance for Indian Child Welfare (CAICW), to continue the removal of Native children, all in the name of "the best interest of the child."

Elizabeth Morris, the co-founder of CAICW, argued that reservations should be redlined as hazardous zones for Native children: "No one, not the federal government, not the tribal government, no one can tell me that these children are being raised in a healthy way. No one can tell me that these children are safe" (Morris, personal interview, 2010). Johnston Moore, a CAICW board member *and* adoptive father of three Native American children, one Black child, and two Latino children wanted to redline certain, but not all, reservations, such as the Leech Lake Reservation: "Leech Lake, and places like that, I don't think that anyone should live there—a dog shouldn't live in some of these places" (Moore, personal interview, 2011). Morris told me a particularly heartbreaking story of suffering and loss as evidence for the need to redline reservations:

> When Michelle hung herself in a closet, that might not mean anything to a congressman, but I knew Michelle. Fifteen years old—she was beautiful, she was intelligent, she was totally messed up, totally depressed. She was gang raped. She was beaten by her mother, she was abandoned by her father, and the closet she hung herself on, the stick in there touched my head. I stood in there and it was right above my head. She was a little taller than me. You know what she did to herself? She strangled herself. She could have stood up.
>
> (Morris, personal interview, 2010)

Michelle's story is heartbreaking. She endured such incredible violence until it broke her, which is something that no human should have to endure. Morris's argument is salient: it engages the desire of all communities to provide children an environment free from violence. Morris levels the blame for Michelle's gang rape, family trauma, and suicide on the reservation, and argues that Michelle could have been "saved" by removal to a white family.

Redlining reservations as uninhabitable for Native children is something the U.S. government has done since boarding schools, the Indian Adoption Project, and the IPP. I asked Jack Trope, the previous director of the Association on American Indian Affairs who worked extensively with Native families and tribal communities, whether there was some truth to Morris' argument that Native children, such as Michelle, should be placed off the reservation in white homes. Trope stated:

> That is just nonsense. You know, tribal programs are placing kids with good families, Indian families, every day. There are plenty of good Indian families everywhere. It is nonsense to say that you can't place a child on the reservation—there are plenty of good families on the poorest reservation in America.
>
> (Trope, personal interview, 2010)

As Trope noted, there are healthy Indian families on every reservation. Even with this information, it is tempting to see Michelle's life as an outgrowth of unfit parents and communities, but her life is part of a larger colonial project of divestiture from Indigenous communities and an investment in whiteness that began over 500 years ago.

This chapter interrogated how the state and white Americans have invested in whiteness: the control of Native women's reproductive freedom through the removal of Native children to white-controlled institutions (boarding schools, the Indian Adoption Project, and the IPP) and white families (foster care and adoption). It argued that the enslavement of Indigenous peoples must be understood as the genesis of this investiture. The continued overrepresentation of Native children in state apparatuses of control such as the child welfare system constitute a violation of Native sovereignty, a group-based harm, and a violation of Indigenous women's reproductive freedom.

Notes

1   Native American is used interchangeably with American Indian, Native, and Indigenous in this chapter.
2   The debate fueled scientific experimentation on and mutilation of Indigenous people, such as the decapitation of Native Americans for measuring cranial capacity to justify the theory of polygenesis, which was a theory that was developed in the 1500s, maintaining there were different races that came from different lineages—different species. The alternate theory was monogenesis, which was the idea the differences between racial groups was not due to humans being different species and linked all humans to a common ancestor (Stannard 1992; Ramirez 2007).
3   American Indians who have heritage of Black and Indian ancestry have been called Black Indians or African Indians, but American Indians who have white and Indian heritage are not called white Indians; they are simply called Indians.

Bibliography

Ablavsky, Gregory. 2011. "Making Indians 'White': The Judicial Abolition of Native Slavery in Revolutionary Virginia and Its Racial Legacy." *University of Pennsylvania Law Review* 159 (1457): 1457–1541.

Anderson, Fred. 2006. *The War That Made America: A Short History of the French and Indian War*. New York: Penguin.

Banks, R. Richard. 1998. The Color of Desire: Fulfilling Adoptive Parents' Racial Preferences through Discriminatory State Action. *Yale Law Journal* 107 (4): 875–964.

Brooks, James. ed. 2002. *Confounding the Color Line: The Indian-Black Experience in North America*. Lincoln: University of Nebraska Press.

Byler, William. 1974. "Statement of William Byler, Executive Director, Association on American Indian Affairs." U.S. Senate (1974) Subcommittee on Indian Affairs of the Committee on Interior and Insular Affairs, Indian Child Welfare Program. Hearings on Problems that American Indian Families Face in Raising their Children and How These Problems are Affected by Federal Action or Inaction, Hearings, April (1974), 93rd Congress, 2nd Session. Washington, DC: Government Printing Office.

Byler, William. 1977. "The Destruction of American Indian Families." In *The Destruction of American Indian Families*, edited by Steven Unger, 1–11. New York: Association on American Indian Affairs.

Carocci, Max and Stephanie Pratt. 2012. *Native American Adoption, Captivity, and Slavery in Changing Contexts*. New York: Palgrave Macmillan.

Carpenter, Kristen A., Sonia K. Katyal, and Angela R. Riley. 2009. "In Defense of Property." *Yale Law Journal* 118 (6): 1022–1125.

De Bourbon, Soma. 2013. "Indigenous Genocidal Tracings: Slavery, Transracial Adoption, and the Indian Child Welfare Act." www.escholarship.org/uc/item/4d22b3fr.

Deer, Sarah. 2010. "Relocation Revisited: Sex Trafficking of Native Women in the United States." *William Mitchell Law Review* 36 (2): 621–683.

Deer, Sarah. 2015. *The Beginning of the End of Rape: Confronting Sexual Violence in Native America*. Minneapolis: University of Minnesota Press.

Deloria, Philip J. 1998. *Playing Indian*. New Haven, CT: Yale University Press.

Deloria Jr., Vine. 1985. *American Indian Policy in The Twentieth Century*. Norman: University of Oklahoma Press.

Deloria Jr., Vine. 2006. *The World We Used to Live In: Remembering the Powers of the Medicine Men*. Golden, CO: Fulcrum Publishing.

Deloria Jr., Vine and Clifford M. Lytle. 1983. *American Indians, American Justice*. Austin: University of Texas Press.

Deloria Jr., Vine and Clifford M. Lytle. 1998. *The Nations Within: The Past and Future of American Indian Sovereignty*. Austin: University of Texas Press.

Deloria Jr., Vine and David Wilkins. 2011. *The Legal Universe: Observations on the Foundations of American Law*. Golden, CO: Fulcrum Publishing.

DeMeyer, Trace A. 2010. *One Small Sacrifice: Lost Children of the Indian Adoption Projects*. Greenfield, MA: Trace DeMeyer.

Ekberg, Carl J. 2007. *Stealing Indian Women: Native Slavery in the Illinois Country*. Champaign: University of Illinois Press.

Fanshel, David. 1972. *Far from the Reservation: The Transracial Adoption of American Indian Children*. Metuchen, NJ: Scarecrow Press.

Fonseca, Felicia. 2017. "New Lawsuits Allege Mormon Church Failed to Protect Children." *U.S. News & World Report*, August 15. www.usnews.com/news/best-states/arizona/articles/2017-08-15/new-lawsuits-allege-mormon-church-failed-to-protect-children.

Forbes, Jack D. 1993. *Africans and Native Americans: The Language of Race and the Evolution of Red-Black Peoples*. Urbana: University of Illinois Press. Printed earlier under the title *Black Africans and Native Americans: Color, Race and Caste in the Evolution of Red-Black Peoples*.

Gallay, Alan. 2009. *Indian Slavery in Colonial America*. Lincoln: University of Nebraska Press.

Gonzales, Angela A. 2009. "Racial Legibility: The Federal Census and the (Trans) Formation of 'Black' and 'Indian' Identity, 1790–1920." In *IndiVisible: African-Native American Lives in the Americas*, edited by Gabrielle Tayac, 57–68. Washington, DC: Smithsonian.

Halliburton, Jr., R. 1977. *Red Over Black: Black Slavery Among the Cherokee Indians*. Westport, CT: Greenwood Publishing Group.

Harris, Cheryl I. 1993. "Whiteness as Property." *Harvard Law Review* 106 (8): 1707–1791.

Hartman, Saidiya. 1997. *Scenes of Subjection: Terror, Slavery, and Self-Making in Nineteenth-Century America*. New York: Oxford University Press.

Heizer, Robert. 1993. *The Destruction of California Indians*. Lincoln: University of Nebraska Press.

Ingersoll, Thomas N. 2005. *To Intermix with Our White Brothers: Indian Mixed Bloods in the United States from the Earliest Times to the Indian Removals*. Albuquerque: University of New Mexico Press.

Johnston-Dodds, Kimberly. 2002. "Early California Laws and Policies Related to California Indians." Sacramento: California Research Bureau.

Jones, Jacqueline, Thomas Borstelmann, Vicki L. Ruiz, Peter Wood, and Elaine Tyler. 2014. *Created Equal: A History of the United States*, 4th edition. New York: Pearson.

Katz, William Loren. 1997. *Black Indians: A Hidden Heritage*. New York: Aladdin Paperbacks.

Littlefield, Daniel F., Jr. 1978. *The Cherokee Freedmen: From Emancipation to American Citizenship*. Westport, CT: Greenwood Press.

Lomawaima, K. Tsianina. 1994. *They Called It Prairie Light: The Story of Chilocco Indian School*. Lincoln: University of Nebraska Press.

Lomawaima, K. Tsianina and Teresa L. McCarty. 2006. *To Remain an Indian: Lessons in Democracy from a Century of Native American Education*. New York: Teachers College Press.

Miles, Tiya. 2005. *Ties That Bind*. Berkeley: University of California Press.

Miles, Tiya. 2009. "Taking Leave, Making Lives: Creative Quests for Freedom in Early Black and Native America." In *IndiVisible: African-Native American Lives in the Americas*, edited by Gabrielle Tayac, 139–150. Washington, DC: Smithsonian.

Miles, Tiya and Sharon P. Holland. eds. 2006. *Crossing Waters, Crossing Worlds: The African Diaspora in Indian Country*. Durham, NC: Duke University Press.

Minges, Patrick Neal. 2004. *Black Indian Slave Narratives: Real Voices, Real History*. Winston-Salem, NC: John F. Blair.

Mohawk, John C. 1992. "Indians and Democracy: No One Ever Told Us." In *Exiled in the Land of the Free: Democracy, Indian Nations, and the United States Constitution*, edited by Oren Lyons and John Mohawk, 43–72. Santa Fe: Clear Light Publishers.

Moore, Johnston. 2011. Phone interview, December 2, 2011.

Moreton-Robinson, Aileen. 2015. *The White Possessive: Property, Power, and Indigenous Sovereignty*. Minneapolis: University of Minnesota Press.

Morris, Elizabeth. 2010. Phone interview, October 10, 2010.

Naylor, Celia E. 2008. *African Cherokees in Indian Territory: From Chattel to Citizens*. Chapel Hill: University of North Carolina Press.

Perdue, Theda. 2009. "Native Americans, African Americans and Jim Crow." In *IndiVisible: African-Native American Lives in the Americas*, edited by Gabrielle Tayac, 21–33. Washington, DC: Smithsonian.

Ramirez, Renya K. 2007. *Native Hubs: Culture, Community, and Belonging in Silicon Valley and Beyond*. Durham, NC: Duke University Press.

Reed, James B. and Judy A. Zelio. eds. 1995. "States and Tribes: Building New Traditions. A Broad Examination of the Condition of State-Tribal Relations and Opportunities for Mutually Beneficial Cooperation as the 21st Century Approaches, from a State Legislative Policy Perspective." Washington, DC: National Conference of State Legislatures.

Riggs, Lynette A. 2008. "The Church of Jesus Christ of Latter-day Saints' Indian Student Placement Service: A History." Dissertation Abstracts International: *Humanities and Social Sciences* 69 (02): 0538.

Roberts, Dorothy. 1997. *Killing the Black Body: Race, Reproduction, and the Meaning of Liberty*. New York: Random House, Inc.

Roberts, Dorothy. 2002. *Shattered Bonds: The Color of Child Welfare*. New York: Basic Civitas Books.

Robin v. Hardaway, 1 Jeff. 109 (Va. Gen. Ct. 1772).

Robinson, Cedric J. 1983. *Black Marxism: The Making of the Black Radical Tradition*. Chapel Hill: University of North Carolina Press.

Rosay, André B. 2016. "Violence Against American Indian and Alaska Native Women and Men: 2010 Findings from the National Intimate Partner and Sexual Violence Survey." Washington, DC: United States Department of Justice.

Ross, Luana. 1998. *Inventing the Savage: The Social Construction of Native American Criminality*. Austin: University of Texas Press.

Sachs, Honor. 2012. "'Freedom By A Judgment': The Legal History of an Afro-Indian Family." *Law and History Review* 30 (1): 173–203.

Sarche, Michelle and Paul Spicer. 2008. "Poverty and Health Disparities for American Indian and Alaska Native Children." *Annals of the New York Academy of Sciences* 1136 (1): 126–136.

Satz, M. and L. Askeland. 2006. "Civil Rights, Adoption Rights: Domestic Adoption and Foster Care, 1970 to the Present." In *Children and Youth in Adoption, Orphanages, and Foster Care*, edited by L. Askeland, 45–61. Westport, CT: Greenwood Press.

Simon, Rita James, Howard Altstein, and Marygold S. Melli. 1994. *The Case for Transracial Adoption*. Washington, DC: American University Press.

"Squaw Slaves in Utah." 1858. *Daily Cleveland Herald*, July 6. http://infotrac.galegroup.com.oca.ucsc.edu/itw/infomark/442/902/149358966w16/purl=rc6_NCNP&dyn=14!start_at?sw_aep=ucsantacruz.

Stannard, David. 1992. *American Holocaust: The Conquest of the New World*. New York: Oxford University Press.

Sturm, Circe. 2002. *Blood Politics*. Berkeley: University of California Press.

Sullivan, Laura and Amy Walters. 2011. "Incentives and Cultural Bias Fuel Foster System." *Native Foster Care: Lost Children, Shattered Families*. National Public Radio, October 25. www.npr.org/2011/10/25/141662357/incentives-and-cultural-bias-fuel-foster-system.

Tallbear, Kimberly. 2009. "DNA and Native American Identity." In *IndiVisible: African-Native American Lives in the Americas*, edited by Gabrielle Tayac, 69–76. Washington, DC: Smithsonian.

Tayac, Gabrielle. ed. 2009. *IndiVisible: African-Native American Lives in the Americas*. Washington, DC: Smithsonian.

Unger, Steven. 1977. *The Destruction of American Indian Families*. New York: Association on American Indian Affairs, Inc.

Unger, Steven. 2004. "The Indian Child Welfare Act of 1978: A Case Study." University of Southern California: ProQuest Dissertations Publishing.

Weller, Kris. 2010. "Defining Human: Species, Sanity, and Legal Subjecthood." PhD dissertation, University of California, Santa Cruz.

Wildeman, Christopher and Natalia Emanuel. 2014. "Cumulative Risks of Foster Care Placement for American Children, 2000–2011." *PLOS ONE* 9: e92785.

Yarbrough, Fay A. 2008. *Race and the Cherokee Nation: Sovereignty in the Nineteenth Century*. Philadelphia: University of Pennsylvania Press.

2

A BODY IS A BODY

THE EMBODIED POLITICS OF WOMEN'S SEXUAL AND REPRODUCTIVE RIGHTS IN CONTEMPORARY IRISH ART AND CULTURE
KATE ANTOSIK-PARSONS

The body politics of women's sexual and reproductive rights in Ireland is firmly embedded in the socio-political landscape that shaped the nation over the last 100 years. Sarah Maria Griffin's poem, "We Face This Land" (2016) boldly reclaimed the body asserting: "A body is a body is a body [...] Not a house. Not a city. Not a vessel, not a country." Yet, over the course of the 20th century and beyond, in hegemonic Irish literary and visual culture, a woman's body has regularly been equated to a vessel and a country (Meaney, 1991; Murphy, 1998; Bhreathnach-Lynch, 2007). Under Article 40.3.3, the Eighth Amendment (1983) to the Irish Constitution (1937), the moment a woman becomes pregnant her body is no longer her own because the fetus is granted equal right to life.[1] Ireland is the only country in the world to have such a provision written into its constitution. Thirty years later, under the Protection of Life During Pregnancy Act (2013) abortion was permitted only in the limited circumstances where to continue the pregnancy would result in maternal death.[2] Under any other circumstance, those who procure an abortion are criminalized and risk facing up to 14 years' imprisonment. The socio-political landscape for reproductive justice in Ireland had reached a critical point.

This chapter examines the power of visual images to address lingering colonial legacies and the subsequent patriarchal, postcolonial conditions that reinforce strict control over women's sexual and reproductive health in

Ireland. Framed by historical context, it analyzes contemporary Irish art, visual culture, and embodied activist gestures, focusing on how these images manifest gendered histories, assert visible resistance and signs of solidarity, and, importantly, reveal hidden journeys women in Ireland take for reproductive healthcare. This chapter, like the art it details, aims to counter the silencing of those impacted by the reproductive injustices in Ireland. On the issue of silencing, it is worth stating at the outset that term 'woman' is used throughout the discussion, though it is meant to be short-hand for women, non-binary people, and transgender men. This can prove problematic as gender is not binary, and non-binary people and transgender men also need access to abortion services. This chapter does not seek to further marginalize non-binary people and transgender men, therefore the term, 'pregnant people' is adopted intermittently. In sum, the discussion that follows will illuminate how artists and activists in the Republic of Ireland engage with feminism, exercise embodied politics to strategically subvert dominant ideologies, histories, and politics, and respond to the continuing struggle for reproductive freedom.

Historical Context

At present Ireland is midway through the 'Decade of Centenaries,' a 10-year period ranging from 2012–2022 during which state-sponsored events commemorate the centenary anniversary of events related to Irish independence. Uncomfortable truths are revealed when the official state-sanctioned 'remembering' is juxtaposed against the peripheral voices of those who have been marginalized by dominant patriarchal historical and political discourses.[3] Although women actively participated in the Easter Rising (1916) and the War of Independence (1922), these conservative Catholic rebellions that overthrew the colonial oppression of the British Empire merely substituted one patriarchal ideology for another. The repressive Catholic ethos that dominated every aspect of Irish political and cultural life carefully policed women's bodies, particularly sexuality and reproduction, as evident by the post-independence legislation that banned divorce (1925), the distribution of literature advocating birth control (1929), and the sale and import of contraceptives (1935). Laury Oaks (1999) argued these legislative restrictions coupled with the assertion in the Irish Constitution (1937) that women's duties best served the nation in the domestic sphere of the home supported "ideology that women should not participate in both 'reproductive' and 'non-reproductive life'" (p. 179). Women's citizenship was intimately tied to their perceived maternal duties and private lives as enshrined under Articles 41.2.1 and 41.2.2 of the Irish Constitution.[4]

In 1983, the Eighth Amendment to the Irish Constitution was passed. It granted equal rights to mother and fetus and was understood as a backlash against the liberalization of a postcolonial Irish society in the late 1970s in the wake of gains by second-wave feminists. Abortion in Ireland became bound to nationalism and a strong desire to imagine Ireland as separate and distinct from Britain. Abortion had already been prohibited under the Offences Against the Person Act (1861) but the Eighth Amendment blocked legalization without further referenda. According to Eardman (2016) the amendment was premised on religious and cultural traditions that historically differentiated Ireland's "sovereignty from England" (p. 44). In the United Kingdom, except Northern Ireland, abortion was legalized under the Abortion Act (1967) up to 22 weeks in cases of maternal life, mental health, health, rape, fetal defects, and/or socio-economic factors. In Northern Ireland it remains illegal under the aforementioned 1861 act and the Criminal Justice Act (Northern Ireland) (1945) meaning women in the North, like those in the Republic, must travel overseas to obtain an abortion. It is with no small irony that the majority of the people from Ireland are forced to travel to England, their former colonizer, to obtain abortions.

Summarizing 'reproductive injustice' in Ireland, Ursula Barry (2015) argued,

> bodily integrity has been displaced by the public physical dissecting of women's bodies; choice has been displaced by calculating risks between a pregnant woman's health and her life; privacy has been displaced by secrecy; compassion has been displaced by the threat of long-term imprisonment; reality has been displaced by denial.
>
> (p. 120)

Secrecy and denial consequently contribute to the silencing of women who seek abortion, as will be discussed in detail later. This concept of reproductive injustice aligns with what Ronit Lentin (2013) termed "the biopolitics of birth," the multiple ways in which Church and state, from the foundation of the Irish Free State to the contemporary pluralist Republic, collude to regulate women's bodies and curtail reproductive freedom. This encompasses the residential institutions like the Magdalene Laundries and mother and baby homes to obstetric violence of medical procedures like non-consensual hysterectomies by Dr. Michael Neary at Our Lady of Lourdes maternity hospital in Droheda and the chilling, long-term effects of symphysiotomy.[5] It includes the policing of pregnant migrant women resulting in the 2004 Citizenship Referendum, a referendum that provided that children born on the island of Ireland to foreign national parents would no longer have a constitutional right to Irish citizenship and, by extension, the present system of direct provision for asylum seekers in Ireland (p. 131).[6] The Eighth Amendment is an extension of the biopolitics of birth, exercising power over the bodies of all pregnant people in Ireland, not only those who seek access to abortion, because the National Consent Policy specifically excludes medical consent in maternity care.

The Embodied Politics of Feminism

The feminist art-historical approach advances that art can facilitate deeper understandings of political, cultural, and social power relations. It scrutinizes imagery bearing in mind, as the second-wave feminist adage asserts, the personal is political, while acknowledging that individual experiences are not universal, nor are structural inequalities distributed evenly. Lucy Lippard (2015) distinguished political art from activist art arguing:

> "political" art tends to be socially concerned and "activist" art tends to be socially involved—not a value judgement so much as a personal choice. The former's work is a commentary or analysis, while the latter's art works within its contexts, with its audience.
>
> (p. 75)

Participatory in nature, activist art aims to empower individuals and communities by actively addressing power structures generated through dialogic processes.[7] While some of the work discussed in this chapter is 'activist,' all can read as 'political' in so far as their subject matter represents the body politics of Irish reproductive justice. Furthermore, the images and gestures are considered in terms of their corporeal or bodily engagement with 'embodied politics,' defined by Natalie Fixmer and Julia T. Wood (2005) as "personal and often physical, bodily action that aims to provoke change by exercising and resisting power in everyday life" (p. 237). For the purposes of this discussion, embodied politics are identified as "personal acts of resistance in local sites where injustices occur" (p. 238). In Ireland, women's bodies are the physical and metaphorical site where injustices occur, deploying them in art, visual culture, and activist gestures constitutes interventionist acts of resistance.

Illustrating Gendered Histories

In 2015, the double volume *The Abortion Papers Ireland* (Smyth, 1992; Quilty, Kennedy, & Conlon, 2015) was released bearing Alice Maher's disquieting large scale charcoal and chalk drawing *Kneeling Girl* (2001) from Maher's aptly titled exhibition *The History of Tears* (2001) on the cover.[8] Against the dark, heavily layered charcoal background rendered on calico fabric, the figure of a young woman has fallen to her knees. Nude, except for the fabric gathered around her hips, she cradles the tears leaking from her eyes gently as they trickle down her body, catching them in the cloth before they flow into a pool of water accumulating in front of her. The futility of her action evident as the seeping bodily discharge evades containment. The tactile surface of the drawing is characterized by a series of erasures, deliberate gestures enabling an accumulation of delicately rendered lines. Although *Kneeling Girl* was not explicitly created in response to the issue of bodily autonomy in Ireland, when the editors of *The Abortion Papers* selected Maher's work for the cover, it deliberately invited consideration about how women's reproductive experiences in Ireland might form their own history of tears; a hidden history, one of stigma and shame underscored by silence and erasure. First released in 1992, *The Abortion Papers Ireland: Volume 1* was dedicated by editor Ailbhe Smyth "to all Irish women who have ever had to travel abroad for an abortion" (p. 6). Between 1980 and 1992 approximately 49,707 traveled abroad to the UK for an abortion. By the end of 2016 a further 118,996 made the invisible journey to access healthcare. In this context, works like *Kneeling Girl* question how art and visual culture contribute to a nuanced understanding of the gendered histories of body politics in Ireland.

Gendered histories are engaged on a number of different levels. Visual artists are vocally engaged with activism, as is evident by the Artists' Campaign to Repeal the 8th, which at present has over 2000 artists living in Ireland who have pledged to support repeal.[9] In direct response to the growing campaign to repeal the Eighth Amendment, the Coalition to Repeal the 8th, representing 50 different organizations throughout the country, was formed. In July 2016, the Artists' Campaign to Repeal the 8th released a special edition print of Jim Fitzpatrick's *Countess Markievicz* (2016). Constance Gore-Booth Markievicz (1868–1927) was an artist, suffragette, and revolutionary nationalist who was a combatant in the Easter Rising and later a politician. Imprisoned on several occasions, Markievicz was sentenced to death for her part in the Rising, though the sentence was commuted because she was a woman. In Fitzpatrick's bust portrait of Markievicz, she wears her Irish Citizen Army military uniform, the strap of her Sam Browne gun belt visible, emphasizing that she was radicalized. This image tangentially references Fitzpatrick's earlier iconic portrait of the Marxist revolutionary Che Guevara (1968), evoking a rebellious spirit. The group's logo, a white '8' inside a gray circle overlaid with a red X, is worn as a badge pinned on her lapel. The notion that Markievicz, amongst her many accomplishments, was also a trained artist, would affirm her professional support for the campaign for repeal fits neatly within the subversive narrative of her gendered, revolutionary activities. Proceeds from Fitzpatrick's poster sales were used to fund the group's continued advocacy.

'Rise and Repeal,' the 5th Annual March for Choice (September 2016), organized by the volunteer organization, Abortion Rights Campaign (ARC), also invoked women's nationalist revolutionary efforts for contemporary reproductive freedom. ARC's signs and pamphlets featured a woman, more specifically a suffragette, holding aloft a 'Rise and Repeal' banner. The figure was appropriated from the masthead of *Bean Na hÉireann* (Women of Ireland), a monthly magazine published by the nationalist, socialist, feminist organization, *Inghínidhe Na hÉireann* (Daughters of Ireland) of which Markievicz was a member, as well as the artist that designed the original masthead for the early 20th century publication. The color and composition of ARC's own logo of yellow, green, and purple draws parallels with the tricolor flag adopted by UK suffragettes that was white, green, and purple. ARC (2016) explicitly framed the march uniting historical efforts for political sovereignty with contemporary bodily autonomy: "The Easter Rising sought sovereignty and self-determination for Ireland. Today, we seek the same control over our own bodies. No longer will the Irish State strip us of our basic human rights" (abortionrightscampaign.ie). Coupling women's historical efforts by referencing the efforts of revolutionary groups like *Inghínidhe Na hÉireann* with contemporary activism demonstrates how the past can be activated in the realm of the visual. By grounding the embodied actions of protest in historical visual culture, ARC established a visual identity that claims a specific lineage to and continuity with Irish feminist concerns from the turn of the 20th century.

'Speaking of IMELDA,' a London-based group engaged in art activism, strategically utilizes humor and satire in interventionist actions to expose critical incongruities, in a similar manner to the Guerrilla Girls. IMELDA

Figure 2.1 Abortion Rights Campaign, Rise and Repeal, 5th Annual March for Choice, September 2016.

stands for Ireland Making England the Legal Destination for Abortion: 'Imelda' was the codeword used to provide information on abortion services to Irish women when it was illegal to do so. *Pro-choice Proclamation* (2015) was staged on the steps of the General Post Office (GPO) during the national broadcaster *Raidió Telifís Éireann*'s (RTÉ) event 'Road to the Rising' which recreated life in 1915 in anticipation of the centenary commemoration of the Easter Rising. In 1916, the Irish Volunteers and Irish Citizen Army seized control of the GPO from the British, on the steps of the captured building the rebels read out their 'Easter Proclamation' (1916). The proclamation was significant for several reasons, but for the purposes of this analysis its importance was that it asserted "religious and civil liberty, equal rights and equal opportunities to all its citizens." This was the first mention of gender equality and was particularly important given that under British colonial law at that time women were not allowed to vote. Although women were active combatants in the struggle for independence, they were subjugated to the patriarchal dictates of the conservative Catholic government after independence. Dressed as suffragettes, entirely in red, Speaking of IMELDA re-enacted the 1916 takeover and chained themselves to a pillar of the GPO for over two hours declaring a proclamation of bodily autonomy, calling on women of Ireland to assert ownership of their own bodies.

Ailbhe Smyth (1992) argued that abortion needed to be considered in the "broad context of reproductive freedom and in the even broader context of women's historical struggle for social and political selfhood" (p. 146). Twenty-five years later, this point is still alarmingly relevant. *Pro-choice Proclamation* drew connections between gender in Irish society, martyrdom, and reproductive freedom. It is notable that just steps from where the women stood, were the sites of two sculptures that depicted masculine heroism. Directly inside the GPO, Oliver Sheppard's bronze statue *Death of Cúchulainn* (1935), the epitome of martyrdom, represents the self-sacrificing Irish mythological hero in his moment of death, his body bound to a pillar in defeat. The visual similarities between the bound bodies are remarkable, demonstrating Speaking of IMELDA's embodied performance reclaimed the vision of equality promised over a century ago. When the bodies of those that Church and state have sought to control are activated in this particular way they disrupt dominant narratives. Meanwhile, across from the GPO once stood the granite capped *Nelson's Pillar* (1809), which bore the likeness of Vice Admiral Horatio Nelson (1758–1805). A tribute to the victorious British naval hero, it visually defined the public streetscape in the colonial era. The presence of the pillar was contentious in the Irish Free State, and in an iconic gesture that unofficially marked the 50-year anniversary of the Easter Rising, it was blown up by expelled Irish Republican Army (IRA) members. Speaking of IMELDA's embodied actions recall the rebellious activities that sought to destroy the pillar as a commemorative symbol of power. *Pro-choice Proclamation*, channeling that insubordinate spirit by directly inserting women's bodies into the public realm, suggested that embodied politics can subvert 'official' histories.

Visualizing Resistance and Solidarity

Visibility is at the heart of the contemporary movement for Irish reproductive freedom and there has been a noticeable shift around openly talking about the abortion issue. Arguably one of the most distinguishable visual contributions to the reproductive justice movement has been Repeal Project, the white letters that boldly proclaim 'REPEAL' against the backdrop of a black sweatshirt. Launched July 2016, creator Anna Cosgrave (2016) cites as inspiration, Gloria Steinem unapologetically wearing an "I had an abortion" t-shirt from the 2004 project by the same name designed by American activist Jennifer Baumgardner in collaboration with Planned Parenthood. Cosgrave's garment "outerwear to give a voice to a hidden problem" aimed to generate conversations about the lack of reproductive freedom in Ireland and initiate a conversation about why the Eighth Amendment should be repealed. Proceeds are donated directly to ARC. Sold initially at a pop-up store, demand was so high that it sold out within an hour. Garnering considerable attention, four months after its release the *University Observer*, University College Dublin's student newspaper, published an article contemplating the sweatshirt as a fashion statement. Adam Lawler (2016) argued "in a campaign about bodily autonomy, a wearable message is all the more powerful." Its popularity with people in their early 20s is not surprising given that the Union of Students in Ireland (USI), representative of 345,000 students in third level education, voted overwhelmingly to support a repeal of the Eighth Amendment (USI, 2017). Images widely circulated on social media of high profile celebrities wearing it, for example Vivienne Westwood, Brendan Courtney, and Rory O'Neill (drag queen Panti Bliss), and, more recently, American presidential candidate Bernie Sanders, further its popularity.

Repeal Project attracted unexpected interest from the advertising industry. In October 2016, Carphone Warehouse, a mobile phone company, debuted a series of controversial 'femvertising' billboards and bus shelter ads that boldly proclaimed "We're Pro-Choice" with the smaller tagline "the only place you get to choose your phone, your plan and your network." One featured an image of a blue button with "we're pro-choice" in white letters pinned on to the chest of a denim jacket. It attempted to embody a DIY, feminist 'activist' aesthetic, while peddling to consumers the freedom to choose the mobile phone suited to their lifestyle. Advertising Standards Authority of Ireland (ASAI) received over 40 complaints and subsequently ruled that Carphone

Figure 2.2 Speaking of IMELDA, *Pro-choice Proclamation,* the GPO Dublin Easter Monday 2015.

Warehouse was to cease using the word 'pro-choice' in advertising campaigns (Murray, 2016). The company stated:

> The campaign features seven topically themed advertisements around the subject of choice. The language and imagery used in the campaign is designed to be deliberately striking, engaging and thought-provoking. We are not making any comment on the current debate in Ireland nor are we seeking to trivialize the issue.
>
> ("This ad ..." *Irish Times*, October 26, 2016)

In no way was the company campaigning for, or making donations to aid, Irish reproductive rights organizations, they were capitalizing upon the momentum of Irish activism for profit. ARC countered:

> selling mobile phones by appropriating the unfortunate struggle for basic human rights belittles our efforts. It's a slap in the face, not only to the thousands of women who travel every day, but the thousands who cannot travel for various reasons.
>
> ("We're Pro-choice," 2016)

Arguably, Carphone Warehouse aimed to leverage the popularity of Repeal Project, indicated by similarities of wearing issues on the body as well as the language used to contextualize each image.

The embodied visibility of the sweatshirt led to a strategic intervention in Irish politics. In a staged action on September 26, 2016, just days after the March for Choice in Dublin, Ruth Coppinger, Bríd Smith, Richard Boyd Barrett, Gino Kenny, Mick Barry, and Paul Murphy, six *Teachtaí Dála* (TDs), members of *Dáil Eireann*, unashamedly revealed their REPEAL sweatshirts. Meanwhile, Coppinger pointedly questioned Taoiseach Enda Kenny:

> You've been here since 1975, but during that time a total of 165,000 women had to travel outside the State for an abortion while you were in the Dáil. Did you ever give those women a second thought when you were making decisions?
>
> (Lord, 2016)

Kenny responded, "while your t-shirts may be black with their writing white the reality is Ireland's abortion law stand-off is not a black and white issue" (O Cionnaith, 2016). Over the following months the sweatshirts caused a desired disturbance as complaints and broader calls for parliamentary dress code reform abounded (Finn, 2016). Their disruptive presence resulted in the live broadcast Dáil TV feed deliberately adopting a sideways view of these representatives to unofficially censor and conceal their sweatshirts ("Calls for…" *Carlow Nationalist*, 2016). This illustrated the subversiveness of the garment when worn in a deliberately provocative manner to participate in acts of resistance, particularly in the seat of legislative political, and importantly patriarchal, power. The embodied politics of reproductive justice seeks to interrupt traditional power demonstrating that it is not just 'business as usual.' Public gestures of activism, protest, and civil disobedience can be understood as 'performances' because they draw upon aesthetics and politics, employing tactical uses of embodiment and symbolic uses of language (Fuentes, 2015).

Nearly one month later in a related embodied gesture, TD Bríd Smith stood to debate the Private Members' Bill, the proposed 35th Amendment to the Irish Constitution. Wearing a plain black sweatshirt bearing a Coalition to Repeal the 8th badge, she engaged in an act of civil disobedience when she produced a packet of illegal abortion pills, defiantly challenging:

> You could arrest me for having it and give me 14 years, but you ain't going to do it because what's on your books and what's in your laws you know that if you dare to implement it you would bring hell-fire and brimstone down on top of this house.
>
> (BreakingNews.ie, 2016)

Holding up illegal abortifacient in *Dáil Eireann*, Smith invoked the spirit of the earlier Irish Women's Liberation Movement (IWLM) and their subversive actions. On May 22, 1971, 49 women from the IWLM traveled from Belfast to Dublin on the train illegally carrying, with intent to distribute, large supplies of condoms. This watershed action in the history of reproductive rights in Ireland was the subject of the recent musical, *The Train* (2015) that celebrated the bravery of the IWLM who flouted the laws to challenge the rigidity of Irish society at that time. Forty-five years later there was a symmetry in Smith's gesture that exposed the hypocrisy of legislation that criminalizes women for importing abortifacients, mifepristone and misoprostol. Though Smith was not charged for blatantly flaunting the law, it would be a mistake to dismiss this law as unenforceable, given the recent cases of the women in Northern Ireland who were charged under similar restrictive legislation for obtaining the abortion pills.[10] When taking this specific context into account, Smith's action was a gesture of solidarity, as well as one of embodied politics, particularly when one considers that Smith is the only TD to have publicly spoken about her own abortion.

The circulation on social media platforms Facebook and Twitter of a cleverly re-appropriated archival photograph of Peig Sayers (1873–1958), the famous Irish language *seanchaí* (or storyteller) of the Blasket Islands, featuring the Repeal Project jumper, encouraged deeper scrutiny of the historical powers of Church and state that seek to render invisible women's experiences. The re-appropriated image depicted the older woman wearing a shawl around her head and shoulders, her hands in her lap, seated in the interior of a traditional Irish cottage, and on the upper half of her body the ubiquitous 'REPEAL.' Famed for her skilled retelling of life on the rugged Blasket Islands, Co. Kerry, Peig's autobiography was compulsory for secondary school students in Ireland and, as a result, often elicits a negative reaction from those who remember the text as laborious. Peig was part of a larger oral tradition of storytelling that was largely dominated by men, and she "strategically borrowed and refashioned male forms" (Radner & Lanser, 1993, p. 12). Sara Baume (2015) valued Peig's contribution to the oral history of Ireland on the basis that she "spoke for generations of poor, uneducated Irish women who never had the opportunity to speak for themselves." Peig's appearance in the jumper alludes to the harsh treatment women in Ireland have faced under conservative, Catholic ideologies. Amid bitter debates about the legalization of contraception and 'politics of procreation in Ireland' Diarmuid Ferriter (2009) detailed:

> an older woman who attended a women's health seminar in Dublin in 1979 organised by the Contraception Action Programme "claimed that the earliest Irish-language editions of Peig Sayers' account of her

Figure 2.3 Kate Antosik-Parsons: Photograph of Repeal Project Sweatshirt, 2018.

life on the Blasket Islands [published in 1936 and regarded as an important autobiography in the context of women's experiences in isolated rural environments] included a reference to a primitive form of cap, or diaphragm, made from sheep's wool." This reference was later purged.

(p. 39)

The notion that Peig, a figure that seemingly embodied the conservative, nationalist vision of womanhood via rural, Catholic Ireland, detailed primitive forms of birth control, strictly forbidden by the Catholic Church, is incredibly subversive. Peig's altered image embodies the current plight of women in Ireland by investing it with the historical efforts to legalize contraception in

1970s Ireland. The image undermines the idealized vision of the monolithic 'Irish woman' enshrined in the Irish Constitution and perpetuated through dominant Irish literary and visual culture.

Solidarity is found in different aspects of the visual imagery created to address the struggle for reproductive rights. On July 8, 2016, an eye-catching mural by Dublin street artist Maser was unveiled on the external wall of the Project Arts Centre located on Essex Street in Dublin's Temple Bar. Against a bright blue background Maser rendered a giant red heart with white text, "Repeal the 8th." The heart form features repeatedly in Maser's art, specifically the print series *Maser Loves You*, and in various guises on his street art. Juxtaposing 'Maser Loves You' with a call to 'Repeal the 8th' the mural

Figure 2.4   Maser, "Repeal the 8th" Mural, Project Arts Centre, July 2016.
Photograph: Project Arts Centre.

deployed the idea of love in relation to bodily autonomy. It was removed after Dublin City Council (DCC) informed the Project Arts Centre that it violated planning permission because it was painted on a permanent structure and was not in keeping with the style of the area (McDermott, 2016). This response was puzzling given that in the prior year the *Yes for Equality* mural referencing the same sex marriage referendum slipped past these restrictions. During the week of its existence, the Project Arts Centre received over 200 letters of support and 50 letters of complaint. Anticipating a backlash, the artist reflected on the documenting of the mural on social media: "Thank God for social media. If we didn't have that I'd be a bit disappointed. It got shared thousands of times, job done" (Freyne, 2016). The controversy surrounding this mural echoes that of another censored Dublin mural, Pauline Cummins's

Figure 2.5   Vanessa Moss, "Repeal the 8th" Manicure, September 2016.

Celebration: The Beginning of Labour (1984), which was painted on the wall at the National Maternity Hospital, Holles Street, and was a commissioned mural that depicted two naked women holding a pregnant woman aloft in what appears to be a joyful moment as she embarks on birthing her child.[11] Known for engaging with women's sexuality, reproductive rights, and 'woman-centered' childbirth in Ireland, one speculates that Cummins's particular representation of pregnant, laboring bodies, presented in a manner that was perceived as a threat to the medical establishment, revealed an uneasiness about images that promote a corporeal, embodied knowledge. Interestingly, when the *Repeal the 8th* mural and *Celebration: The Beginning of Labour* are placed in proximity, it is evident that visual images promoting women's reproductive autonomy provoke strong responses when placed in the public realm. This suggests the subversive power of embodied actions, particularly when women's bodies engage in strategic acts of resistance.

After its removal, the mural was 'rebirthed' through acts of resistance when its image went viral, reproduced on silk-screened t-shirts, co-opted by Facebook users for profile pictures, displayed in shop fronts, and emblazoned on women's manicured nails by the Dublin based nail bar, Tropical Popical. The mural countered the isolation that women that have had abortions experience, for comedian Tara Flynn it represented "giving the oppressed a voice, saying: you're not on your own" (O'Brien, 2016). Outraged by the censorship, Grace Fitzgerald and Katie O'Kelly staged a protest in front of the Project Arts Centre encouraging people to gather with their faces painted blue, the same color that was used to cover the original mural, while some held photographs of its former existence. Protest has been a valuable tool of resistance throughout the history of the struggle against reproductive injustices, particularly in Ireland as detailed in the aforementioned gestures of the IWLM. Deploying their bodies in this act of resistance, the protestors demonstrated that erasure of the mural would not serve to erase the realities pregnant people face in the shadow of the Eighth Amendment. One protestor was cognizant of this: "Blue paint will not get rid of the stories of women having to go abroad in order to get medical treatment" (Devine, 2016). Maser's heart functioned as a visual call to arms, a reminder that despite efforts to suppress its message, much like the suppression that women from Ireland face in trying to access abortion, the grassroots movement will continue to mobilize against efforts to deny reproductive justice.

Documenting Hidden Journeys

Social media, a powerful tool to distribute information across broad audiences, has played an important role in the campaign for reproductive rights. On August 19, 2016 the hashtag #TwoWomenTravel began trending on the microblogging site, Twitter. Composed of 23 tweets, the biography for

@TwoWomenTravel read "Two Women, one procedure, 48 hours away from home": it documented in real time the journey of a woman and her friend to Liverpool for an abortion. Each publicly visible tweet was directly sent to @EndaKennyTD, the Twitter account of then current Taoiseach. This recalled comedian Grainne Maguire's (2015) earlier live tweeting of her period to Kenny. Each aimed to render visible women's corporeality in the public sphere to highlight the restrictions of women's bodies in Ireland. The monotony of the long days were draining for @TwoWomenTravel: "Feel might collapse from exhaustion. No sleep. Friend calm. Brave." The singular corporeal journey temporarily converged with other bodies as they encountered others from Ireland: "Forced to leave Ireland, @EndaKennyTD joined by more Irish in waiting room, waiting for our loved ones." Emphasizing the support of loved ones, @TwoWomenTravel brought a different perspective to this divisive issue, elaborating upon the idea 'someone you know' has had an abortion. It compelled people to question how they might support a woman in this situation. The trending hashtag reached the notice of celebrities including comedian James Cordon: "Today, @TwoWomenTravel but you're not on your own in this. So many people are with you. X" (JKCorden, 2016). With over nine million followers Cordon's message had enormous potential to bring the plight of @TwoWomenTravel and the women of Ireland to an audience nearly double the entire population of the Republic. Irish Minister for Health, Simon Harris, responded directly to the account: "Thanks to @TwoWomenTravel for telling story of reality which faces many. Citizens Assembly—a forum to discuss 8th & make recommendations" (Harris, 2016). This message was the only public acknowledgement of this journey made by a member of the Fine Gael, the majority political party.

The images depicted the mundane: the view from a bus window; the floor of a waiting room in a clinic; a television on the wall of a café; curtains blocking the light from a hotel window. They were evocative because they did not depict an identifiable person, or the body in its entirety. One knee, the smallest tip of a finger, these were visible reminders of the women behind this account. Unlike the imagery utilized by anti-abortion protestors where the fetus is completely disembodied from the maternal body, the @TwoWomenTravel's images called attention to the invisibility of these women. Furthermore, one doesn't need to have knowledge of her reasons for terminating her pregnancy to empathize with her. The implied gaze of the camera's lens, that of her friend, enabled the viewer to identify with the position of the waiting friend. These images are reminiscent of Emma Campbell's *When They Put Their Hands Out Like Scales* (2012), a video work and photographs that depict voyages women from Northern Ireland make to terminate pregnancies. Prefacing the most powerful image by @TwoWomenTravel: "Not the first or the last bleeding woman about to face the long treck [sic] home." It revealed rumpled hotel bedsheets, stained with the faint wash of her blood as it seeped from her tired post-abortion body. This highly affective image captured the cruelty of exiling women for their healthcare choices. The stain on the sheet suggested that no sanitizing of Irish history could completely erase the invisible stain of the reproductive injustices committed.

It is significant that in recent years an increasing number of artworks have identifiable subject matter that relates specifically to abortion journeys. *Renunciation* (2015), a performance, one of the only to mention trans men, by home|work Collective inspired by the Angelus detailed different experiences of those who travel. Siobhán Clancy's participatory workshop 'Choosing Choice: Packing up abortion stigma' invited six people who traveled for abortions to share their personal accounts and create collage cardboard suitcases representative of their experiences. *Case Studies* (2013) was both the process and the resulting artwork meaning the work existed as both the safe space for the dialogic exchange of experiences as well as the material objects each participant created over the course of the workshop. *Case Studies* provoked an understanding of the complexities of individual experiences as well as how visual art can enable a sense of solidarity when activating embodied experiences. The suitcases represented 'abortion tourism,' a phrase that describes the phenomenon of women traveling to jurisdictions where abortion is legal. This stark understanding of 'tourism' is compounded by the fabrication of a holiday

Figure 2.6   Siobhán Clancy, *Case Studies*, 2013, Mixed Media.

for pleasure to conceal the true purpose, as evidenced by a tag on the suitcase: "Scheduling annual leave and holiday pay. Counting the hours and days the pounds and cents ... waiting, anxiously 'Looking forward' to our abortion/ holiday seeing the sights—inside the clinic." It contained a pregnancy test, a urine sample cup, and a pair of heart-shaped sunglasses. Another case bore a painted yellow submarine, juxtaposing the reference to Liverpool as a holiday destination for Beatles fans with that of its more somber destination for abortion seekers. The importance of *Case Studies* is twofold: it revealed hidden stories of travelling for abortion—the planning, the emotional and financial hardship, the secrecy and lies—while it created a space where those who had abortions could share their stories without fear of condemnation. Clancy (2013) aimed to bring a nuanced understanding to the subject by avoiding the "type of sloganeering they may typically associate with political discourse on the subject of abortion." Similarly, Katie Gillum's *Women Have Abortions Everyday: It's Just One Choice* (2013), a short film funded by the Irish Family Planning Association and the International Planned Parenthood Federation, dispelled myths about abortion placing it within the larger framework of life's decisions and pathways. Likewise, Melissa Thompson's earlier documentary *Like a Ship in the Night* (2006) focused on four, anonymous women, as they unpacked their reasons behind their decisions to end their pregnancies. Putting these stories in the public realm with compassion and sensitivity enabled these artworks and embodied gestures to counter the stigma and cultural silencing of those who chose to terminate a pregnancy.

The symbolism of the suitcase, in an Irish context, also represented the hundreds of thousands of Irish women and men who have emigrated from the Irish shores.[12] Furthermore a connection can be drawn between the figure of the emigrant and women who must travel abroad for abortions. The *X-ile Project* (2015 to present), a series of photographic portraits depicting women who have traveled for abortions underscores this point, while the 'X' in the title drew parallels with the X-case (which will be discussed later in this chapter). The image of an exiled woman whose reproductive freedom is forsaken by her nation is a powerful one. Similarly, Sarah Pierce's *Between the Devil and the Deep Blue Sea*, a crisp, solitary ferry rail ticket from Dublin port to London terminals also addressed the issue of exile from the Irish nation. It is dated April 24, 2016, Easter Monday, 100 years after the Easter Rising that signaled the beginning of the armed struggle for Irish Independence. Though the single ticket does not disclose the purchaser's circumstances, its presentation in a glass display case, a nod to 'break glass in case of emergency' and, by extension, the UK's role as a pressure release valve for Irish women seeking terminations, also suggested the sobering, solitary journey.

Ben Hickey's *Pearl* (2016), a photograph of a woman seated on a suitcase with the Dublin Poolbeg towers in the background similarly referenced travel and the legacy of colonial history. The image alluded to John Lavery's *Portrait of Lady Lavery as Kathleen Ni Houlihan* (1928) the iconic image of Hazel Lavery in the guise of the literary figure that personified Ireland as an old woman who calls her sons to take up arms. Lavery's image featured on Irish banknotes from 1928–1970, the metaphorical commodification of women's bodies. In *Pearl*, a suitcase bearing airline destination luggage tags was substituted for the emblematic Irish harp, implying that her travel has already occurred. Considering *Pearl*, with its historic references to money, alongside that of *Case Studies*, the *X-ile Project*, and *Between the Devil and the Deep Blue Sea*, different factors associated with traveling for abortions emerge, including cost, absence from work, and the feelings of physical and psychological exile of women. It is important to note that the right to travel only extends to certain types of women. These works provocatively question how hierarchies of class, race, age, ability, economic status, and immigration status function to divide women into two groups, those who can travel for abortions and those who cannot.

In terms of contemporary cultural production visualizing reproductive injustices, at present the author is unaware of any artworks that overtly address Irish experiences of the abortion pill. It has been illegally imported by people in Ireland for at least 13 years, as the Dutch organization Women on Waves (WOW) has supplied pills to women in Ireland since 2004. This reflects the double marginalization of women who cannot travel and put themselves at great legal risk to take illegal abortion pills. Áine Phillips's performance *Aspiration* (2014) addressed 'backstreet abortions' in addition to bodily experience and visibility when she physically wrestled with 700 clothing hangers. The hangers symbolized 'back-street,' unsafe and illegal abortion methods in which women use a sharp object or wire such as a knitting needle or clothes hanger to break the amniotic sac, signifying desperation and the potential danger women risk to control fertility. For Phillips, 700 represents 1% of 70,000 women worldwide that die annually from backstreet abortions (Singh, Wulf, Hussain, Bankole, & Sedgh, 2009, p. 32) linking national and global reproductive issues. The title *Aspiration* denotes the action of drawing fluid by suction from a vessel or cavity: a gynecological procedure that is associated with abortion. Aspiration also represents desire, hope, or focus toward a goal, suggestive of the goal of recognizing the bodily autonomy of reproductive bodies in Ireland. At various points of the performance, Phillips repeatedly sang 'a song for X.' The symbolism of this is that X was the anonymous name given to the 14-year-old girl at the heart of the X case (1992), the landmark case that tested the Eighth Amendment, resulting in further referendums, notably the 13th Amendment that clarified women had a right to travel to obtain abortions.[13] X also bears a more sinister Irish reference, for in the early 1950s an Irish woman referred to as 'Mrs. X' in the newspapers,

later revealed as Mamie Cadden, was sentenced to 56 years in prison for procuring abortions for eight women (Conroy, 1992, p. 128). At protests Irish
pro-choice campaigners frequently place two pieces of black tape in an X over
their mouths referencing the X case and the continued silencing of women
with regards to reproductive control of their own bodies. When Phillips
raised her voice in this way, she united the specific struggles for reproductive
control of women's bodies in Ireland with ongoing global struggles, in doing
so her embodied protest was a refusal to be silenced.

Pairing hangers with the maternal figure, *Aspiration* can be read against
the iconic scene from the cult film *Mommie Dearest* (1981), Christina Crawford's autobiographical account of child abuse she endured at the hands of her
adopted mother Joan Crawford. In the scene, Joan Crawford, played by Faye
Dunaway, discovered Christina has hung up her clothes on wire hangers.
Crawford exclaimed "No Wire Hangers," ripped the clothes from the closet
and then beat her daughter with a hanger. Though a symbol of abortion, the
wire hanger, framed in the context 'bad mothers,' provokes examination of
the perceived dichotomy between good and bad mothers. Lentin (2013),
paraphrasing Gerardine Meaney, argued, "Ireland has a long history of pitch-
ing 'Good (Catholic, Married) mothers' versus 'Bad (Unmarried) mothers'"
(p. 133). Potentially more transgressive is the deliberate decision not to
become a mother, for as Smyth (1992) argued "In a society where motherhood remains virtually the only secure source of canonised validation for the
vast majority of women, the decision not to be a mother is deeply subversive
and risky" (p. 144). It is relevant that UK 2016 statistics show nearly half of
women (47%) from Ireland accessing abortion are those who are already
mothers (p. 79). This problematizes the constructed binary of good/bad
mothers, for when women who are already mothers terminate a pregnancy,
they are likely prioritizing the lives of their children. The interlocking hangers
of *Aspiration*, nearly impossible to separate out as individual forms, suggested
the nuances and the tangled complexities of women's reproductive lives. This
work, like the others discussed, demonstrates the power of the visual to negotiate the ever-changing socio-political climate in Ireland.

Conclusion
This chapter argued that embodied politics is a feminist strategy utilized by
those advocating for access to abortion in Ireland. Although only a handful of
examples from Irish art and visual culture that visualize reproductive rights
have been examined, the sheer number of artworks, exhibitions, illustrations,
dance, and theatre productions identified in the course of the research for this
chapter indicates Ireland is in the midst of an important cultural shift. The
intersections of gendered histories and activism in several images including
Pro-choice Proclamation drew upon the physical and metaphorical bodies of

Figure 2.7 Áine Phillips, *Aspiration*, 2014, Performance, Catalyst Arts Gallery, Belfast.
Photograph: Jordan Hutchings.

women aligning the personal with the political. The Repeal Project and related imagery illustrated how a simple word, worn on the body, can provoke discussion of reproductive rights. Out of Maser's censored mural came acts of public solidarity and resistance as well as one of the most recognizable symbols associated with the contemporary reproductive justice movement in Ireland. The live tweeting of an abortion journey by @TwoWomenTravel made the personal political by rendering visible the invisible journeys for reproductive healthcare. Entanglements of visual art and body politics in *Case Studies* and *Aspiration*, amongst other works, represented the complexities of decision-making and lived experiences, while countering the cultural denial and erasure of those experiences. It is particularly striking how most of the images examined highlight the gaps and silences of the stories of those who have left Ireland to exercise autonomy over their pregnant bodies; the journey itself is an act of embodied politics. Although embodied politics strategically employ resistance, it is important to acknowledge that structural changes are needed to produce societal change on a larger scale in Irish society. While the reproductive rights movement has momentum behind it, now is not the time for complacency. Patriarchy is persistent, ever shifting, and adapting in a bid to maintain power. Art and visual culture highlights the pressing need for meaningful conversations about abortion access in Ireland. It offers innovative ways of fleshing out the nuances and complexities of women's reproductive lives, encouraging examination of the reasons why reproductive freedom is of paramount importance in Ireland.

Post Script: In early March 2018 the referendum bill was introduced and debated by both houses of the *Oireachtas*. Receiving majority support, the bill was passed despite opposition from anti-choice legislators who sought to deny the people of Ireland from even having their democratic say on the issue. On May 25, 2018, the 36th Amendment to the Irish Constitution was passed by an overwhelming majority of 66.40% Yes (1,429,981) to 33.6% No (723,632), revoking the Eighth Amendment and replacing it with the clause "Provision may be made in law for regulation of termination of a pregnancy." I campaigned alongside fellow activists in my local constituency group Dublin Bay North Repeal the 8th, a member of the Coalition to Repeal the 8th and the Together for Yes campaign. Dublin Bay North returned a resounding Yes vote (74.7%) with the second highest voter turnout (71.6%) in the country. The personal stories women shared about the impact of the Eighth Amendment on their reproductive lives in relation to abortion access, miscarriage, and autonomy in child birth while canvassing for votes on the doorsteps and more broadly on social media was a major defining feature of this campaign.

Notes

1 The state acknowledges the right to life of the unborn and, with due regard to the equal right to life of the mother, guarantees in its laws to respect, and, as far as practicable, by its laws to defend and vindicate that right.

2 This legislation resulted from the tragic death of Savita Halappanavar (October 28, 2012). She attended National University Hospital, Galway with a miscarriage; however when was clear the pregnancy could not be saved she requested a termination. This request was denied, as she was told "This is a Catholic country." She developed septicemia and died of multiple organ failure. See Holland and Cullen (2012).

3 The Department of Arts, Heritage, Regional, Rural and Gaeltacht Affairs is responsible for state-sponsored events advised by a non-partisan expert board composed mainly of academic historians.

4 Article 41.2.1: "In particular, the State recognises that by her life within the home, woman gives to the State a support without which the common good cannot be achieved." Article 41.2.2: "The State shall, therefore, endeavour to ensure that mothers shall not be obliged by economic necessity to engage in labour to the neglect of their duties in the home."

5 During symphysiotomy the pubic bone is sawed in half to widen the pelvis during childbirth. It was carried out without consent on birthing women in Ireland (1950–1980), long after it was used in Western Europe. It was advocated by Catholic-run maternity hospitals instead of caesareans in order to prevent limiting the number of births. Women who underwent symphysiotomies suffered incontinence, difficulty walking, and chronic pain.

6 In Ireland, asylum seekers are institutionalized in direct provision where they reside until refugee status is granted. They cannot work, or obtain state funding for third level education or social welfare benefits. They often live in appalling conditions, sometimes an entire family housed in a single room with shared cooking facilities, and sometimes they are unable to cook their own meals, eating what the direct provision facility provides them (see O'Brien, 2013).

7 Joseph Beuys, Adrian Piper, Suzanne Lacy, and Tania Bruguera are associated with dialogic activist art.

8 *The Abortion Papers Ireland: Volume 1* was re-released with the publication of the second volume in 2015.

9 Artists Cecily Brennan, Eithne Jordan, Alice Maher, and writers Paula Meehan, Lia Mills, Mairead O'hEocha, and Rachel-Rose O' Leary founded 'The Artists' Campaign to Repeal the 8th.'

10 In 2015 a 21-year-old woman was charged and found guilty for supplying poison to induce a miscarriage and unlawfully procuring an abortion. The case was brought after her housemates reported her to the police citing her lack of regret. In another a mother who purchased and distributed abortion pills to her 15-year-old daughter was charged under the NI legislation (Bell, 2016).

11 On Cummins' work see Antosik-Parsons (2015).

12 See Antosik-Parsons (2014) on visualizing migration in contemporary art.

13 Article 40.3.3: "This subsection shall not limit freedom to travel between the State and another state."

References

Antosik-Parsons, K. (2014). Mobility, migrancy and memory: Visualizing belonging and displacement in Jaki Irvine's *The Silver Bridge* (2003). In R. Boyd & D. S. Nititham

(Eds.), *Heritage, diaspora and the consumption of culture: Movements in Irish landscapes* (135–158). London: Ashgate.

Antosik-Parsons, K. (2015). The development of Irish feminist performance art in the 1980s and the early 1990s. In A. Phillips (Ed.), *The history of performance art in Ireland* (174–207). London: Live Art Development Agency and Reaktion Books.

Barry, U. (2015). Discourses on foetal rights and women's embodiment. In A. Quilty, S. Kennedy, & C. Conlon (Eds.), *The Abortion Papers Ireland: Volume 2* (118–132). Dublin: Attic Press.

Baume, S. (2015, March 15). In praise of Peig Sayers. *Irish Times*. Retrieved from www. irishtimes.com/culture/books/in-praise-of-peig-sayers-by-sara-baume-1.2124500.

Bell, G. (2016, January 14). "Abortion Pill" case leads to Belfast protests by pro-choice campaigners. *Irish Times*. Retrieved from www.irishnews.com/news/northernireland news/2016/01/14/news/-abortion-pill-case-leads-to-belfast-protests-by-pro-choice-campaigners-382767/.

Bhreathnach-Lynch, S. (2007). *Ireland's Art, Ireland's History: Representing Ireland, 1845 to Present*. Omaha, NE: Creighton University Press.

BreakingNews.ie. (2016, October 25). TD Bríd Smith produces packet of abortion pills in Dáil. *Breaking News*. Retrieved from www.breakingnews.ie/ireland/watch-td-brid-smith-produces-packet-of-abortion-pills-in-dail-761011.html.

Calls for "Censorship" to stop as "REPEAL" jumpers cut from Dáil TV feed (2017, March 8). *Nationalist*. Retrieved from www.carlow-nationalist.ie/2017/03/08/two-tds-wore-repeal-jumpers-to-dail-amid-complaints/.

Clancy, S. (2013). *Case studies: Abortion artefacts*. Dublin: The Exchange. Exhibition information handout.

Conroy, P.J. (1992). Outside the jurisdiction, Irish women seeking abortion. In A. Smyth (Ed.), *The Abortion Papers Ireland: Volume 1* (119–137). Dublin: Attic Press.

Cosgrave, A. (2016, August). Repeal Project founder Anna Cosgrave: Repeal Project is my micro contribution to a movement spanning decades. Retrieved from www.her.ie/ repeal/repeal-project-founder-anna-cosgrave-repeal-project-is-my-micro-contribution-to-a-movement-spanning-decades/308025.

Devine, C. (2016, July 26). Putting blue paint over it won't make it go away: Protest held over the removal of Repeal the 8th mural at Temple Bar. *Irish Independent*. Retrieved from www.independent.ie/irish-news/news/putting-blue-paint-over-it-wont-make-it-go-away-protest-held-over-the-removal-of-repeal-the-8th-mural-at-temple-bar-34913 753.html.

Eardman, J. (2016). The politics of global abortion rights. *Brown Journal of World Affairs* 22(2), 39–57.

Ferriter, D. (2009). *Occasions of sin: Sex and society in modern Ireland*. London: Profile Books.

Finn, C. (2016, October 17). Examining the dress code of other parliaments is ridiculous. *Journal*. Retrieved from www.thejournal.ie/dail-dress-3027188-Oct2016/?utm_source= shortlink.

Fixmer, N., & Wood, J.T. (2005). The personal is still political: Embodied politics in Third Wave Feminism. *Women's Studies in Communication* 28(2), 235–257.

Freyne, P. (2016, November 18). Maser the street artist: I did the Brown Thomas windows for the wedge. *Irish Times*. Retrieved from www.irishtimes.com/culture/music/maser-the-street-artist-i-did-the-brown-thomas-windows-for-the-wedge-1.2868946.

Fuentes, M. (2015). Performance, politics, and protest. In D. Taylor & M. Steuernagel (Eds.), *What is performance studies?* Durham, NC: Duke University Press. Retrieved from http://scalar.usc.edu/nehvectors/wips/index.

Griffin, S.M. (2016, September 21). We face this land. *Irish Times*. Retrieved from www.irishtimes.com/culture/books/we-face-this-land-a-poem-by-sarah-maria-griffin-1.27 99708.

Harris, S. (2016, August 21). @SimonHarrisTD, Twitter, 3:58 p.m.

Holland, K., & Cullen, P. (2012, November 14). Woman "denied termination" dies in hospital. *Irish Times*.

JKCorden. (2016, August 20). Today, @TwoWomenTravel but you're not on your own in this. So many people are with you. X [Tweet]. Retrieved from https://twitter.com/JKCorden/status/766903540069507072.

Lawler, A. (2016, October 16). Repeal jumpers: When trend becomes statements. *University Observer*. Retrieved from www.universityobserver.ie/otwo/repeal-jumpers-when-trends-become-statements/.

Lentin, R. (2013). A woman died: Abortion and the politics of birth in Ireland. *Feminist Review 105*, 130–136.

Lippard, L. (2015). Trojan horses: Activist art and power (1984). In H. Robinson (Ed.), *Feminism art theory 1968–2014* (69–79). London: Wiley Blackwell.

Lord, M. (2016, September 27). Yes, Taoiseach, abortion is not black and white. *Irish Times*. Retrieved from www.irishtimes.com/news/politics/oireachtas/miriam-lord-yes-taoiseach-abortion-is-not-black-and-white-1.2807930.

McDermott, M. (2016, July 25). "Repeal the 8th" mural in Project Arts Centre in Temple Bar removed. *Irish Times*. Retrieved from www.irishtimes.com/news/environment/repeal-the-8th-mural-in-project-arts-centre-in-temple-bar-removed-1.2733842.

Maguire, G. (2015, November 16). Why I decided to live tweet my menstrual cycle to Enda Kenny. *Irish Times*. Retrieved from www.irishtimes.com/life-and-style/people/grainne-maguire-why-i-decided-to-live-tweet-my-menstrual-cycle-to-enda-kenny-1.2431917.

Meaney, G. (1991). *Sex and nation: Women in Irish culture and politics*. Dublin: Attic Press.

Mommie Dearest. (1981). Director Frank Perry, Paramount Pictures.

Murphy, P. (1998). Madonna and maiden, mistress and mother: Woman as symbol of Ireland and spirit of the nation. In J.C. Steward (Ed.), *When time began to rant and rage: Figurative painting from twentieth-century Ireland* (90–101). Berkeley: University of California Press.

Murray, C. (2016, December 16). Carphone Warehouse told to stop controversial "pro-choice" adverts. *Irish Independent*. Retrieved from www.independent.ie/irish-news/carphone-warehouse-told-to-stop-controversial-prochoice-adverts-35299144.html.

O Cionnaith, C. (2016, September 27). "Repeal" wearing TDs to face disciplinary action after breaking rules. *Irish Examiner*. Retrieved from www.irishexaminer.com/breaking news/ireland/repeal-wearing-tds-to-face-disciplinary-action-after-breaking-rules-756 723.html.

O'Brien, C. (2013, October 28). State fears reform of system will attract asylum seekers. *Irish Times*. Retrieved from www.irishtimes.com/news/social-affairs/state-fears-reform-of-system-will-attract-asylum-seekers-1.1575210.

O'Brien, H. (2016, August 8). How the Maser mural galvanised the Movement to Repeal the 8th. *Hot Press*. Retrieved from www.hotpress.com/Maser-Mural-Repeal-the-8th/features/reports/How-the-Maser-mural-galvanised-the-Movement-to-Repeal-the-8th/17935211.html.

Oaks, L. (1999). Irish trans/national politics and locating fetuses. In L. Morgan & M. Michaels (Eds.), *Fetal subjects, feminist positions* (175–195). Philadelphia: University of Pennsylvania Press.

Protection of Life During Pregnancy Act (2013). Irish Statute. Retrieved from www.irish
    statutebook.ie/eli/2013/act/35/enacted/en/pdf.
Quilty, A., Kennedy, S., & Conlon, C. (Eds.). (2015). *The Abortion Papers Ireland: Volume
    2*. Dublin: Attic Press.
Radner, J.N., & Lanser, S.S. (1993). Strategies of coding in women's cultures. In J.N.
    Radner (Ed.), *Feminist messages: Coding in women's folk culture* (1–27). Chicago: Univer-
    sity of Illinois Press.
Singh, S., Wulf, D., Hussain, R., Bankole, A., & Sedgh, G. (2009). *Abortion worldwide: A
    decade of uneven progress*. Guttmacher Institute. Retrieved from www.guttmacher.org/
    sites/default/files/pdfs/pubs/AWWfullreport.pdf.
Smyth, A. (1992). The politics of abortion in a police state. *The Abortion Papers Ireland:
    Volume 1* (138–148). Dublin: Attic Press.
The Train. (2015). Arthur Riordan and Bill Whelan, Rough Magic Theatre Company
"This ad is being blasted on social media, but is it offensive?" (2016, October 26). *Irish
    Times*. Retrieved from www.irishtimes.com/news/social-affairs/this-ad-is-being-blasted-
    on-social-media-but-is-it-offensive-1.2844457.
Two Women Travel. (2016). Two Women Travel [Twitter]. Retrieved from https://
    twitter.com/twowomentravel?lang=en.
Union of Students in Ireland. (2017). *Citizens Assembly presentation*. Retrieved from www.
    citizensassembly.ie/en/Meetings/Union-of-Students-in-Ireland-s-Paper.pdf.
"We're Pro-choice" Carphone Warehouse advertisements: What do you make of it? (2016,
    October 24). *Abortion Rights Campaign*. Retrieved from www.abortionrightscampaign.
    ie/2016/10/24/were-pro-choice-carphone-warehouse-advertisements-what-do-you-
    make-of-it/.

3

POPULATION DISCOURSE, FAMILY PLANNING POLICIES, AND DEVELOPMENT IN COLOMBIA, 1960–1969

ALISA SÁNCHEZ

Over the course of a few short years in the 1960s, Colombia seemingly transformed from a traditional, staunchly Catholic country to a modernizing country at the forefront of research and action on what many leaders and experts worldwide considered a grave threat to humanity: rapid population growth. Scientific experts in medicine, demography, agriculture, and sociology, across multiple countries, characterized rapid population growth as a serious global problem and brought it to public attention. Political and non-profit leaders championed the message and helped make the population "crisis" visible, using their powerful positions to make speeches and support funding for population initiatives. National governments, scientific experts, private foundations, and non-governmental organizations joined together to advance population research and implement family planning policies. The Catholic Church debated family planning extensively, from the highest level at the Vatican to parish priests and lay Catholics. Beyond theological concerns, many Latin American Catholics, along with nationalists across the political spectrum, criticized family planning as a US imperialist plot to reduce the numbers of Latin Americans.

Despite concerns about the Colombian Catholic Church's reaction, in 1966 Colombian President Carlos Lleras Restrepo implemented the country's first family planning policy, which funded family planning training for 1200 physicians. In 1969, Colombia became the first country in South America to

incorporate a population policy of lowering fertility into its national development plan. Population leaders and experts in the late 1960s and since charac-
terize Colombia as an unexpected success for having developed family
planning policies in a highly Catholic context. For example, two highly
respected population researchers active since the 1960s remark, "The Colombian case is such an outstanding success story that imagining a better scenario
is hard" (Measham and López-Escobar 133).

This chapter draws out the crucial role that opposition to abortion played
in motivating and legitimating Colombia's family planning policies. In
studying the discourses surrounding family planning in 1960s Colombia,
focusing on a close reading of 1967 Colombian Senate hearings attacking the
first national family planning policy, I show how proponents for family planning policies presented contraceptive education and access as a crucial intervention for decreasing abortions among Colombian women. Although those
for and against family planning policies disagreed over a great deal—whether
lowering the fertility rate was necessary to achieve social and economic development, to what extent the state should be involved in the family—they were
largely united in condemning abortion as unsafe and immoral, which ultimately helped justify family planning initiatives.

The chapter makes a larger argument about how the role of abortion in
this period reveals the chauvinist biopolitics of the time, analyzing three areas
of discourse around family planning: first, a transnational population discourse, which communicated urgent concern over the population "crisis" and
spread the idea of lowering fertility; second, discourse focused specifically on
Latin American abortion rates; and, finally, discourse among Colombian
political elites, centered on 1967 Colombian Senate hearings in which
Colombian government agency officials defended the first national family
planning policy. A close reading shows that the government distanced itself
from population discourse, instead aligning itself with Catholic Church
philosophy to defend its 1966 policy and general interest in population.

Religious and bureaucratic arguments for contraceptives as abortion prevention helped establish family planning policies that increased women's
reproductive autonomy. However, in making these arguments against abortion, male politicians and researchers also rejected and silenced women's
voices about their reproductive lives and decision-making. Through this study
of the first national family planning policy in Colombia, we see how what
women need and want with regard to reproduction is assumed, interpreted on
the basis of insufficient evidence, and disregarded; and yet, nevertheless, is
treated as unassailable knowledge, which is then used to justify reproductive
policies and norms profoundly affecting women's reproductive autonomy.

This chapter reveals how 1960s family planning policy in Colombia
pursued goals rooted within the narrow lenses of population crisis discourse

and Catholic ideology, rather than seeking to understand people's experiences of life, reproduction, and death in order to improve their lives with their input and dialogue. The chapter situates the story of abortion rights and family planning in Colombia within a feminist analysis to account for how economic, social, and political aspects shape abortion and reproductive actions more broadly. In the process, it shows the importance of including women in policy making not simply as biopolitical subjects, but also as leaders in interpreting and explaining their experience.

The 1966 Policy and the Colombian Population Context

As elaborated below, participants in 1960s population discourse recommended lowering fertility as the best solution to what they called the population "crisis," or that rapid population growth would outpace government and environmental capacity to meet people's basic needs. Population leaders and experts were excited at recent technological advances in contraceptives, especially the long-acting intrauterine device (IUD) and new forms of birth control pills. Widespread family planning, defined as the ability of parents to control the timing and spacing of having children, seemed within reach. Those concerned with overpopulation became avid proponents of national-scale family planning programs.

In Colombia, population policies and family planning programs were the product of partnerships across multiple entities: the Colombian government; the Colombian Association of Medical Schools (ASCOFAME) and its Division of Population Studies (DEP); PROFAMILIA (an affiliate of the International Planned Parenthood Federation); the Ford Foundation; and the Population Council. ASCOFAME and the Ford Foundation were early partners in stimulating Colombian population research, co-sponsoring a 1964 conference "for the study of Colombian demographic problems" that "was most successful" (Delgado García 251). At this meeting, ASCOFAME founded the DEP (*División de Estudios de la Población*). The DEP began conducting research in fertility, family planning, abortion, and socio-demography in January 1965 under the leadership of Hernán Mendoza Hoyos, a physician (Mendoza Hoyos "The Colombian Program" 827). In addition to research activities, DEP also arranged for Colombian professionals to receive training at home and abroad in demography and family planning (Delgado García 252; Mendoza Hoyos "The Colombian Program" 827–828). Mendoza was by all accounts a formidable advocate for family planning policies as a response to Colombia's accelerating population growth (Ott 3; Measham and López-Escobar 125).

The year 1965 also saw the founding of PROFAMILIA, an affiliate of the International Planned Parenthood Federation (IPPF) led by two Colombian physicians who hoped to make contraceptives (especially the IUD) available to women of lesser means and in rural areas. PROFAMILIA clinics dramatically increased women's health services in the country; the non-profit "quickly became the most outstanding IPPF affiliate and a recognized pioneer in the delivery of community-based family planning services" (Measham and López-Escobar 124).[1] DEP and PROFAMILIA operated independently but shared a broad mission of increasing Colombians' family planning knowledge and contraceptive use. DEP focused on research and training Colombian professionals, while PROFAMILIA provided family planning services to Colombian women. Both organizations also developed family planning educational materials and promoted family planning media coverage in press, radio, and television. With dedicated leaders and international funding, DEP and PROFAMILIA helped transform the Colombian family planning landscape between 1965 and 1969. Finally, international institutions, largely based in the US, were vital to DEP and PROFAMILIA's work. Private foundations, non-profits, and universities provided funding and training for Colombian family planning research and services (Delgado García 252).

DEP and PROFAMILIA's activities encouraged a receptive Colombian government to develop family planning policies. President Carlos Lleras Restrepo (1966–1970) was an economist who entered the presidency already concerned with deleterious effects of population growth (Measham and López-Escobar 124). Lleras Restrepo authorized his Minister of Health, Antonio Ordoñez Plaja, to work with DEP to develop the 1966 and 1969 family planning policies and to defend the government's involvement in family planning as needed. Although Lleras Restrepo and Ordoñez supported family planning policies, the Lleras Restrepo administration allowed DEP and PROFAMILIA to publicly advocate family planning—or in the words of some scholars, serve as "convenient lightning rods to deflect criticisms" (Measham and López-Escobar 125, see also Ott 3).

Policies are sets of guidelines and rules that a government sets out to pursue a specific goal. Policies differ from laws in that the former are not subject to the legislative process. The nature of these actions as policies reflects both the extremely sensitive nature of the topic in Colombia at this time, which was handled more quietly than legislation or judicial decision.

The 1966 policy was the Colombian government's first financial and programmatic commitment to family planning. This policy consisted of a contract between the Colombian Ministry of Health and ASCOFAME, in which the Ministry of Health committed the use of the United States Agency for International Development (USAID) counterpart[2] funds to train 1200 public hospital physicians in family planning; ASCOFAME was charged with designing and carrying out the training (*Anales* 251; Ott 3; Stycos *Ideology* 147). The contract thus created a partnership between the Colombian government and a non-profit association to train doctors as frontline family planning educators to the wider public. It signified President Carlos Lleras Restrepo's vision that family planning was important for curbing population growth and achieving economic and social development, a vision he expressed in multiple statements during his presidency (*Anales* 275; Sanders "Family Planning" 3). At the same time, the 1966 policy created some distance between the government and actual service delivery on family planning, since ASCOFAME was in charge of training. Scholars note that Lleras Restrepo was careful to keep some distance between the Colombian government and family planning during the first years of his presidency, as he sought to pass constitutional reforms and wished to avoid backlash over a controversial topic like family planning (Ott 4). Nevertheless, there was vociferous backlash against the 1966 policy from the Colombian Catholic Church and its conservative supporters, which came to a head during 1967 Senate hearings attacking government involvement in family planning. To understand both how the 1966 policy, the first of its kind in Colombia, came to be and how it was able to succeed, we now take a closer look at the discourses surrounding family planning in 1960s Colombia.

Population Discourse and Explaining the Population "Crisis"

I use the term "population discourse" to describe discourse concerned with population growth based on scientific assessments of how population growth rates would affect economic and social development, especially in "developing" countries. Population discourse began in the 1950s postwar era and was firmly established as a leading knowledge worldwide during the 1960s. This is evidenced by the worldwide explosion of writing, conferences, training programs, aid programs, policies, and laws during the 1960s on assessing population growth, predicting its impact, and developing initiatives to slow rapid growth. Participants in population discourse included politicians, technocrats at government agencies, physicians, demographers, sociologists, and nonprofit and philanthropic staff, among others. I refer to this group as "population leaders and experts" to emphasize the great number who are political leaders or trained specialists.

To develop a sense of the transnational population and development discourse at this time, I studied a range of primary documents from Colombia, the United States, and the United Nations, published in Spanish and English. These documents included articles from demography and population journals; proceedings of population and development conferences; writings of Colombian academics in medical demography; speeches from Colombian and US presidents; US Senate and Colombian Senate sessions; and speeches from the United Nations and private US foundations. From studying these sources, I identified lines of argument and concerns representative of population discourse during 1960–1969.

An example of the collaboration among institutions and countries that characterized 1960s population discourse is the United Nations' "Declaration of Population," issued on Human Rights Day, 1966. The one-page "Declaration of Population" consists of three short statements urging action on rapid population growth. In order, the statements are by United Nations Secretary General U Thant; 12 heads of state, including Colombian President Carlos Lleras Restrepo, the only Latin American signatory; and John D. Rockefeller the third, a US philanthropist and Chairman of the Board of the Population Council. Rockefeller proclaims the heads of state "deserve our admiration and respect" because they "have recognized the seriousness of this sensitive problem and are actively facing up to it" (1). The Declaration's show of unity, in statements like Rockefeller's and in the fact of its joint authorship, demonstrates the authors' conviction that population increase is an issue to confront together, that crosses national and organizational boundaries. A leading family planning researcher of the time, J.M. Stycos, called the Declaration "[p]erhaps the most remarkable document of the century" for bringing together motley parties to assert population increase was a grave matter for all the world over ("Prospects" 277).

Origins of the "Crisis": Diminished Death and Abundant Life
In the opening speech at the 1965 Pan-American Assembly on Population, held in Cali, Colombia, former Colombian president Alberto Lleras Camargo explains the population crisis rose due to a dramatic drop in mortality rates. Death had been, he observes, "master and lady of humankind": "a galaxy of illnesses" had "kept life expectancy very low in the underdeveloped countries" (611). However, science and funding had transformed death into a problem that researchers, governments, and donors could tackle. Lleras elaborates,

> extremely effective chemical ... methods [of killing disease vectors such as mosquitoes] were cheap and the international team placed took up the charge of spreading them to those places where if it were up to indigenous peoples, they would never have arrived.
>
> (611)

Lleras credits the perseverance of an "international team" to having reduced disease using scientific weapons. His statement is representative of a common tenet in population crisis discourse, namely, that developed countries were largely responsible for global lowered mortality rates, since their scientific expertise and financial contributions sustained developing countries' public health campaigns combating common and lethal diseases. And yet, population leaders and experts determined that the mortality decline had rendered life into a problem.

Lowered mortality translated to more children surviving to reproductive age, resulting in greater numbers of people having children each generation. Children who would have died before "beginning or concluding their period of fecundity" were now multiplying beyond themselves (Lleras Camargo 611). Leona Baumgartner, a physician and high official at USAID from 1962–1965, personalizes exponential population growth through the figure of an individual "girl baby":

> As someone has recently written, "the girl baby spared from death in early childhood contributes not only her own life to the world's people but the lives of the children she produces as she moves through her reproductive years, followed in turn by the lives of the children's children, and so on."
>
> (280)

The quotation conveys an image of cascading offspring starting from the survival of one female infant. This image raises the stakes of the girl's reproduction; every single number counts—not only the baby just born, but also the future offspring that this baby will add to the world during her reproductive years, for endless future generations. While population leaders and experts are by no means calling for a return to higher infant mortality rates, they explicitly desire fewer numbers of lives.

Science, donor aid, and government intervention are perceived as key elements for addressing the problem of "life," similar to how the problem of "death" had been handled. To lower fertility, population leaders and experts would turn to family planning.

Stakes of the "Crisis": Peace and Prosperity
Population experts and leaders worried about the implications of an exponentially increasing population. A frequently discussed concern was how such great numbers of people would be fed. While UN Secretary General U Thant warns of future food scarcity "over the two or three decades immediately ahead," expert statements during the 1966 US Senate sessions on the global population crisis reveal a belief that developing countries were already on the brink of food crisis ("Declaration" 1). James Roosevelt, the eldest son of Franklin Delano and Eleanor Roosevelt, and then-US ambassador to UNESCO (United Nations Educational, Scientific, and Cultural Organization), warned that developing countries are only scraping by: "In the developing regions as a whole, food production has bearly [*sic*] kept pace with the population increase" (S.1676 (5) 1067, exhibit 148 by James Roosevelt).[3] Roosevelt portrays a situation in which developing countries are living from hand to mouth, mired in meeting their population's food needs with no release in sight. Like

U Thant and Roosevelt, other population leaders and experts argued for "moderating" population growth based on a concern that many people would starve if growth continued unabated.

Shortages in food (and jobs, housing, education, and other items necessary for decent and productive human lives) are problematic not only because of the human misery they imply, but also, according to population leaders and experts, because social and political turmoil follows from widespread depriva- tion. This causal logic, from lack to uprising, can be said to be a tenet of the population crisis discourse. Various population leaders and experts worry over the "political unrest" (Dorn 290) and "the social conflicts that naturally emerge" from scarcity (Mendoza Hoyos *Sobrepoblación* 18). In population discourse, the concern with food production and other basic human needs, due to growing population, becomes a security issue. When population growth, scarcity, and unrest are linked, the situation appears to be a crisis requiring swift intervention. As María Margarita Fajardo Hernández, a historian of the Colombian medical demography field, points out, "Before such distressing panoramas, taking action would appear to be more of a duty than a choice" (229).

Scarcity raised a second dilemma, according to population leaders and experts: if developing countries were spending all their capital to satisfy the basic needs of their increasing populations, they would miss an opportunity to save and reinvest capital in national modernizing projects such as infrastruc- ture or to participate in the global market. Economic development was a key goal for developing countries during the 1960s, touted as the way to improve living conditions, expand capitalist markets, and prevent Communist eco- nomic and political models from spreading. Following a linear model of eco- nomic growth, US foreign aid and United Nations development programs sought to move developing countries through the stages of economic growth to achieve an end point of "capitalistic modernization," focused on growing industries and markets (Portocarrero 14). Family planning became a major *development* initiative because of the perceived threat population growth posed to capitalist economic growth.

In Latin America, the population's age distribution, with a so-called "youth bulge," is perceived as exacerbating the challenge of economic growth. The US diplomat Thomas Mann[4] explains the difficulties posed by Latin American population structure in detail:

> Latin America is a developing area. The composition of the population is quite different from that in the United States. For example, about one-fourth of the population is less than ten years old. A large portion of the population therefore contributes little to production; rather it is essentially a consumer ... Because a higher percentage of production

must be consumed on the necessities of life, there is less available to invest in farms and factories that are needed to increase production. This is truly one of the dilemmas of the Alliance: how can we best achieve adequate levels of production so essential to social justice and political stability and at the same time meet the desire of the people that production be distributed immediately so that it can be consumed.
(S.1676 (5) 1059, Exhibit 146, Mann, US Coordinator for Alliance for Progress, at Planned Parenthood Conference NYC 1964)

Concerned with increasing production and capital, children become a problematic population category in population crisis discourse. In the quote above, children are translated into economic terms and apprehended as a consumer class, not producers. This reflects anthropologist Arturo Escobar's observation that people become abstracted in development discourse, for the purpose of technical assessment: "Development was—and continues to be for the most part—a top-down, ethnocentric and technocratic approach, which treated people and cultures as abstract concepts, statistical figures to be moved up and down in the charts of 'progress'" (Escobar 91). From the population experts' viewpoint, the barrier to economic growth and prosperity in Latin America is that the continent has too many children; like the archetype of the numerous poor family, the nation has too many dependent mouths to feed. Population leaders and experts seek to transform developing countries' fertility practices as part of a plan to improve their economic standing.

Transnational population discourse assumed a divide between "developed" and "developing" countries, where developing countries needed to curb their fertility for the sake of their own modernization and international peace. While avoiding social unrest and economic development were very motivating for Colombian population leaders and experts, the Colombian government would invoke a third objective, specific to Latin America, to defend the 1966 family planning policy: decreasing abortions.

Latin America, Abortion, and Methodological Innovation
In population discourse, abortion came to represent women's "unmet need" for family planning education and services. Studies on current reproductive practices formed a knowledge base from which Latin America was characterized as having high abortion rates, and abortions were interpreted as women's "unmet need" for family planning education and services. The studies represent an intellectual and funding network dedicated to learning the knowledge, attitudes, practices, and vital statistics of the population with regard to fertility. This section describes the role of population experts' knowledge production in identifying Latin America as a region with excessive abortions and interpreting abortion as women's "unmet need" for family planning education

and services. This had the effect of legitimating transnational investment in Latin American population studies and family planning, and motivating national population policies centered on family planning education and services.

Population researchers spearheaded new methods of collecting data that allowed them to describe reproduction within a specific population. Researchers considered especially important the "KAP" survey, or "sample surveys of *knowledge, attitudes, and practices* with regard to fertility matters" (Berelson 655, my emphasis). The KAP survey filled a gap in the existing types of data available to researchers. Prior to the KAP survey, population researchers relied on censuses to gather information about birth rates. However, as W. Parker Mauldin, the Population Council's Associate Director of the Demographic Division, noted, censuses offered limited information, providing "data about fertility levels, not about attitudes toward family size nor practices of birth control" (2). The KAP survey became the tool to collect such information on attitudes and practices. Questions focused on attitudes toward family size; knowledge about reproduction, contraception, and the recent decline in infant mortality; and reproductive practices, including abortion experiences (Berelson 656). KAP surveys were administered in-person by trained interviewers. In most countries, non-profit national medical associations or universities conducted KAP studies, with technical and financial support from US foundations (Mauldin 2). Celebrating their "objective and scientific" character, population researchers relied on KAP studies to "secure a reliable picture of the present [reproductive] situation" and help design family planning programs (Berelson 665–666).

In Colombia, as throughout Latin America, KAP surveys revealed that Latin American women had low knowledge of family planning and often turned to abortion to control their fertility (Miró 632; Requena 789–790). Reviewing Colombian abortion studies to date in late 1967, Mendoza Hoyos concludes, "that among the communities studied the ideal number of children is achieved and maintained mainly by means of induced abortion" ("Research Studies" 226–227). This held true for women across social classes, education levels, and current family sizes.

Population leaders and experts became concerned that too much abortion was happening in Latin America, even though they were at the same time worried about overpopulation. Latin America, as a region, was characterized as having high abortion rates. Nearly every time "Latin America" appears in population discourse during the 1960s, a mention of the numerous abortions there seems to follow. What follows is a small sampling: the "Final Report" of the 1965 Pan-American Assembly on Population in Cali urges Latin American governments to address their countries' "high incidence of criminal abortion" (Delgado García 255–256). Mauldin writes, "there is a growing and widespread concern, especially about the problem of abortion, which seems to be increasing rapidly among Latin American populations" (2). Mendoza Hoyos also warns in 1968 that "the incidence of abortion seems to be in a progressive upsurge" in Colombia ("Research Studies" 233). Hernán Romero, a Chilean physician and advisor to the largest Chilean family planning non-profit organization, laments, "Nothing exasperates this group [of Chilean physicians] more than the ever increasing disaster of illegal abortions in Chile" (237). Mariano Requena, a leading Chilean population researcher, reports in 1968 that "In the majority of Latin American countries, induced abortion still constitutes the most widely used method or practice to avoid live births" and "In the objectives of all programs related to fertility, the struggle against induced abortion is always mentioned, sometimes to the extent of being pointed out as the central objective" (785).

Population leaders and experts deplored the use of abortion to control fertility. That abortion was illegal throughout Latin America (except for socialist Cuba as of 1965) meant many women suffered through unsafe abortions, experiencing complications often resulting in hospitalization or death. For example, the Colombian DEP studies found abortion complications to be the number one cause of maternal mortality at many hospitals (Mendoza Hoyos "Research Studies" 224). Latin American physicians saw firsthand how unsafe abortions harmed women and reliably supported contraceptive access to decrease abortions (Measham and López-Escobar 122). In addition to women's health, population leaders and experts lamented the high medical costs expended on women's postabortion care (Seltzer and Gomez 9). For example, the Chilean physician Hernán Romero calculates the resources used to treat incomplete abortions at a Santiago hospital during 1960:

> They [women receiving postabortion care] comprise 35% of all opera-tions performed in maternity cases and require 17% of the transfusions and 26.7% of the volume of blood used by emergency services ... they represented 184,000 bed-days and produced, by this single fact alone, an expenditure exceeding $1million. Each survivor of *Clostridium perf-ringens septicemia* [septic abortion] costs over $3,000.
>
> (245)

Romero's calculations reflect a concern for using medical resources. Decreas-ing the number of abortions would free up medical resources to be used else-where. In population discourse, abortion was regarded as dangerous and inefficient.

Abortion was also understood by population leaders and experts as a clear message of "unmet need" for effective contraceptives. An IPPF report com-ments that in Latin America, "the prevalence of wide scale induced illegal abortion is so evident that there can be no question of any lack of motivation to curb fertility" (Deverell 577). In this statement, and others like it, the high incidence of abortion becomes an incontrovertible expression of women's desire to have fewer children. Mendoza also regarded high abortion rates and KAP studies results as women calling for family planning. Across his writings, Mendoza used the phrase *necesidad sentida*, or "felt need," to refer to what he determined abortions signified—namely, women's want of contraceptives (Ott 7). For example, in a 1968 article, Mendoza declared that the knowledge gained from KAP studies demonstrates a "felt need" for family planning: "This knowledge, in turn, has made it possible to show the country its own reality: the existence of a serious population problem and of a strongly felt need for information and services that should be satisfied without delay" ("The Colombian Program" 827).

Occasionally, population researchers raised the question whether women might not want safe, legal abortions in addition to contraceptives (Davis 733, 736). By and large, however, population researchers avoided the topic of legal abortion as too controversial. Abortion would become an important common target during the 1967 Colombian Senate hearings on Colombia's orientation toward population matters.

The 1966 Policy and Response

Objections from the Catholic Church and Conservative Senators

While population leaders and experts wondered whether family planning would fare poorly in Colombia because of a "formidable" Catholic Church, the Church did not express a formal stance toward family planning until the papal encyclical *Humanae Vitae* was issued on July 26, 1968. Before 1968, Church hierarchy and laypersons followed the general admonition to consult their own conscience (Sanders "The Relationship" 3). Individual Colombian priests varied widely on whether they encouraged, accepted, or counseled against their parishioners using contraceptives (Stycos *Ideology* 80–84). The Church's delay in assuming a formal position against contraceptives allowed many people to learn and adopt family planning methods, which people continued even after an official Church position became clear (Sanders "Family Planning" 3; Stycos *Ideology* 76–77).

However, some individuals and groups in the Colombian Catholic Church began publicly attacking family planning once the 1966 policy was announced. The attacks consisted of regular articles against family planning in the most prominent Colombian Catholic periodical, the weekly *El Catolicismo*, from January through August 1967, and a Lent Pastoral Letter by the Colombian Cardinal read in all Bogotá Archdiocese churches during Holy Week, in May 1967 (Mendoza Hoyos "The Colombian Program" 830–831; Stycos *Ideology*

151; Stycos "Prospects" 277). The arguments against family planning were not only based in interpretations that Catholicism repudiated contraceptives, but also in the idea that family planning was a US imperialist plot to intervene in Colombia and reduce the number of Latin Americans. A typical sentiment appears in this *El Catolicismo* article from January 22, 1967:

> One of the most regrettable aspects of the [family planning] campaign is the fact that it amounts to play into the hands of President Johnson, who is determined to sterilize underdeveloped countries in an effort to stop a population growth that implies so many political and financial difficulties for his own country.[5]

The US imperialism argument judged family planning as US elites' convenient solution to a fear of being outnumbered by less-better-off neighbors. The Colombian Catholic Church's campaign against family planning thus rejected the tenets of population discourse and the very idea that rapid population growth was intrinsically problematic. Above all, the Church rejected the idea that the state should be involved in fertility, in contrast to how population discourse justified state intervention given the predicted consequences of "overpopulation" on national development and international peace.

The closest the 1966 policy came to congressional review was two intensive weeks of Senate hearings. During February 1967, two Conservative senators initiated hearings under the title, "Subpoena to the Ministers of Health and Education in order to inform the honorable Senate about Government policy on so-called fertility control" (*Anales* 169). The hearings lasted from February 2 to February 16 and consisted of senators' speeches and questions to the Minister of Health, Antonio Ordoñez Plaja, and the Minister of Education, Gabriel Betancur Mejía. The two senators who convened the hearings were Diego Tovar Concha and Manuel Bayona Carrascal, both stalwarts of the Conservative party.[6]

A close reading of the hearings shows that Conservative senators rejected tenets of population discourse and the idea that Colombia had to accept family planning for social and economic development. Conservative senators emphasized the line of argument in *El Catolicismo* articles, namely that the US was thickly involved in Colombian family planning research and programs with nefarious aims. In an article detailing the backlash to the 1966 policy, Mendoza observed that the "theme of 'BIRTH CONTROL, A NEW WEAPON OF IMPERIALISM' was repeated again and again" during the Senate hearings ("The Colombian Program" 829). Mendoza himself was attacked by some senators as a US pawn, politically driven scientist, or obsessed with power (*Anales* 186, 203). The hearings aired an extensive array of arguments against family planning or state involvement in family planning via policy, with arguments of US imperialism and disrespect to the *Concordato* agreement with the Catholic Church occupying the most time.

A summary of the February 7 session describes Tovar Concha raising the issue of "foreign advisors who intervene in possible solutions to the problem of Colombian fertility" (*Anales* 186). These foreign advisors, Tovar Concha laments, are "converting into the planners of what methods will be adopted" and are "hoping to dictate law for future national demography" (*Anales* 186). He criticizes Mendoza for wielding science to support outsiders' interest in demonstrating that Colombia has a population problem. Tovar Concha claims, "they [demographers] are not developing a scientific investigation, trying to find the truth of the demographic phenomenon, but operate a methodology destined to produce determined effects previously calculated by those who have suggested the survey" (*Anales* 186). It is unclear who the referent is for "those" in Tovar Concha's statement, the "those who have suggested the survey." However, the context indicates that Tovar Concha is thinking here of both Colombian and foreign population experts.

Tovar Concha and Bayona Carrascal also rejected the idea that increasing population growth would stall social and economic development. Considering how to improve Colombians' living conditions, Tovar Concha announces, "the problem is not to be like Herrod, but to redistribute national income" (*Anales* 567). In comparing fertility planning to being like Herrod, Tovar Concha regards family planning akin to slaughter. Herrod was the biblical figure who killed all boys under age two in the Bethlehem "Massacre of Innocents" to protect his throne from a prophesied usurper (Jesus).[7] Tovar Concha suggests rethinking how national income is used as an alternative; he does not elaborate this idea, but his suggestion shows how those opposed to family planning were still considering how Colombia could improve its situation. Bayona Carrascal similarly recognizes the pressures of a growing population, but totally repudiates family planning as the answer:

> Because we cannot accept, to the contrary we greatly reject with horror and limitless indignation this abusive, inhuman, incredible assertion [made] in the century of science and advancements of all kinds, that we must avoid people being born because the Colombian population each day has growing desires and because there are not sufficient resources to give them adequate food, clothing, housing and education.
>
> (*Anales* 567)

Bayona Carrascal expresses faith in scientific advancements to address the challenges of meeting a growing population's basic needs. For Bayona Carrascal, family planning would mean a loss of humanity, not only literally (fewer births), but also philosophically; to accept family planning is to reject those humans who would have been born and deny that humans could resolve their problems at a lesser cost than preventing life. He contends that, if anything, family planning would impede development by diverting doctors' attention and services from vital medical services, such as treating common diseases:

> they [doctors] will not be able to return to their health clinics, because they will be ever more interested in being some hawker of death, some Herrods [*herrodes*] financed by the State so that the Colombian population will not augment in the phantasmagorical form in which they believe it is augmenting.
>
> (*Anales* 567)

Bayona Carrascal intimates there is an allure to family planning, a power of life and death, magnified by a sense of heroism in combating what is believed to be an epic problem. His vivid imagery attacks any family planning doctors' self-importance and undercuts the supposed gravity of a rapidly growing population.

Senators also criticized the Lleras Restrepo administration for potentially violating the *Concordato*, a 1886 international treaty between the Holy See and Colombia that recognized the Catholic Church as the guardian of Christian morality in Colombia and bound Colombia to respect and cooperate with the Church.[8] During Betancur Mejía's questioning, Tovar Concha asks three times, increasingly pressingly, "if the program, the theories, the modus operandi, the development of the program, in the judgment of the Minister of Education is yes or no adhering to the norms of the *Concordato*" (*Anales* 483).

Government Response
To refute charges that the government is contravening the Church, the subpoenaed Ministers, Ordóñez Plaja and Betancur Mejía, affirmed the government's family planning goals are ones the Church also shares. Betancur Mejía draws on a recent presidential statement to show how Lleras Restrepo is principally concerned with the moral aspects of overpopulation. The statement reports on a February 8 summit at the presidential palace among Lleras Restrepo; the Ministers of Health and Education; and two high-ranking Church officials, the President and Vice-president of the Episcopal Conference, the Archbishop of Pamplona and Bishop of the diocese of Sonsón. At the summit, Lleras Restrepo and the Church officials each shared prepared statements about their orientation toward family planning. Lleras Restrepo's opening sentences portray overpopulation as primarily a moral issue: "excessive population growth, occurring with little or no responsibility, creates, above all, grave problems of a moral character" (*Anales* 275). He elaborates

that high population affects both children and parents: many children in a family can place strain on the parents such that their parenting suffers, with the result that the parents fail to provide proper parental guidance (*Anales* 275). "All this constitutes a serious problem," Lleras Restrepo declares, "principally in a country where neither the State has the resources to replace" parental guidance, "nor do sufficient private organizations exist that can fill this gap" (*Anales* 275). Hence, Lleras Restrepo maintains that family planning promotes responsible parenthood. Supporting couples to choose their number of children will enable couples to be better parents and ensure more children grow up with sufficient parental care. Lleras Restrepo's rendering of population growth as a dilemma of irresponsible parenthood and children's welfare matches the Church's concern that married couples are intentional about becoming parents (*Anales* 275). The first principle in the Church officials' statement is, "A couple's inalienable right to determine the number of children, in accordance with their conscience and moral norms, must be protected" (*Anales* 275). This principle protects parents from any imposed methods, but also recognizes parents should be thoughtful about conceiving children. Even after the Church decided against artificial contraception in 1968, the Church continued to allow couples to practice "natural" methods (such as the rhythm method, abstaining from sex during a woman's fertile period) to approach parenthood responsibly.

Betancur Mejía further aligns government and Church by signaling how the government's family planning philosophy matches the Pope's recent statement on fertility. He reads Pope Paul VI's recent statement on fertility, "*Constitución Pastoral sobre Iglesia de Hoy*" and notes the opening lines recognize population as a government matter (*Anales* 483). The Church's current position on family planning methods is vague, Betancur Mejía notes; the only guidance is for "all to abstain from those solutions promoted privately or publicly and even sometimes imposed, that contradict moral law" (*Anales* 483). The Pope does not elaborate on which, if any, methods, are acceptable or unacceptable under "moral law." The Pope concludes his statement affirming the right of married couples to decide with "well-formed conscience" the number of children to have, and that it is important for couples to have information about scientific progress in methods that can help them make their choice (*Anales* 483). Betancur Mejía asserts this is precisely the government's position: "[The government] is taking advantage of new methods and informing people about the methods they can adopt to plan their families" (*Anales* 483). Overall, Betancur Mejía follows Lleras Restrepo's lead (as set in the summit report) in using Church vocabulary and positions to describe the government's own family planning approach.

During his questioning, Ordoñez Plaja emphasizes family planning as a solution to Colombia's morally troubling high abortion rate. He rejects the

Senate's use of the term "fertility control" (*control de la natalidad*) instead of "family planning" (*planificación familiar*), for example, because the former may envelop abortion. The term "fertility control," he explains,

> implies adopting all methods, even those condemned not only by morality, but also by most religions and the law, if not by simple common sense; like abortion which is a method of fertility control; but in no instance is that method considered a means of family planning.
>
> (*Anales* 259)

Ordoñez Plaja makes very clear that abortion is not a part of "family planning" and that the government views abortion as problematic in multiple aspects. He reminds the Senate that both he and Betancur Mejía have used the term "family planning" throughout the hearings.

The call to intervene in abortion practices is not a top-down governmental imposition, Ordoñez Plaja continues, but comes from doctors on the frontlines with patients. Family planning policy is responding to "doctors' concern in the sense of limiting the number of children, requested by their patients," accompanied by the fact that "provoked abortions, with their criminal and dangerous consequences, were occurring" (*Anales* 259). Ordoñez Plaja underscores how family planning can support couples as well as prevent dangerous, illegal abortions. He concludes, "[Family planning] tries, respecting the inalienable right of each marriage, to help choose a method that would overcome those ineffective and dangerous methods that they [couples] have been practicing in a criminal way" (*Anales* 259). Naming couples' current methods as "criminal" indicates that Ordoñez Plaja refers to abortion here, which was the only outlawed fertility method. While the Church was vague on acceptable family planning methods, it was indubitable that the Church disapproved of abortion. In relating how the government's family planning policy would diminish abortion, Ordoñez Plaja establishes shared values and goals among the government, Conservative senators, and the Church.

The Ministers' statements during the Senate fertility control hearings show how the Lleras Restrepo administration navigated challenges to family planning. Although the Lleras Restrepo government maintained that rapid population growth challenged Colombia's economic and social development, and that fewer births via family planning were key to slowing population growth, the Ministers and Lleras Restrepo did not announce these viewpoints. Instead, they echoed the Catholic Church's vocabulary and reasoning on fertility matters, emphasizing responsible parenthood and abortion prevention. Lleras Restrepo also distanced the government from ASCOFAME, private doctors, and non-profit organizations involved in family planning in the summit statement:

The President and his Ministers cannot know, naturally, all the details of the manner in which the Medical School Association [ASCO-FAME] is carrying out the contract [of the 1966 policy], and much less the activities others may be carrying out of their own initiative.

(*Anales* 275)

The government reveals it is attentive to the political environment and adept at handling various positions in order to pursue the 1966 policy.

The Senate hearings' outcome was the creation of a committee to study population growth and family planning programs in Colombia. The Senate voted 59 in favor and 7 against to create the committee and granted the committee 90 days to report its findings (*Anales* 306). The committee's report, made public in October 1969, was "favorable to the national program" and the Senate did not pursue the topic further (Mendoza Hoyos "The Colombian Program" 830; Stycos *Ideology* 154).

Opposition toward family planning policies continued in other venues from a range of political and ethical positions. Beginning in 1968, leftist university students mounted a fierce critique of family planning policies and programs, on the basis that family planning was a US imperialist project.[9] Nationalist elites on the left and right espoused the same US imperialist line of argument in books and editorials.[10] Some in the Colombian Catholic Church, particularly clergy in the heavily Catholic department of Antioquia, continued to disapprove of family planning. Nevertheless, the 1969 policy incorporated family planning as a response to rapid population growth in the national development plan. The policy states its "immediate objectives" are to "obtain a better territorial distribution of the population and alter the present rate of population growth by lowering fertility" (Colombia *Planes* 5; also, see Ott 5). The Conservative president following Carlos Lleras Restrepo's term not only continued lowering fertility as part of population policy in the national development plan, but even expanded upon it. Over time, the Colombian Catholic Church also came to accept some government involvement in promoting family planning, to the extent that it posted representatives to a government advisory committee on population and family planning matters, formed in 1970.

The Absence of Women's Voices on Abortion

We can look back now and know that the fertility rate did not continue to grow exponentially, but that since the 1960s, there has been an ongoing fertility decline in Latin America. During the 1960s, however, population researchers and leaders predicted the most dire possibilities for families, countries, and the globe due to increasing numbers of people and the needs they called for. Especially in the newer postwar spirit of human rights, leaders were calling for every human being, in principle, to live a dignified, enriched life, and yet this was precisely at the moment when the increase in numbers of people were, in their eyes, threatening this possibility.

Population discourse constructed the problem of the population "crisis" and its most promising solution—family planning to lower fertility rate. The attention, financial and technical resources, and sense of urgency attending the population "crisis" helped establish family planning research and programs in many countries. Through population discourse, family planning became tied to a national and global stable and prosperous future; family planning would allow countries, especially developing countries, to pursue economic development that would advance social development. In this way, a state's interest in population matters and support for family planning programs became associated with being a modern state. In Colombia, key policy partners such as DEP participated in population discourse, but the government took a more cautious stance that echoed the Catholic Church's position (at the time) toward family planning. Emphasizing how family planning could diminish abortions was key for gaining government, Church, and broader public support.

Researchers interpreted the high abortion rate as demonstrating women's desire for contraception, reading abortion statistics to determine women's needs and desires. This research was touted as cutting-edge, using new survey methods to capture the current reality of women and families' reproductive experiences. And yet, the way that researchers interpreted abortion statistics left a looming gap in understanding women and abortion. Women were "heard" and known through their bodies, with little opportunity to guide policy making about reproductive medicine.

The DEP's studies which found a "felt need" for family planning laid the groundwork for Colombia's 1966 and 1969 policies. As Mendoza asserted,

> The Division of Population Studies of the Colombian Association of Medical Schools believes that when someone is capable of forcibly [*sic*: forcefully] and vehemently demonstrating the existence of a serious and threatening phenomenon, it is possible to create a favorable national reaction. This, in turn, leads to the possibility of reaching the goals suggested.
>
> (Mendoza Hoyos "The Colombian Program" 835)

For Mendoza and other population leaders and experts, the goal was achieving family planning at the policy level. The 1960s were a turning point for women's reproductive lives in making family planning education and services more available than ever before. At the same time, widespread cultural rejection of abortion played an important role in legitimating family planning.

It might seem that high-abortion-rates-signify-women's-desire-for-contraceptives is a logical conclusion for population leaders and experts to draw. After all, women who abort (unless coerced) do so to avoid having a child. Yet, this logic treats women's reproductive actions as constituting their voice: researchers gather, record, and assess what women need based on their bodies' experiences, as transformed into statistics. In its disinterest with women's voices, 1960s population research misses how women's reasons for seeking abortion may be more complicated than having lacked contraception during sex. As Colombian sexologist and psychologist María Ladi Londoño observed from her practice during the 1970s and 1980s, women may want a child but pursue an abortion because of changes in their health, relationships, prospects, or economic conditions (163–164). It is just as plausible to interpret abortion rates as women's "felt need" for protection from sexual violence or job security during pregnancy (not legally established in Colombia until 1991). The population experts' assumption, however, is that women who abort pregnancies would not get pregnant if they could avoid it. In limiting abortion prevention to contraceptives, population experts miss the greater context of women's reproductive decision-making. Instead of inquiring further with women about their reproductive experiences, or welcoming women to take part in policy making, population leaders and experts claimed knowledge of women's needs and desires through reading demographic data on abortions.

In Colombia and many other countries, during the 1970s and by the 1980s, family planning shifted from a demographic issue to a women's health issue. This occurred in large part as women organized against the paternalistic and often misogynistic medical establishment of the 1960s. Family planning would become much less about national demographic control to center on women's health and well-being.

Notes

1 PROFAMILIA has continued to be a transformative service provider in Colombia since its founding. Writing in 1987, one scholar concludes, "Profamilia has surpassed any private family planning association in Latin America in terms of the numbers of clients reached and program innovation" (Roper 340).

2 Counterpart funds refer to the local currency generated from selling aid commodities, such as food, or from foreign exchange received as aid (see Bruton and Hill 4–5).

3 All references cited in this manner (beginning with S.1676) are drawn from the entry noted in the References as "United States Congressional Senate. Hearings before the Subcommittee on Foreign Aid Expenditures of the Committee on Government Operations, United States Senate, 89th Congress, 1966."

4 Thomas Mann served in the US Foreign Service and was considered an expert on Latin America. Mann served as Coordinator for the Alliance for Progress, a Latin American intensive aid program started by President John F. Kennedy. Mann prioritized US interests to the extent of supporting regime change in Latin American

countries, and for this remains a controversial figure in US and Latin American politics. However, for a different perspective on Mann's legacy, see Tunstall Allcock (2013).

5   The English translation of this Spanish-language source is from Mendoza "The Colombian Program" (829).

6   For political biographies of Diego Tovar Concha and Manuel Bayona Carrascal, see Ayala Diago (337–338, 344–345).

7   Tovar Concha and Bayona Carrascal often refer to Mendoza as "*herrodista*," or "Herodist." They refer to Mendoza as "Herod-like" during the hearings.

8   The *Concordato* was renewed in 1973.

9   For literature on leftist and nationalist family planning opposition in Colombia, see Ott (6–9); Sanders' "Opposition," and "The Relationship"; and Stycos *Ideology*.

10   Arguably the most renowned of these nationalist figures was Hernán Vergara, a psychiatrist and psychology professor, who argued that the US promoted family planning "to slow down—or end, who knows—the procreation of racially mixed, tropical and Catholic Latin Americans" in his 1968 book *El Complejo del Layo* (102). The English translation of this quote is from Stycos (*Ideology* 51).

References

Anales del Congreso de Colombia 169, año X, no. 13, febrero 2, 1967.

Anales del Congreso de Colombia 186, año X, no. 14, febrero 7, 1967.

Anales del Congreso de Colombia 203, año X, no. 15, febrero 8, 1967.

Anales del Congreso de Colombia 251, año X, no. 18, febrero 14, 1967.

Anales del Congreso de Colombia 259, año X, no. 19, febrero 15, 1967.

Anales del Congreso de Colombia 275, año X, no. 20, febrero 16, 1967.

Anales del Congreso de Colombia 306, año X, no. 22, febrero 21, 1967.

Anales del Congreso de Colombia 483, año X, no. 33, marzo 15, 1967.

Anales del Congreso de Colombia 567, año X, no. 38, marzo 30, 1967.

Ayala Diago, César. *La explosión del populismo en Colombia: Anapo y su participación política durante el Frente Nacional.* Universidad Nacional de Colombia, 2011.

Baumgartner, Leona. "Family Planning Around the World." *Family Planning and Population Programs: A Review of World Developments*, edited by International Conference on Family Planning Programs and Bernard Berelson, University of Chicago Press, 1966, pp. 277–294.

Berelson, Bernard. "KAP Studies on Fertility." *Family Planning and Population Programs: A Review of World Developments*, edited by International Conference on Family Planning Programs and Bernard Berelson, University of Chicago Press, 1966, pp. 655–668.

Bruton, Henry and Catherine Hill. *The Development Impact of Counterpart Funds: A Review of the Literature.* Agency for International Development, 1991.

Colombia. *Planes y Programas de Desarrollo, 1969–1972.* Printing Office of the National Administrative Department of Statistics (DANE), 1969.

Davis, Kingsley. "Population Policy: Will Current Programs Succeed?" *Science*, vol. 158, no. 3802, November 10, 1967, pp. 730–739.

"Declaration of Population." *Studies in Family Planning*, vol. 1, no. 16, January 1967, p. 1.

Delgado García, Ramiro. "Latin America." *Family Planning and Population Programs: A Review of World Developments*, edited by International Conference on Family Planning Programs and Bernard Berelson, University of Chicago Press, 1966, pp. 249–257.

Deverell, Colville. "The International Planned Parenthood Federation: Its Role in Developing Countries." *Demography*, vol. 5, no. 2, 1968, pp. 574–577.

Dorn, Harold F. "World Population Growth: An International Dilemma." *Science*, vol. 135, no. 3500, January 26, 1962, pp. 283–290.

Escobar, Arturo. *Encountering Development: The Making and Unmaking of the Third World*. Princeton University Press, 1995.

Fajardo Hernández, María Margarita. "La comunidad médica, el 'problema de población' y la investigación sociodemográfica en Colombia, 1965–1970." *Historia Crítica*, no. 33, enero-junio 2007, pp. 210–235.

Lleras Camargo, Alberto. *Primera Asamblea Panamericana de Población*, agosto 11, 1965, Cali, Colombia. Opening address.

Londoño, María Ladi. *Prácticas de libertad en sexualidad y los derechos reproductivos*. Talleres Gráficos de la Impresora Feriva, 1991.

Mauldin, W. Parker. "Fertility Studies: Knowledge, Attitude, and Practice." *Studies in Family Planning*, vol. 1, no. 7, June 1965, pp. 1–10.

Measham, Anthony R. and Guillermo López-Escobar. "Against the Odds: Colombia's Role in the Family Planning Revolution." *The Global Family Planning Revolution: Three Decades of Population Policies and Programs*, edited by Warren C. Robinson and John A. Ross, The World Bank, 2007, pp. 121–135.

Mendoza Hoyos, Hernán. "Research Studies on Abortion and Family Planning in Colombia." *Milbank Memorial Fund Quarterly*, vol. 46, no. 3, July 1968, pp. 223–236.

Mendoza Hoyos, Hernán. *Sobrepoblación en los países en desarrollo (Elevada densidad social en Colombia)*. Asociación Colombiana de Facultades de Medicina—División de Estudios de Población, 1966.

Mendoza Hoyos, Hernán. "The Colombian Program for Public Education, Personnel Training and Evaluation." *Demography*, vol. 5, no. 2, 1968, pp. 827–835.

Miró, Carmen. "Some Misconceptions Disproved: A Program of Comparative Fertility Surveys in Latin America." *Family Planning and Population Programs: A Review of World Developments*, edited by International Conference on Family Planning Programs and Bernard Berelson, University of Chicago Press, 1966, pp. 615–634.

Ott, Emiline Royco. "Population Policy Formation in Colombia: The Role of ASCO-FAME." *Studies in Family Planning*, vol. 8, no. 1, January 1977, pp. 2–10.

Portocarrero, Patricia. "Old Dreams and New Visions. From Women to Gender: A Change in the Concept of Development." *Women and Local Democracy in Latin America: Notebook of the Local Government Training and Development Center*. IULA/CELCADEL, 1994.

Requena, Mariano. "The Problem of Induced Abortion in Latin America." *Demography*, vol. 5, no. 2, 1968, pp. 785–799.

Romero, Hernán. "Chile." *Family Planning and Population Programs: A Review of World Developments*, edited by International Conference on Family Planning Programs and Bernard Berelson, University of Chicago Press, 1966, pp. 235–247.

Roper, Laura E. "The Management of Family Planning Programs: Profamilia's Experience." *Studies in Family Planning*, vol. 18, no. 6, November/December 1987, pp. 338–351.

Sanders, Thomas. "Family Planning in Colombia." *American Universities Field Staff Reports*, vol. 17, no. 3, January 1970, pp. 1–6.

Sanders, Thomas. "Opposition to Family Planning in Latin America: The Non-Marxist Left." *American Universities Field Staff Reports*, vol. 17, no. 5, March 1970, pp. 1–7.

Sanders, Thomas. "The Relationship between Population Planning and Belief Systems: The Catholic Church in Latin America." *American Universities Field Staff Reports*, vol. 17, no. 7, April 1970, pp. 1–12.

Seltzer, Judith and Fernando Gomez. *Family Planning and Population Programs in Colombia: 1965–1997. POPTECH Report No. 97-114-062*. Population Technical Assistance Project, 1998.

Stycos, J. Mayone. *Ideology, Faith, and Family Planning in Latin America*. McGraw-Hill Book Company, 1971.

Stycos, J. Mayone. "Prospects for World Population Control." *World Population: The View Ahead*, edited by Richard N. Farmer, John D. Long, and George J. Stolnitz, Bureau of Business Research, 1968, pp. 271–284.

Tunstall Allcock, Thomas. "Becoming 'Mr. Latin America': Thomas C. Mann, Reconsidered." *Diplomatic History*, vol. 0, no. 0, 2013, pp. 1–29.

United States Congressional Senate. Hearings before the Subcommittee on Foreign Aid Expenditures of the Committee on Government Operations, 89th Congress, 1966.

Vergara, Hernán. *El Complejo del Layo*. Tercer Mundo, 1968.

II

THE STATE, THE LAW, AND SEXUAL AND REPRODUCTIVE JUSTICE

4

INDIGENOUS REPRODUCTIVE JUSTICE AFTER *ADOPTIVE COUPLE V. BABY GIRL* (2013)

KRISTA L. BENSON

For indigenous youth on Turtle Island (what many call North America), the notion of home is often a fraught concept. Due to settler colonization, displacement, and limited sovereignty, the homes that have been available to Native youth after settler contact are always tainted by ongoing colonization. As Native Studies scholars inform us, ongoing settler colonization—wherein the colonizers dispossess and displace indigenous people from their lands with the intent of staying and taking over that land—requires that indigeneity be erased, elided, or at the very least assimilated (e.g., Deloria, 1969; Simpson, 2014; Wolfe, 1999). Once indigeneity is erased or at least limited to only being racial difference and not related to sovereignty, then logics of multicultural inclusion insist that race no longer matters. Native people "therefore ostensibly vanish twice: first, they are erased as sovereign peoples with rightful claims to the land on which they live or once inhabited, and second, they disappear in the embrace of contemporary multicultural inclusion" (Goldstein, 2014, p. 1078). Native Studies scholars and indigenous scholars insist that it is important to consider settler colonization as an ongoing process, not a discrete event in the past (Wolfe, 2006).

As a part of the ongoing justification of settler colonization in the United States, U.S. officials focused on removal of Native children from family and tribal homes to disrupt indigenous communities as a part of assimilation and elimination. The primary systems of child removal have been compulsory education in the late-19th to mid-20th century (Adams, 1995; Child, 1998; Ellis, 2006; Lomawaima, 1995), foster care and adoption into white families

(Briggs, 2012; Cotter-Busbee & DeMeyer, 2013; Jacobs, 2011; Jacobs, 2014), and the juvenile justice system (Benson, 2017).

In this chapter, I analyze the U.S. Supreme Court decision *Adoptive Couple v. Baby Girl* (2013) to remove a Native child from her Native father's custody and place her with a non-Native adoptive family chosen by her non-Native birth mother. This decision radically changed U.S. courts' interpretations of the application of the Indian Child Welfare Act of 1978 (ICWA) to children from sovereign Native nations. The ICWA provides a set of guidelines intended to protect Native children from aggressive removal from indigenous communities and highlights the importance of the ability for Native communities to parent their children, a response to the aggressive removal of Native children through compulsory education and adoption into white homes from the 1880s to the 1970s. Using reproductive justice as a lens, I explore the 2013 Supreme Court decision as an erosion of the ICWA's ability to protect the reproductive justice of Native communities. If the ICWA were to really address the problems outlined in its framing, I argue that the ICWA would have to extend beyond being a mere family protection bill. Effective legislation to address centuries of child removal of Native children would need to provide protection for Native parents to have their children parented in indigenous homes and directly address ongoing settler colonization. The Supreme Court's decision in *Adoptive Couple v. Baby Girl* (2013) shores up the foundations of a U.S. legal system which developed in part out of a need to erode Native sovereignty and self-determination. Adoption of Native children, I argue, is an issue of reproductive justice, of the ability of Native families to parent Native children, and to assert sovereignty over their communities.

From Reproductive Rights to Reproductive Justice
The framework and articulation of reproductive justice emerged in 1994 from the Illinois Pro-Choice Alliance Conference, when a group of black feminists formed the Women of African Descent for Reproductive Justice. This group critiqued the limited language of choice at the conference as not being inclusive of the three central rights, "the right to have a child, … the right not to have a child, and … the right to parent the children we have" (Ross, 2006, p. 14). This led to a larger collection of women of color and indigenous women coalescing around the limitations of feminist organizations' too-narrow focus on abortion as an individual right. Activists joined together on a variety of collaborative projects that advocated for reproductive justice through organizing. These projects were based on the premise that women of color and indigenous women "negotiate their reproductive lives in a system that combines various interlocking forms of oppression" (Ross, Gutiérrez, Gerber, & Silliman, 2016, p. 11). When these interlocking systems of

oppression are recognized, the framework of "choice" so often invoked in mainstream discourse of reproductive rights becomes troubled. In the context of ongoing settler colonization in a country that has been founded on the enslavement of African people, genocide and land dispossession of Native people, and American empire writ large, the framework of individual choice ignores structural inequalities. For indigenous women in the United States, who often experience neglectful or insufficient reproductive health care (Gurr, 2014) and who live in communities with the highest rates of unemployment in the United States (U.S. Bureau of Labor Statistics, 2014), "choices" are constrained.

As explored in *Undivided Rights: Women of Color Organize for Reproductive Justice* (Ross et al., 2016), there are coalitional activist organizations engaged in reproductive justice work at the ground level. These include the National Black Women's Health Project, African American Women Evolving, the Native American Women's Health Education Resource Center, the Mother's Milk Project, Asians and Pacific Islanders for Reproductive Health, the National Asian Women's Health Organization, the National Latina Health Organization, and the Colorado Organization for Latina Opportunity and Reproductive Rights. A shared commitment to comprehensive reproductive justice guides the work of these organizations. As the framework of reproductive justice spreads, women of color continue to conceptualize struggles for reproductive rights as embedded and intertwined with issues of racism, classism, and sexism, among other oppressions (Asian Communities for Reproductive Justice, 2005; Ross, 2006).

Reproductive justice has been used as a productive framework to look at the real impacts on women of color, indigenous women, and women from developing countries when considering abortion (Wallis, 2013; Chen, 2013), ableism in technologies that facilitate the manipulation or control of genetics (Jesudason & Kimport, 2013; Jarman, 2015), the use of women of color in developing countries as surrogates (Bailey, 2011; Fixmer-Oraiz, 2013), prenatal and postpartum care (Sagrestano & Finerman, 2012; Johnston-Robledo & Murray, 2012), and the overlaps between transnational adoption and surrogacy (Cuthbert & Fronek, 2014). Importantly, Loretta Ross (2006) emphasizes the positive rights under a reproductive justice framework—the right to decide whether or not to have a child and the right to parent one's children.

This set of rights and the ways that structural racism, classism, ableism, heterosexism, and other sets of privilege and power deny different communities access to them can be seen when considering adoption and the ways that children become available for adoption. Though adoption is rarely mentioned by reproductive justice activists and has never to my knowledge been formally studied as a reproductive justice issue by scholars, I insist—alongside other Adoption Studies scholars and adult adoptees—that adoption is a reproductive justice issue. In a roundtable conversation about reproductive justice and technology, Laura Briggs writes that,

> [a]doption, as the transfer of children from the impoverished to those who are middle class, from the global South to the United States, Europe, Canada, and a handful of other places, and from the young to older parents, should trouble us more than it does, as a place where violence, coercion, and power meet (usually single) mothers and their children.
>
> (Briggs et al., 2013, p. 121)

Adoption Studies scholar and adult adoptee Kimberly McKee concurs and emphasizes that reproductive justice requires that we assess which parents are able to assert their right and capability to parent. She argues that adoption is a commodified market which disintegrates first families and creates new families. Through this process, transnational adoption privileges white adoptive parents' reproductive destines over those of the transnational, often of-color birth families (McKee, 2018). Adoption, then, cannot be extracted from other issues of reproductive justice.

In addition to rarely looking critically at adoption, reproductive justice is a framework that has been infrequently applied to indigenous communities within academic scholarship. It is important that any application of reproductive justice in indigenous communities recognizes the specificity of the context of both race *and* sovereignty when considering issues of parenting, justice, and reproduction for indigenous people of Turtle Island. Scholars such as Barbara Gurr (2014) and Elizabeth Hoover (Hoover et al., 2012), in collaboration with indigenous youth and organizations invested in environmental justice have begun to apply the framework to address issues of health care for Native women and the impacts of environmental health risks as they relate to reproductive justice. Gurr emphasizes the ways that gender, sexuality, and racialization are tied up in the construction of the settler state:

> Nation building, the productive of a (fictive) collective ethnicity, is always already gendered; patriarchy is not merely a social system, it is the very idiom through which the racialized State is constructed. Because patriarchy relies on the control of women's bodies, motherhood, as a site of physical and cultural identity, is targeted for control in the production of the nation.
>
> (Gurr, 2014, p. 29)

I agree, though in this chapter I focus on parenting as an entire category, addressing the aspects of fatherhood's relationship to settler colonization which Gurr gestures toward and marks as an area of future research.

Though scholars have only recently begun to explore the specificity of reproductive justice for indigenous communities in settler colonial states, indigenous communities and activist groups have embraced the framework of reproductive justice. This can be seen in the Native American Women's Health Education Resource Center of the Yankton Sioux Reservation in South Dakota and the Mother's Milk Project of the Akwesasne of the St. Regis Mohawk Reservation in New York highlighted in *Undivided Rights* (Ross et al., 2016). Importantly, the most effective mobilization of reproductive justice as a political framework in Indian Country is Native activists and organizers within their own communities and in collaboration with one another.

These activists and organizers work with transnational and pan-tribal organizations that operate from a reproductive justice framework. Such organizations also advocate at the national level for changes in treatment of Native peoples and land. One such program is the Native American Women's Health Education Resource Center's Reproductive Justice Program. This program brings together roundtables of indigenous women from across the United States to discuss indigenous women's sexual and reproductive health and to issue reports, including on a lack of standardized policies in the Indian Health Service (IHS) for sexual assault treatment, IHS violations of Native women's right to pregnancy prevention, and reproductive health care ("Reproductive Justice Program," n.d.). It applies a reproductive justice framework—one which arises from the racialization of Native people—that is specifically contextualized within issues of sovereignty, relationships between members of federally recognized tribes, the IHS and other U.S. federal government systems, and calls for justice for Native people.

Another program is the Native Youth Sexual Health Network (NYSHN), a transnational organization of Native youth on Turtle Island. They engage in political advocacy and public education about the relationship between environmental violence and sexual and reproductive health, rights, and justice ("Environmental Violence & Reproductive Justice," n.d.). Focusing largely on the practice of extractive natural resource industries such as mining, gas, oil, and logging, they create media arts justice projects which are shared on social media, submit testimony to the Canadian government to resist oil pipelines ("NYSHN statement to the National Energy Board regarding Line 9 Pipeline Proposal," 2013), and create public education videos and public declarations about indigenous reproductive justice and environmental devastation ("Environmental Violence & Reproductive Justice," n.d.). Through supporting activism and developing the wisdom of Native youth and young adults, the NYSHN reproductive justice program engages in complex intellectual production that is working to disrupt settler states' practices of environmental devastation and explicitly connecting those practices to the reproductive justice of indigenous communities.

These organizations' work shows the degree to which reproductive justice is embedded in the activism of many indigenous women and their understandings of the connected importance of reproductive health, reproductive justice, and the health of indigenous communities. However, these interconnections are not always apparent in the scholarship and activism of non-indigenous people in the United States. I argue that reproductive justice movements and scholarship in the United States need to grapple with the differences of citizenship status in the settler state and racialization of Native women as connected to but *distinct* from other women of color. Native women's relationship to the settler state is a gendered and racialized one. However, it is also always seated in the context of settler colonization and the state dispossession of land and culture. Though I would encourage more engagement with settler colonization and the state in all reproductive justice scholarship, that engagement must be central to any application of reproductive justice in indigenous communities.

For the remainder of this chapter, I use reproductive justice as a framework to engage in a critical analysis of the U.S. settler state and its investments in Native child removal. I argue that adoption of Native children into non-Native homes is an issue of reproductive justice and is a product of the settler state's dispossession of indigenous land, knowledge, and ways of life. In the next section, I turn to outline the U.S. government's long history of removal of Native children from their family and tribal environments and connect this history to the U.S. Supreme Court decision in the case of *Adoptive Couple v. Baby Girl* (2013).

Legacies of Child Removal and the Case of Baby Veronica

Indigenous communities in the United States have a complex road to realizing reproductive justice and freedom. Like other racialized communities in the United States, indigenous people experience a number of governmental, medical, and legal constraints to their ability to decide when and how to parent, to keep their children safe and healthy, and to build communities of support. Some of these constraints are overt. Many scholars have written about long histories of forced and coerced sterilization of Native women by doctors in the IHS in the 1960s and 1970s (Gurr, 2014; Lawrence, 2000; Torpy, 2000; Rutecki, 2011) resulting in the sterilization of 25% of Native women between the ages of 15 and 54. These histories are deeply connected to issues of reproductive justice of Native women and families. Forced sterilizations, much like coerced adoption into white families, prevent Native women from having access to the full range of ability to have, raise, and parent their children.

Child removal through education and adoption are issues of reproductive justice and have a much longer history than the adoption of the individual child at the center of the *Adoptive Couple v. Baby Girl* (2013) decision. The history of indigenous child removal through adoption and education projects—explored more in depth later in this chapter—is elided in much of the discussion of the case. This omission is despite the fact that child removal was central to the U.S. Congress establishment of the law that the decision addresses, the ICWA. The removal of indigenous children from their family and tribal environments is a core part of federal policy in both the United States and Canada.

In the United States, removal of Native children started in the late 19th century with the passing of the Compulsory Indian Education Act of 1887. According to the act, all indigenous children were required to be educated in day schools and boarding schools established or funded by the U.S. government and nearly entirely staffed with non-Native teachers and administrators. The goal of this project was to force assimilation of Native youth and the elimination of their indigenous knowledge, languages, and cultural practices. As famously framed by General Richard Pratt, founder of the first federal boarding school, the goal of this project was to "kill the Indian to save the man" (Pratt, 1892). Teachers and administrators at boarding and day schools attempted not only to instruct Native youth in academic subjects, but also in vocational skills which would train young Native men to be farmers and heads of the household and Native women to tend to a European style home and family. The education into these white, Western understandings of labor and relation were explicitly developed to disrupt Native communities and to eliminate indigenous kinship structures. This project was unevenly successful in this goal and, in the mid-1950s, the Bureau of Indian Affairs (BIA) partnered with the Child Welfare League of America to develop the Indian Adoption Project.

Launched in 1958, the Indian Adoption Project was designed to replace the compulsory education project, as boarding and day schools were rapidly closing or being turned over to tribal control. Concerned about the number of indigenous children who would be returned to their home communities and a presumed life of poverty, BIA officials worked with child welfare agencies and social workers to place indigenous children with non-Native families. At the same time, social welfare agencies began to recognize institutional living—including the boarding schools—as detrimental to children's health and recommended adoption as a preferable option (Fanshel, 1972). The connection of adoption to the compulsory education period was not only recognizable through government intent, but also sometimes led to parents who had been educated in boarding schools to think their children would be better off if they were raised outside their tribes. For example, a member of the Cherokee tribe described the following:

worried sets of parents would come to the clinic begging for help in securing placement in a boarding school for their eight or nine-year old child. This puzzled me, and it soon became clear that it was a heart-breaking matter for them to part with the child, yet they know nothing else to do. They had never known family life from the age of school entrance. Their parents have never known life from the age of school entrance. There were no memories and no patterns to follow in rearing children except the regimentation of mass feeding, mass sleeping and impersonal schedules.

(93rd Congress, session II, on April 8 and 9, pp. 483–484. Testimony of C. Attneave, member of the Cherokee Nation, cited in Palmiste, 2011)

The relationship between compulsory education programs and adoption, as we can see here, extends beyond the goals and designs of the framers of the Indian Adoption Project. Because compulsory education—especially board-ing schools—so thoroughly disrupted many indigenous people's under-standings of family, kinship, and child rearing, some survivors of the project felt unable to parent their own children. They genuinely believed that adop-tion into white families would be better for their children because they were raised without familial examples around them. Both the framing of the Indian Adoption Project as well as some members of indigenous communities point out the deep connections between the two.

Although a limited number of children were formally adopted through the Indian Adoption Project, the project encouraged social workers, BIA officials, and judges to change the way that indigenous youth's best interests were con-sidered in home placement during child welfare hearings. The promotion of out-of-culture placements of Native children opened the door for validating adoptions of Native children into white families even when not pursued through the Indian Adoption Project. As former Child Welfare League of America Director Shay Bilchik (Director, 2000–2007) acknowledged in a keynote presentation at the National Indian Child Welfare Association Conference,

the BIA and [Child Welfare League of America] actively encouraged states to continue and expand the practice of "rescuing" Native children from their own culture, from their very families. Because of this legiti-mizing effect, the indirect results of this initiative cannot be measured.

(Bilchik, 2001)

The practice of rescue replaces the language of "assimilating" found in the education project, but the mechanisms are startlingly similar. This program also increased white families' willingness to consider the adoption of Native children.

The numbers of Native children adopted out-of-culture across the United States at this time were large. As of 1979, scholars estimated that anywhere between 20% and 35% of all indigenous children had been or were currently separated from their families in adoptive or foster homes (Barsh, 1979, p. 1290; Guerrero, 1979, p. 53; Mannes, 1995) and states placed 85% of Native children with non-Native families (Plantz, Hubbell, Barrett, & Dorbrec, 1989). The consistent removal of children from Native communities through foster care and adoption, following up on large-scale removal of Native children through compulsory education, had significant impacts on the Native youth removed, their families, and their communities. Tribal leaders expressed concern about the impacts of these removals and the safety of their children throughout the Indian Adoption Project and their leadership was vital to ongoing efforts to force the federal government to change adoption policy. Advocates for Native child welfare called for federal government action, resulting in the ICWA. The ICWA is the U.S. federal government's attempt to promote the stability of indigenous families and tribes in response to the demonstrated risk of removal of children from tribal and parental homes by both private child welfare agencies and the government. The ICWA grants both the birth parents and the tribe the right to intervene in state proceedings involving Native children, and was intended to prevent social workers and judges from placing indigenous youth in non-Native homes.

Unfortunately, studies of indigenous child welfare after passage of the ICWA did not show a significantly improved situation for indigenous children in out-of-home care. In 1998, Graham noted that 20% of indigenous children were still placed in out-of-home placements, which she attributed to "courts, welfare agencies, and attorneys failing to follow the letter of [the ICWA]" (p. 2). Donald, Bradley, Critchley, Day, & Nuccio (2003) also noted a higher-than-representative proportion of indigenous youth in out-of-home foster care and found that indigenous children are likely to go into the foster care system younger than non-Native children, are generally from single-parent homes, and the majority live in poverty. In general, poverty is a predictor of out-of-home child placements (Albers, Reilly, & Ritter, 1993; Belsky, 1993; Cross, Earle, & Simmons, 2000; Rosenfeld et al., 1997), and welfare reforms have made it possible that poor people are more likely to have their children either taken out of home or to voluntarily relinquish them (Donald et al., 2003, p. 268). This has a disproportionate impact on indigenous youth because their families are statistically poorer than non-indigenous families in the same area.

Additionally, indigenous family structures have frequently not been recognized and honored through the U.S. government's systems of child welfare.

Extended family networks, care for children by extended family members, and family structures which do not mirror the heterosexual and nuclear families permitted by white American culture are all potential targets for negative attention by BIA agents and child welfare officials. As Graham (1998) notes, "for many Native American nations, 'family' denotes extensive kinship networks that reach far beyond the Western nuclear family" (1998, p. 5). This extensive kinship network can (and in many situations, does) mean that there is a strong interplay between community responsibility and individual responsibility for children that is difficult to represent in U.S. courtrooms and child welfare decisions, creating difficult relationships between indigenous people and settler state family welfare systems. Donald et al. (2003) highlight how changes in federal child welfare policy to move toward adoption and permanent foster placement of youth ignore that "tension exists between dominant society and American Indian definitions of permanency" (p. 268). Due to this tension, indigenous concepts of permanency may include things like kinship care, a common form of familial foster care for many Native people, which non-Native judges and social workers may not recognize. The "Existing Indian Family" doctrine highlights this failure. The Existing Indian Family doctrine is a judicially created exemption to the ICWA enacted in some states wherein the ICWA does not apply to an infant raised outside an indigenous family environment. This judge-created doctrine, first enacted in 1982, allows judges the opportunity to assess whether they think that the child or their parents have significant social, cultural, or political relationship with their tribes (Jaffke, 2006), which the majority of non-Native judges would have no ability to do accurately.

Child Removal and the Case of Baby Veronica
Limitations to the ICWA and the history of child removal from indigenous homes provide a key background when turning to a recent Supreme Court decision considering application of the ICWA, *Adoptive Couple v. Baby Girl* (2013), popularly known as the "Baby Veronica" case. In 2009, a white, non-indigenous couple sought to adopt a child whose father—Dusten Brown—was an enrolled member of the Cherokee nation and whose biological mother—Christy Maldonado—was Latina and non-indigenous. At birth, the baby—alternately known as Veronica and Ronnie by her various families—was placed by her mother with Melanie Duncan and Matthew Capobianco and lived with the couple from 2009 to 2011. Although her birth mother discussed the adoption for months before the birth with the adoptive couple, Brown was not informed of the adoptive placement and planned adoption proceedings. Four months after Veronica's birth, Duncan and Capobianco served Brown with notice of a pending adoption. Brown immediately contested the adoption on the grounds that he was not notified of the adoption

in accordance with the ICWA and won in both trial court and on appeal to the South Carolina Supreme Court. Veronica lived with her father from 2011–2013. In June 2013, the Supreme Court issued a five–four decision on the case, reversing the previous courts' decisions and returning custody to the adoptive parents. The majority based their decision on the Court's holding that a non-custodial father does not have rights under the ICWA. In September 2013, her biological father turned Veronica over to her adoptive parents and her biological father dropped proceedings within the Cherokee and Oklahoma courts and is currently "in communication" with Veronica, though it's not clear how or how often that communication happens (Overall, 2014).

Legal scholars have critically analyzed this case's logic and impacts on the legal bounds and applications of the ICWA. Some of this analysis focuses on ongoing problems with implementation of the ICWA, including a lack of repercussions for states failing to adhere to the ICWA (Burke, 2014), as well as the impact of weakening the application of the Existing Family Doctrine in enforcement of the ICWA, which was applied by the South Carolina Supreme Court when they placed Veronica with Brown (Zug, 2014). Other scholars are concerned less with the practical impacts of the decision and instead cite cultural and historical contexts that provide concerning framing for the legal and cultural reasons for the Supreme Court ruling. According to Jessica Di Palma (2013), the Court's decision oversimplified the actual text of the ICWA and ignored the impetus behind its passage and resulting protections. She argues that the majority distorted the language of the ICWA to decide what they felt was *morally* right, not what was in adherence to the law. Both Di Palma (2013) and Dustin C. Jones (2014) cite concern that the repercussions of this decision could result in more Native parents being excluded from being protected under the ICWA and that the Court effectively created a second class of parenting citizens—absentee indigenous parents—solely through the logic that there was no way that the ICWA would have meant to protect them. Jones asks: why would the ICWA not have been intended to apply to absentee parents? Absentee parents still have other custody and parenting rights.

Additionally, some scholars are concerned about how this case relates to ongoing colonization and systems of racialization in the United States. Bethany R. Berger (2015) argues that this case was a "microcosm of anxieties about Indianness, race, and the changing nature of parenthood" (p. 295). These anxieties were focused on condemnation of poor single mothers, class divides in parenting, and racialized stereotypes of Native people. Though the majority claimed that the decision was in the interest of the child, the decision supports policies and procedures that undermine Native children's interests. Alyosha Goldstein (2014) concurs, arguing that the majority's decision is fundamentally about the right of white people to possess due to white heter-onormativity. Goldstein connects this right of possession as associated with whiteness and as important to a cultural denial of culpability for ongoing settler colonization and racial violence.

Racism, settler colonization, and white supremacy do more than frame how the majority justices approached this case, however. Arguably, these frameworks shaped how the judges understood the very facts of the case. Though the majority opinion paints Brown as a non-custodial parent who did not seek custody or parental rights until long after the child's birth, scholars contest this framing. Drawing on both published and unpublished records and testimony, Berger (2015) establishes that Brown sought to parent his daughter as soon as he found out that the mother was pregnant. He was pre-vented from doing so because the adoptive parents and their attorneys actively hid the adoption plan from him. This conflicts with the Court's representa-tion of Brown in the decision. Rather than being a negligent father who abandoned his child, Brown sought custody and the right to parent his child at every opportunity.

Indigenous Reproductive Justice

A specific history of racialization *and* sovereignty frames reproductive justice for indigenous people, intertwined with unique issues for indigenous com-munities on Turtle Island. Taken in the context of child removal, family and community disruption, and attempts to "kill the Indian to save the man," adoption becomes incredibly complex. Reproductive justice is a necessary framework when considering the removal of Native children and how U.S. settler state agents facilitate that removal.

Reproductive justice is a framework most often applied with the concerns and needs of women of color and indigenous women at the center. In this case, however, I am applying an indigenous reproductive justice framework to the removal of a child who has a non-Native mother and a father who is an enrolled member of the Cherokee Nation. When we consider the history of the settler state and its histories of framing indigenous families as unfit to raise their children it becomes clear that reproductive justice and adoption in indigenous communities are as much a community issue as an individual one. This narrative of unfitness is part of what facilitated the logics that led to the final decision and majority opinion in *Adoptive Couple v. Baby Girl*.

Reproductive justice also provides grounds for a lens of skepticism in the interests and possibilities for justice that the settler state can provide. This skepticism is productive when considering the role of the federal government and the Supreme Court in the final decision to place Veronica with her adop-tive parents to the objections of her paternal family and the Cherokee Nation. Reproductive justice scholars have long insisted that the state cannot be a place where women of color and indigenous women can easily place their trust. After all, this is the same state that authorizes uranium mining on Tewa Pueblo land, leaching uranium into groundwater and drinking water (Landa & Gray, 1995), and that tested sterilization procedures on coerced and uninformed women in Puerto Rico (Briggs, 2003). There is no reason for people of color and indigenous people to see the settler state as a neutral figure, nor to trust its representatives to care for their reproductive justice.

This critical eye to the state is important to apply in the case of *Adoptive Couple v. Baby Girl* (2013). From the beginning of the implementation of the ICWA, legal scholars expressed concern about what they saw as statutory and legal weaknesses in the text of the law. They were concerned—rightfully so—that the law would not be as effective as advocates hoped if clearer language about application was not added and if training and funding requirements were not added to the bill. The weaknesses of the ICWA, the law attempting to protect Native families, were never addressed.

The federal government, even in attempts to address a long history of child removal and community disruption, failed to create a law that adequately protected indigenous families. And yet, this should not be a total surprise. Individual agents of the government may work for conditions under which indigenous communities and families can flourish, but the federal government as a whole cannot. The very validation of the settler state in part comes from the domination of indigenous communities. From this view, the Supreme Court decision to weaken the ICWA and to return Veronica to her adoptive family is less surprising. In fact, we can see the logics of settler colonialism and justifications for child removal throughout the majority decision.

The majority opinion of the Supreme Court decision, written by Justice Samuel Alito, begins by minimizing Veronica's relationship to the Cherokee people. Justice Alito describes her as "classified as an Indian because she is 1.2% (3/256) Cherokee" (*Adoptive Couple v. Baby Girl*, 2013). Here, the majority opinion begins by focusing on Veronica's "blood quantum," or the percentage of her DNA that can be traced to a specific federally recognized tribe. Alito tacitly trades on popular non-Native understandings of membership within tribes as predicated upon this "percentage" of heritage. However, the imposition of blood quantum on tribal membership is a facet of indigenous community belonging—now understood as tribal registration—that indigenous studies scholars have emphasized was a result of colonization. Tribes integrated blood quantum into some tribal agreements with the U.S. government to allow the U.S. government to limit the number of members of the tribes (Harmon, 2001; TallBear, 2003). More importantly, blood quantum is not a part of how the Cherokee Nation recognizes and enrolls members. Rather, they determine tribal enrollment according to documented connection to an enrolled lineal Cherokee Nation ancestor who is listed on the Dawes Roll, taken between 1899 and 1906 of citizens and freed people in Indian Territory, which is now northeast Oklahoma (Cherokee Nation Tribal Registration, n.d.).[1] At the very outset of the decision, Justice Alito relies on historically racist constructions of Native identity to call into question the very legitimacy of Veronica's ties to her indigenous community trying to claim custody. These questions are grounded in mechanisms of colonization which further a colonial agenda.

Alito again brings up Veronica's blood quantum when describing Brown's authority to object to the adoption placement. "It is undisputed that, had Baby Girl not been 3/256 Cherokee, Biological Father would have had no right to object to her adoption under South Carolina law" (*Adoptive Couple v. Baby Girl*, 2013), as consent of a biological father is not required under South Carolina adoption law. The repetition of the "percentage" of Veronica's heritage—despite it being meaningless to her relationship to the Cherokee Nation—reiterates settler investments in blood quantum and the racialization of Native people. Alito references blood quantum to dismiss Veronica's connection to her family and tribe.

Alito also cites the requirement of the ICWA that any adoption must show that there had been attempts made by the state and adoption agents to prevent the breakup of the Native family. Alito highlights this to emphasize the majority reading of this statue as applying "only in cases where an Indian family's 'breakup' would be precipitated by the termination of the parent's rights" (*Adoptive Couple v. Baby Girl*, 2013). The quotes around breakup here are significant, as they emphasize that the court majority does not see the removal of an indigenous infant as a family breakup. Additionally, though the Court focuses on the fact that Brown had no parental rights upon Veronica's adoption, they ignore the fact that their decision *does* terminate his parental rights, obtained when lower courts found in his favor. The Supreme Court justices are in the process of removing those rights and removing Veronica from her family home while emphasizing that he did not have those rights upon her initial placement. The U.S. legal system's intention to protect Veronica and her family from family breakup are so deeply intertwined with settler state investments that they have a limited ability to protect indigenous children and families. As a result, the Cherokee Nation has set up a firm set of guidelines for adoption of Cherokee children intended to work in tandem with the ICWA.

Even if Brown and his parents had not been willing to care for Veronica, it is very unlikely that the Cherokee Nation would have approved Duncan and Capobianco as prospective adoptive parents had they gone through the correct channels. If either they or the birth mother followed the guidelines in the ICWA, Duncan and Capobianco should have worked with the Cherokee Nation to adopt Veronica. However, the Cherokee Nation likely would have rejected them as potential adoptive parents immediately based on requirements found clearly on their Child Welfare website. In addition to needing to be willing to submit to a background check, being in appropriate mental and physical health to care for a child, and other relatively standard child welfare requirements, the Cherokee Nation requires the enrollment of the potential adoptive parent or their spouse "as a member of Cherokee Nation or another federally recognized Indian tribe, or a relative of a child in the custody of the tribe or state" ("Qualification of Placement Resource Homes," 2017). They do note that the Child Welfare office reserves the right to deviate from the standards to serve the best interest of the child. This process, more clearly invested in family and community cohesion and without the investment of the settler state, should have been effective for Veronica. So, one wonders: why did this process not work for Veronica and her family?

When Veronica's birth mother initially selected Duncan and Capobianco as adoptive parents, her attorney contacted the Cherokee Nation to determine whether Brown was formally enrolled. However, because the inquiry letter misspelled Brown's first name and included an incorrect birth date, the Cherokee Nation responded to the attorneys that they could not confirm that individual as a registered tribal member (*Adoptive Couple v. Baby Girl*, 2013). Due to a mistake in paperwork, the authority of the Cherokee Nation was bypassed and the U.S. government gained jurisdiction over the final decision. These kinds of mistakes—ones which resulted in Native families not being allowed to raise their children—are riddled throughout the historical record, showing how tightly tied Brown's experience is to that of other indigenous families who had children removed through adoption.

The specific histories of child removal and complexities of racialization and sovereignty are highlighted by considering the adoption of Veronica and the final decision in *Adoptive Couple v. Baby Girl* (2013) as connected through reproductive justice. Reproductive justice emphasizes that citizenship is a vital part of understanding reproductive justice and the relationship that many women of color and indigenous women have to the state. Loretta Ross emphasizes that we must understand citizenship as extending beyond the sphere of legal citizenship and formal rights. She argues that this limited understanding of citizenship "ignores the intersectional matrix of race, gender, sovereignty, class and immigration status that complicates debates on reproductive politics in the United States for women of color" (2006, p. 62). Reproductive justice in the United States must also recognize the differences of actual citizenship and sovereignty for Native women as distinct from other women of color. Reproductive justice in Native communities must always highlight and recognize the complexities of sovereignty and racialization for Native people, as well as the ways that relationship to the settler state is unique to indigenous people.

Indigenous reproductive justice also allows a shift in understanding of reproductive politics. No longer can we think of reproductive politics as solely about individual rights. Rather, reproductive politics and justice in indigenous communities must always consider reproductive rights and justice of individuals as connected to the rights and justice of communities. This is particularly important for Native women because of the long history of Native women and communities being targeted as a group for things such as inadequate health care through the IHS (Gurr, 2014) and sterilization (Lawrence, 2000; Ralstin-Lewis, 2005).

Conclusion

The decision of the Supreme Court in *Adoptive Couple v. Baby Girl* (2013) was more than a judicial decision that—depending on your orientation toward the case—either reunited or decimated a family. It was a result of more than a century of federal policies and child welfare practices which facilitated the ongoing removal of massive numbers of indigenous children in the United States from their family and tribal environments. It was also a moment when the U.S. federal government was clear about the degree to which indigenous families can find safety within the settler state. In the decision that the ICWA did not apply to Dusten Brown and his custody of his daughter, the court both confirmed fears of the ICWA's inefficacy and validated previous child removal and family disruption projects.

The ability to parent your children is an issue of reproductive justice, as reproductive justice activists and scholars have been highlighting for decades. The adoption of Native children into non-Native homes is an issue of reproductive justice that is specific to indigenous communities due to their histories of child removal and relationship to the U.S. government. The case of *Adoptive Couple v. Baby Girl* (2013) confirms what many people in indigenous communities have long known—they cannot trust the U.S. government to protect their interests or the wellbeing of their families. Indigenous communities continue to advocate for the interests with their communities in issues of reproductive justice. In the future, I hope to see reproductive justice scholars, indigenous community members, and adoption studies scholars working together to address the specific social and policy issues that need to be addressed to adequately deal with the role of settler colonization in racialization of Native people and disruption of Native families. All of the factors that contribute to understanding Native families as unfit, white families as inherently better, and Native children as targets for removal must be accounted for. Only then will effective policies to protect Native families be possible.

Note

1   It is worth noting that the citizenship of the descendants of Cherokee Freedmen—people whose ancestors were held in slavery by members of the Cherokee Nation and who were granted citizenship in the Cherokee Nation upon the abolishment of slavery—in the Cherokee Nation of Oklahoma has been fraught. Stripped of their tribal citizenship by popular vote in 2007, the descendants of the Cherokee Freedmen sued the Cherokee Nation and, on August 31, 2017, a U.S. federal court judge ruled that these descendants had citizenship rights within the tribe (Chow, 2017).

References

Adams, D. W. (1995). *Education for extinction: American Indians and the boarding school experience.* Lawrence: University of Kansas Press.

Adoptive Couple v. Baby Girl, 133 S. Ct. 2552 (2013).

Albers, E. C., Reilly, T., & Ritter, B. (1993). Children in foster care: Possible factors affecting permanency planning. *Child and Adolescent Social Work Journal, 10*(4), 329–341.

Asian Communities for Reproductive Justice. (2005). *A new vision for advancing our movement for reproductive health, reproductive rights and reproductive justice.* Oakland, CA: ACRJ. Accessed May 25, 2017 at http://reproductivejustice.org/assets/docs/ACRJ-A-New-Vision.pdf.

Bailey, A. (2011). Reconceiving surrogacy: Toward a reproductive justice account of Indian surrogacy. *Hypatia, 26*(4), 715–741.

Barsh, R. L. (1979). Indian Child Welfare Act of 1978: A critical analysis. *Hastings Law Journal, 31,* 1287–1336.

Belsky, J. (1993). Etiology of child maltreatment: A developmental–ecological analysis. *Psychological Bulletin, 114*(3), 413–434.

Benson, K. (2017). *Generations of removal: Child removal of Native children in eastern Washington state through compulsory education, foster care, and juvenile justice.* Unpublished doctoral dissertation.

Berger, B. R. (2015). In the name of the child: Race, gender, and economics in *Adoptive Couple v. Baby Girl. Florida Law Review, 67,* 295–362.

Bilchik, S. (2001, April 24). [Keynote address]. Working together to strengthen supports for Indian children and families: A national perspective. Speech presented at the 19th Annual Protecting Our Children Conference, Anchorage, AK.

Briggs, L. (2003). *Reproducing empire: Race, sex, science, and US imperialism in Puerto Rico.* Berkeley: University of California Press.

Briggs, L. (2012). *Somebody's children: The politics of transracial and transnational adoption.* Durham, NC: Duke University Press.

Briggs, L., Ginsburg, F., Gutierrez, E. R., Petchesky, R., Rapp, R., Smith, A., & Takeshita, C. (2013). Roundtable: Reproductive technologies and reproductive justice. *Frontiers: A Journal of Women's Studies, 34*(3), 102–125.

Burke, J. (2014). Baby Veronica case: Current implementation problems of the Indian Child Welfare Act. *Wayne Law Review, 60,* 307–328.

Chen, C. (2013). Choosing the right to choose: *Roe v. Wade* and the feminist movement to legalize abortion in martial-law Taiwan. *Frontiers: A Journal of Women Studies, 34*(3), 73–101.

Cherokee Nation Tribal Registration. (n.d.). Accessed January 10, 2017 at www.cherokee.org/Portals/0/Documents/2012/8/31660Application_Instructions.pdf.

Child, B. J. (1998). *Boarding school seasons: American Indian families, 1900–1940.* Lincoln: University of Nebraska Press.

Chow, K. (2017, August 31). Judge rules that Cherokee Freedmen have right to tribal citizenship. Accessed October 3, 2017, at www.npr.org/sections/thetwo-way/2017/08/31/547705829/judge-rules-that-cherokee-freedmen-have-right-to-tribal-citizenship.

Cotter-Busbee, P., & DeMeyer, T. A. (2013). *Two worlds: Lost children of the Indian Adoption Project.* Greenfield, MA: Blue Hand Books.

Cross, T. L., Earle, K. A., & Simmons, D. (2000). Child abuse and neglect in Indian country: Policy issues. *Families in Society, 81,* 49–58.

Cuthbert, D., & Fronek, P. (2014). Perfecting adoption? Reflections on the rise of commercial off-shore surrogacy and family formation in Australia. In A. Hayes & D. Higgens (Eds.), *Families, policy, and the law: Selected essays on contemporary issues for Australia,* pp. 55–66. Melbourne: Australian Institute of Family Studies.

Deloria, V. (1969). *Custer died for your sins: An Indian manifesto.* Tulsa: University of Oklahoma Press.

Di Palma, J. (2013). *Adoptive Couple v. Baby Girl*: The Supreme Court's distorted interpretation of The Indian Child Welfare Act of 1978. *Loyala Law Review, 47,* 523–538.

Donald, K. L., Bradley, L. K., Critchley, R., Day, P., & Nuccio, K. E. (2003). Comparison between American Indian and non-Indian out-of-home placements. *Families in Society: The Journal of Contemporary Social Services, 84*(2), 267–274.

Ellis, C. (2006). "We had a lot of fun, but of course that wasn't the school part": Life at the rainy mountain boarding school, 1890–1923. In C. E. Trafzer, J. A. Keller, & L. Sisquoc (Eds.), *Boarding school blues: Revising American Indian Educational Experiences,* pp. 65–98. Lincoln: University of Nebraska Press.

Environmental Violence & Reproductive Justice. (n.d.). Accessed May 25, 2017 at www.nativeyouthsexualhealth.com/environmentalviolenceandreproductivejustice.html.

Fanshel, D. (1972). *Far from the reservation: The transracial adoption of American Indian children.* A Study Conducted Under the Auspices of the Child Welfare League of America, New York.

Fixmer-Oraiz, N. (2013). Speaking of solidarity: Transnational gestational surrogacy and the rhetorics of reproductive (in) justice. *Frontiers: A Journal of Women Studies, 34*(3), 126–163.

Goldstein, A. (2014). Possessive investment: Indian removals and the affective entitlements of whiteness. *American Quarterly, 66*(4), 1077–1084.

Graham, L. M. (1998). "The Past Never Vanishes": A contextual critique of the existing Indian family doctrine. *American Indian Law Review, 23*(1), 1–54.

Guerrero, M. P. (1979). Indian Child Welfare Act of 1978: A response to the threat to Indian culture caused by foster and adoptive placements of Indian children. *American Indian Law Review, 7*(1), 51–77.

Gurr, B. (2014). *Reproductive justice: The politics of health care for Native American women.* New Brunswick, NJ: Rutgers University Press.

Harmon, A. (2001). Tribal enrollment councils: Lessons on law and Indian identity. *Western Historical Quarterly, 32,* 175–200.

Hoover, E., Cook, K., Plain, R., Sanchez, K., Waghiyi, V., Miller, P., Dufault, P., Sislin, C., & Carpenter, D. O. (2012). Indigenous peoples of North America: Environmental exposures and reproductive justice. *Environmental Health Perspectives, 120*(12), 1645–1649.

Jacobs, M. (2011). *White mother to a dark race: Settler colonialism, materialism, and the removal of indigenous children in the American west and Australia, 1880–1940.* Lincoln: University of Nebraska Press.

Jacobs, M. (2014). *A generation removed: The fostering and adoption of indigenous children in the postwar world.* Lincoln: University of Nebraska Press.

Jaffke, C. (2006). The "Existing Indian Family" exception to the Indian Child Welfare Act: The states' attempt to slaughter tribal interests in Indian children. *Louisiana Law Review, 66*(3), 733–762.

Jarman, M. (2015). Relations of abortion: Crip approaches to reproductive justice. *Feminist Formations, 27*(1), 46–66.

Jesudason, S., & Kimport, K. (2013). Decentering the individual and centering community: Using a reproductive justice methodology to examine the uses of reprogenetics. *Frontiers: A Journal of Women Studies, 34*(3), 213–225.

Johnston-Robledo, I., & Murray, A. (2012). Reproductive justice for women and infants: Restoring women's postpartum health and infant-feeding options. In J. C. Chrisler (Ed.), *Reproductive justice: A global concern*, pp. 269–288. Santa Barbara, CA: Praeger.

Jones, D. C. (2014). *Adoptive Couple v. Baby Girl*: The creation of second-class Native American parents under the Indian Child Welfare Act of 1978. *Law and Inequality: A Journal of Theory and Practice, 32*, 421–449.

Landa, E. R., & Gray, J. R. (1995). US Geological Survey research on the environmental fate of uranium mining and milling wastes. *Environmental Geology, 26*, 19–31.

Lawrence, J. (2000). The Indian health service and the sterilization of Native American women. *American Indian Quarterly, 24*(3), 400–419.

Lomawaima, K. T. (1995). *They called it prairie light: The story of Chilocco Indian School*. Lincoln: University of Nebraska Press.

McKee, K. (2018). Adoption as a reproductive justice issue. *Adoption and Culture, 6*(1), 74–93.

Mannes, M. (1995). Factors and events leading to the passage of the Indian Child Welfare Act. *Center for Social Research and Development, 25*, 350–357.

NYSHN statement to the National Energy Board regarding Line 9 Pipeline Proposal. (2013, October 18). Accessed May 25, 2017 at www.nativeyouthsexualhealth.com/october182013.pdf.

Overall, M. (2014, September 21). One year later, Baby Veronica case still resonates. *Tulsa World*. Accessed March 29, 2016 at www.tulsaworld.com/news/courts/one-year-later-baby-veronica-case-still-resonates/article_2b85eeef-72c5-50cb-b3e8-74f9dfe7355e.html.

Palmiste, C. (2011). From the Indian Adoption Project to the Indian Child Welfare Act: The resistance of Native American communities. *Indigenous Policy Journal, 22*(1), 1–10.

Plantz, M., Hubbell, T., Barrett, B., & Dorbrec, A. (1989). Indian child welfare: A status report. *Children Today, 18*(1), 24–29.

Pratt, R. (1892). Kill the Indian, save the man. In *Official report of the nineteenth annual conference of charities and correction*, Washington, DC (pp. 46–59).

Qualification of Placement Resource Homes (Standards). (2017). *Cherokee Nation Indian Child Welfare*. Accessed May 26, 2017 at www.cherokeekids.org/How-To-Become-A-Home/What-To-Expect-Copy.

Ralstin-Lewis, D. M. (2005). The continuing struggle against genocide: Indigenous women's reproductive rights. *Wicazo Sa Review, 20*(1), 71–95.

Reproductive Justice Program. (n.d.). Accessed May 25, 2017 at www.nativeshop.org/programs/reproductive-justice.html.

Rosenfeld, A. A., Pilowsky, D. J., Fine, P., Thorpe, M., Fein, E., Simms, M. D., Halfon, N., Irwin, M., Alfaro, J., Saletsky, R., & Nickman, S. (1997). Foster care: An update. *Journal of the American Academy of Child and Adolescent Psychiatry, 36*(4), 448–458.

Ross, L. J. (2006). Understanding reproductive justice. *Off Our Backs, 36*(4), 14–19.

Ross, L., Gutiérrez, E., Gerber, M., & Silliman, J. (2016). *Undivided rights: Women of color organize for reproductive justice*. Chicago: Haymarket Books.

Rutecki, G. W. (2011). Forced sterilization of Native Americans: Later twentieth century physician cooperation with national eugenic policies? *Ethics and Medicine, 27*(1), 33.

Sagrestano, L. M., & Finerman, R. (2012). Pregnancy and prenatal care: A reproductive justice perspective. In J. C. Chrisler (Ed.), *Reproductive justice: A global concern*, pp. 201–230. Santa Barbara, CA: Praeger.

Simpson, A. (2014). *Mohawk interruptus: Political life across the borders of settler states.* Durham, NC: Duke University Press.

TallBear, K. (2003). DNA, blood, and racializing the tribe. *Wicazo Sa Review, 18*(1), 81–107.

Torpy, S. J. (2000). Native American women and coerced sterilization: On the trail of tears in the 1970s. *American Indian Culture and Research Journal, 24*(2), 1–22.

U.S. Bureau of Labor Statistics. (2014, November). Labor force characteristics by race and ethnicity, 2014. *BLS Reports.* Accessed May 26, 2017 at www.bls.gov/opub/reports/race-and-ethnicity/archive/labor-force-characteristics-by-race-and-ethnicity-2014.pdf.

Wallis, E. V. (2013). "The verdict created no great surprise upon the street": Abortion, medicine, and the regulatory state in Progressive-era Los Angeles. *Frontiers: A Journal of Women Studies, 34*(3), 48–72.

Wolfe, P. (1999). *Settler colonialism and the transformation of anthropology.* London: Cassell Press.

Wolfe, P. (2006). Settler colonialism and the elimination of the Native. *Journal of Genocide Research, 8*(4), 387–409.

Zug, M. A. (2014). The real impact of *Adoptive Couple v. Baby Girl*: The Existing Indian Family Doctrine is not affirmed, but the future of the ICWA's placement preferences is jeopardized. *Capital University Law Review, 42*, 327–360.

5

PASSING FOR REPRODUCTION

HOW LESBIANS IN TAIWAN USE ASSISTED REPRODUCTIVE TECHNOLOGIES
SZU-YING HO

Introduction

With the increase in gay and lesbian parenting, a number of studies have noted the "lesbian baby boom" or "gay baby boom" phenomenon in the United States (Patterson, 1992; Weston, 1997). Other studies have discussed the relation between the popularization of self-insemination (SI) techniques and lesbian procreation (Klein, 1984; Wikler & Wikler, 1991). While reproduction has long been medicalized and reproductive technology monopolized by medical professionals (Oakley, 1984; Rothman, 1984), SI has emerged as a process of demedicalizing reproductive technology and a successful strategy for women to regain autonomy in regard to their bodies. It has even been characterized as a form of "lesbian empowerment" (Wikler & Wikler, 1991; Agigian, 2004; Mamo, 2007).

However, most of the literature on lesbian procreation focuses overwhelmingly on experiences in the United States and some European countries (particularly Britain) (Donovan, 2000; Haimes & Weiner, 2000; Klein, 1984; Weston, 1997). Little research has explored other regions of the world. Is SI a panacea for all lesbians who want to be parents? Or does this configuration of "lesbian empowerment" function only in special cultural and social contexts rather than as a successful and universal model that can be promoted in all parts of the Earth? How has SI spread in countries with varying social and historical contexts? And is the technique even well known in other regions? For example, as Herrera (2009) notes, despite the fact that some lesbians in Chile did not understand exactly how the SI process works, they still *perceived* it, compared to heterosexual sex and adoption, as the best alternative way to have children. In other words, not all lesbians are familiar with this technique or clearly understand how to practice it. While Grzanka (2008) asserts that SI has already traveled through generations and networks of women, in general, the extent of the lesbian appropriation of assisted reproductive technologies (ARTs) in non-Western regions is still largely unknown and uninvestigated. Given these concerns, the major goal of my research is to explore and deepen our understanding of how lesbians[1] appropriate ARTs, including SI, in regions outside the United States and Britain. This chapter focuses in particular on Taiwan.

According to Grzanka (2008), one of the cruxes of queering reproduction is the decoupling of heterosexuality from reproduction. Furthermore, as Mamo (2007) argued, by gaining access to ARTs, "lesbians have destabilized the dichotomy between heterosexual and homosexual experience and the institution of the family." Such lesbian actors overcome a variety of interwoven barriers, such as legal regulations, physicians' moral concerns, and inscribed discrimination in medical environments. Consequently, this research adopts Mamo's (2007) "queering reproduction" as the major analytical concept in this research.

Queering Reproduction in Transition: From Demedicalization to Biomedicalization

The effect of ARTs on women has become a topic of heated debate among feminist scholars in recent decades. Some contend that ARTs may exacerbate the medicalization of reproduction and that ARTs serve only the patriarchy's desire for descendants (Crowe, 1990; Rothman, 2000). For example, the descendants inherit the blood lineages, properties, and, in the Taiwanese context, the most important thing—the family name (Shieh, 2003). In addition, there is concern that ARTs may menace the notion of the natural, holy, unified, women-only experience of maternity (Corea, 1986). In contrast, some feminists argue that ARTs have the potential to emancipate women because they challenge the naturalized concept of unified maternity by interrupting the consistency of genetic, gestational, and social motherhood. As Firestone (1970) argues, the biological division of labor in reproduction is the root cause of male domination and the ensuing gender inequality. Consequently, Firestone contends that the "artificial womb" can emancipate women from biological motherhood and help to eliminate female subordination.

However, these two approaches are only partly accurate because they rely on oversimplified reasoning, ignore how ART practices are embedded in social contexts, and neglect the diversity of the users of such technologies. As Farquhar (1996) aptly puts it, to move beyond this dichotomy, we need to forge a third way in order to explore the diversity of users as well as those who cannot even qualify as users. We need to explore the social and historical contexts in which users adopt ARTs to embody their reproductive agency. In the past, ARTs served only privileged groups, such as white, heterosexual, middle-class, infertile couples (Rowland, 1987). However, more alternative users have chosen procreation by ARTs in recent decades. Among them are single women and gay or lesbian couples. Farquhar argues that by tracing these ART users' experiences, we can find what prejudices and discrimination are inscribed in these techniques and how non-normative users challenge such assumptions, re-create, and redefine the meanings of ARTs.

The SI practices used by lesbians in the United States and the UK in the 1970s are often praised as a successful example of demedicalization and lesbian empowerment, especially because lesbians were denied access to ARTs in the United States due to the fundamental prejudices and exclusionary policies of the medical community (Agigian, 2004; Raboy, 1993). In 1994, the Ethics Committee of the American Fertility Society—a major professional association for practitioners of the American Society for Reproductive Medicine (ASRM)—officially claimed the privilege of using ARTs for heterosexual married couples and announced that it supported physician gatekeeping practices (Ethics Committee of the American Fertility Society, 1994). Likewise, lesbians in the UK were historically denied access to ARTs by clinics and most medical systems (Morgan & Lee, 1991). Furthermore, although the UK's Human Fertilisation and Embryology Act does not directly exclude lesbians from access to ARTs, it asks physicians to consider "the welfare of any child", including the need for a father, before providing such treatments (Saffron, 1994).

In this context, restrictions on access to ARTs drive women to seek other ways to conceive. In the United States, early women's health movements focused on teaching women to understand medical information, learn to know their own bodies, and control their own health and reproductive choices. In 1978, the first SI self-service group appeared and feminist organizations began to run women's health clinics (Ruzek, 1978). The next year, 1979, the first edition of the book *Lesbian Health Matters!* devoted a chapter to "alternative reproduction".

Similar cases occurred in England around the same time: many lesbians who wished to conceive formed SI self-help groups. These groups enabled women to talk about the SI process in public and to gather information about this technique (Hornstein, 1984). One article that clearly represents the political atmosphere of feminism at the time loudly announced, "Do it ourselves!" The article, entitled "Doing It Ourselves: Self Insemination," described in detail the formation of a self-help group, which distributed brochures to teach people how to perform SI (Klein, 1984). As Agigian (2004) argues, the

emergence of such demedicalized SI practices challenged the medical mono-
poly over artificial insemination and further reduced the power of physicians
to exert social control by deciding who could or could not become pregnant.
Furthermore, Wikler and Wikler (1991) note that SI techniques are now
"familiar to a wider public" (p. 17). But, how widely is this technique adopted
beyond the United States and UK?

Lesbians' use of ARTs has changed over the past decade. As Agigian
(2004) notes, most lesbians' practice of artificial insemination is usually high-
tech and professionally mediated. Additionally, Mamo (2007) argues that
there has been an "escalation of medical interventions" in the lesbian reproductive process. This transition could be understood as a process of biomedicalization. According to Clarke, Shim, Mamo, Fosket, and Fishman (2003),
"biomedicalization" refers to the more complicated, multi-sited, multidirec-
tional process of medicalization that has been extended and reconstituted in
the interaction between new social forms and increasingly technoscientific
biomedicine.

As Rose (2007) maintains, new biopolitics bring new possibilities, but
individuals are also forced to make choices at every moment. According to
Rose, "every act of choice opened up by the new biomedicine does indeed
involve a judgment of value in a field of probabilities shaped by hopes." Such
hopes are based on the idea that people cannot only control their lives but
also transform them. Consequently, involuntary childlessness is not necessarily a grief that LGBT (Lesbian, Gay, Bisexual, Transgender) people must
bear. New reproductive technologies have the potential to bring new choices
to this group but also lead to new issues and disputes. For example, Mamo
notes, "the initial step of performing at-home insemination appears to be
slowly disappearing" (2007, p. 164). In addition to concerns regarding the
success rate of ARTs, the diversity of ARTs provides more possibilities for
lesbian conception practices. For example, more lesbians have recently under-
taken reception of oocytes from their partner (ROPA) for conception because
it is a way of allowing both partners in a lesbian couple to participate in biological motherhood. In this procedure, one partner provides the eggs, which
are fertilized with donated semen, and the other receives and gestates the
embryos (Marina et al., 2010).

Altogether, Mamo (2007) concludes three main features of queering
reproduction. First, by gaining access to ARTs, "lesbians have destabilized
the dichotomy between heterosexual and homosexual experience and the
institution of the family." Second, Mamo notes that lesbian actors must overcome a variety of interwoven barriers, including legal restrictions, physicians'
moral concerns, and inscribed discrimination in medical environments. Third,
Mamo proposes hybrid technology practices, suggesting that lesbian actors
consciously mix high-tech/low-tech and medical/nonmedical knowledge.

Mamo argues that lesbians consciously combine techniques and knowledge learned from different groups and areas.

While most literature of lesbian procreation focuses overwhelmingly on the United States and some European countries, this study is the first to examine lesbians' appropriation of ARTs in Taiwan. Furthermore, while most Western countries have not clearly restricted access to ARTs for single women and lesbians in law, this research is the first to explore how lesbians in Taiwan appropriate ARTs despite the country's restrictive legislation against non-heterosexual, unmarried users.

The Case of Taiwan: Restrictive Regulations and Vibrant Lesbian Parenting Desires

Taiwan is an interesting and theoretically abundant case study because it is situated in a special social and cultural intersection. On one hand, Taiwan enjoys some of the most progressive gender equality policies of any East Asian country. Furthermore, Taiwan is believed to be the first country in Asia to legalize same-sex marriage (Horton, 2016). According to a study released by the World Bank (2011), while 28 of the 30 high-income Organisation for Economic Co-operation and Development countries grant parental leave, only two nations in East Asia and the Pacific region grant parental leave. Taiwan is one of them.

On the other hand, Taiwan has enacted restrictive eligibility requirements for ART users. According to a survey conducted by the International Federation of Fertility Societies (IFFS), only 13 of 62 countries have required marriage status as an absolute prerequisite for ARTs. Seven of those are Southeast Asian (Hong Kong, Japan, Philippines, Singapore, Vietnam, China, and Taiwan) (Nygren, Hirshikesh, Le Roux, & Sullivan, 2013).

Interestingly, in the IFFS survey in 2010, 12 Islamic countries and seven Southeast Asian countries permitted only heterosexual married couples to use ARTs (Jones, Cooke, Kempers, Brinsden, & Saunders, 2010). With the loosening of regulations in the Islamic world, Southeast Asia has become the most prominent region in the world in which only married couples are legally qualified to use ARTs. Furthermore, while a number of studies have explored the practice of ARTs in Islamic regions (Inhorn, 2012), there is still little research in the use and development of ARTs in Asia. Despite such strict regulations, the first lesbian parenting social group in East Asia emerged in Taiwan.

According to Wu (2011, 2012), one of the features for donor insemination in Taiwan is a physician-dominated trajectory. Taiwan's physicians highly regulate the practice of ARTs. Before the legislation of the Artificial Reproduction Act in 2006, physicians could decide the "suitable" users of ARTs in clinical settings. This situation corresponds to Daniels and Golden's (2004) observation regarding "surrogate fathers." Before the rise of the private sperm bank market in the United States, the united management of sperm enabled doctors to decide how their patients could make use of ARTs. They exercised great control over the selection of sperm and controlled the process of insemination. Similarly, medical professionals played crucial roles as gatekeepers and "surrogate fathers" before the passage of the Assisted Human Reproduction Act in Taiwan in 2007.

Data and Methods

Gay and lesbian respondents in studies about parenting may fear exposure because it may cause them to lose employment or custody (Haimes & Weiner, 2000), so access is a crucial issue in this kind of study. I conducted fieldwork by participating in the Taiwan Lesbian Mothers Association (also known as Taiwan LGBT Family Rights Advocacy [TLFRA]) from 2007 to 2014. Research participants were recruited from this organization through personal contacts and snowball sampling.

Fourteen self-identified lesbians were interviewed in this research, including five couples. Thirteen of them are biological mothers or co-mothers; one had tried SI twice, but it had not worked by the time of the last interview. Eight of the 14 respondents or their partners had tried SI; however, none of them had conceived by this technique. Ten of the respondents or their partners had experienced intrauterine insemination (IUI). Five couples had pursued ARTs abroad (two in Canada and three in Thailand), and three had used ROPA to conceive. The interviews were semi-structured and ranged from one hour to three hours; all were taped and transcribed; and all participants' names have been changed to protect their privacy. The respondents' children ranged in age from one year to 12 years old. In addition to the interviews, I analyzed the text from the Lesbian Mothers Association newsletter, website, and blog, and attended activities and colloquiums held by TLFRA.

Queering Reproduction in a Prohibited Context: Lesbian Appropriation of ARTs in Taiwan

Classified by different historical periods, community resources, and types of lesbian appropriation of ARTs, this research generally divides Taiwan lesbians' ART practices into three stages, which will be discussed separately in the following sections.

Passing for Reproduction Period (1990s to Early 2000s): Seeking Ways into the Existing Medical System

The Taiwan LGBT movement began to emerge and flourish in the early 1990s. Its main focus was on issues of coming out and LGBT identities. Little attention was paid to gay and lesbian parenting. The scarcity of discussion of lesbian parenting limited lesbians' imagination and actions regarding having children.

One volume published in 1997 of *Girlfriend*, the first journal exclusively for lesbians in Taiwan, described lesbians' lament in not being able to bear children:

> There are some regrets same-sex couples have to bear. Among all, not being able to have our own child is the most unbearable for me and my partner, Sisy. I can't help envying those who keep their cats and dogs and treat them as their own babies.
>
> (Wen, 1997)

Additionally, there was a lack of discussion of SI at this time and lesbians' ideas of how to have children were still restricted to heterosexual intercourse or relationships. Another article in *Girlfriend* repeats this complaint: "Is the only way for lesbians to have biological children by sleeping with a man?" (Garfield, 2001). These comments reflect a general lack of imagination about using ARTs to realize parenting desires among Taiwan lesbian communities from the 1990s to the beginning of the 2000s.

Furthermore, in this period, gay identity and identity as a parent were almost mutually exclusive. For example, Cheng's (1997) book *Lesbian Circle*, the first anthropological work about the Taiwan lesbian community, reports lesbian partner relationships and heterosexual marriage experiences, but the "mother" and "lesbian" identities almost did not exist simultaneously. Most lesbians in this period faced the dilemma of embracing lesbian life and identity or staying in a heterosexual marriage with children. Gian (1997) contends that although lesbian mothers were a growing phenomenon in Western countries, women's disadvantaged socioeconomic status in Taiwan meant a lesbian could not afford a child or a dependent child would limit her career development. During this period, parenting was viewed as occurring only in heterosexual marriage and there was almost no discussion of how to use ARTs to conceive. Therefore, given the relative scarcity of resources and limited imagination, passing as a married or as a heterosexual single woman and "smuggling" oneself into the existing health care system in the current social context was considered a more viable option.

For example, one respondent, Xiao-Yuen, a 47-year-old self-identified butch lesbian, found ways into the existing health care system to conceive through an ART and gave birth to a baby boy. Her partner at the time was 23 years older than she was. Worried that her partner would die before her, she had a strong desire for a blood relative. When asked how she wanted to get pregnant, Xiao-Yuen said the first thing that came to her mind was a pseudo-marriage with a gay man. She said, "That is why I had to get pseudo-married!

At least your ID card shows the name of my spouse." The legal marital status enabled her to enter the medical institution and obtain assisted reproduction. In this way, ARTs thus offered an opportunity to distinguish "reproduction" from "intercourse." Xiao-Yuen describes herself and her partner as "interviewing" multiple gay couples to seek an appropriate one for the pseudo-marriage:

> It's for sure. I don't want to have real "sex" with the gay [man]. My partner didn't want me to do so. I myself, as a lesbian, am not willing to, either. We had blind dates ... and the first couple were ... devastating. Because we would ask them one by one, and if they were not against having actual sex with us, their points would right away plummet beneath zero.

This comment demonstrates how important non-sexual reproduction was for Xiao-Yuen. In her narrative, as a pseudo-marital partner, a gay man who was not opposed to heterosexual sex would "plummet beneath zero." Originally, Xiao-Yuen used her gay husband's sperm to practice SI at home. After several failed attempts, she sought assisted reproduction through the medical establishment. Xiao-Yuen's case illustrates, while only legal heterosexual couples were allowed to adopt ARTs, gay men and lesbians circumvented the law by pretending to be heterosexual couples in order to gain access to those services.

Ting-Ting, a 32-year-old femme, adopted a different method from Xiao-Yuen, she consciously tried to be recognized as a married woman. More precisely, she presented a fake marriage certificate that she had made herself. Ting-Ting and her partner, Mai-Ken, tried to use Mai-Ken's brother's sperm for SI, but Ting-Ting had some problems with the health of an oviduct, so their three attempts failed. After that, Ting-Ting went to the hospital and alleged that she was married and had infertility issues with her husband. Ting-Ting brought Mai-Ken's brother's sperm and asserted that it was her husband's, and the clinical staff did not ask for proof before agreeing to provide artificial insemination services for her. Taiwan's Artificial Reproduction Act does not regulate artificial insemination using a husband's semen; only artificial insemination using a donor's semen must be reported to the Department of Health. However, Ting-Ting's gynecological problems still caused her to have difficulty conceiving and she transferred to another medical center to pursue access to ARTs. Because her spouse's name did not appear on her ID card, the medical center asked her to present her marriage certificate. Ting-Ting calmly argued with the staff of the medical center:

> They asked me when we got married and why my spouse's name is blank ... I said we got married in 2007 because the civil law was amended in 2008; you only need to have a wedding ceremony to get

legal married status, but after that, you need to register at the Household Registration Administration ... When they said the marriage certificate could be submitted later and only needed to be faxed to them, I
almost hurrahed in my mind because the fake certificate is just so easy
to make.

Thus, Ting-Ting "passed" as a married heterosexual woman by presenting a
fake marriage certificate in order to access services.

Similarly, some of my interview respondents "passed" as single heterosexual women to gain access to ARTs. Although single women were denied
the use of ARTs generally, doctors typically recognized them as more "legitimate" users than lesbians. Dora, a femme in her 30s, recalled that she and her
partner went to the ob-gyn to say that they wished to use ARTs but were
repeatedly rejected. When the doctors recognized their lesbian relationship,
some rejected them immediately and some ridiculed them as "unusual" and
"immoral."

Dora realized that if she continued to visit doctors with her partner, she
would be rejected because of their lesbian identity. Therefore, after being
turned down several times, she went to a doctor and put her request as a
single woman, based on the assumption that she was heterosexual. She
asserted that she had stable work and economic ability and wanted to have a
child. The doctor asked why she did not find a husband or boyfriend, and her
response was "Men are all unreliable." Finally, the doctor was willing to help
Dora conceive. However, in order to let her use the sperm supplied by the
sperm bank for an infertile couple, the doctor charged Dora 200,000 NT, a
price almost 10 times higher than the usual one.

Dora, as a self-identified femme, enables her to pass as a heterosexual
woman by the doctors, who are the moral "gatekeepers" in the clinical setting.
One way to avoid stigma is to control personal social information (Goffman,
1963). When she proclaimed that she could afford to bring up a child as a
lesbian, it was regarded as "abnormal." However, when she claimed to be a
single heterosexual woman, she obtained the doctor's help.

In Xiao-Yuen's case, gay men and lesbians married each other to acquire a
legal identity in order to gain access to ARTs. However, in Dora's story, we
see that in addition to the law, the doctor's moral concern played a large part.
Neither single women nor lesbians were allowed access to ARTs by law. But,
in the doctor's own moral hierarchy, single women were "superior" to lesbians. For example, the Taiwanese Society for Reproductive Medicine advocated to include single women as qualified users for ARTs in a draft of their
official statement, but not single or coupled lesbians (Wu, 2002).[2] Taken
together, these stories demonstrate how the medical system imagines "suitable" ART users and how medical professionals play roles as gatekeepers and

"surrogate fathers" (Daniels & Golden, 2004). In addition, these stories also illustrate how lesbians use creative ways to circumvent the rules and regulations of heteronormativity and get access to ARTs.

It is also worth noting that the Assisted Human Reproduction Act was passed in 2007 in Taiwan. Both Xiao-Yuen and Dora used ARTs before 2007, when the regulations provided only a guideline and no clear punishment for doctors who violated it, thus providing considerable latitude for doctors. Since the passage of the law, illegal practice of ARTs may result in a revocation of a physician's license, making it harder to find a doctor to take such a risk.

Self-Insemination Period (2006–2012): The Emerging Network of Self-Insemination and Its Limits

Many scholars note that most SI has been performed and spread in the context of the feminist health movement and extended self-help groups (Wikler & Wikler, 1991; Agigian, 2004; Mamo, 2007). However, health and body issues have been less prevalent in the feminist movement in Taiwan (Wu, 2012) than in Western movements, and discussion of SI did not emerge until 2006. It is notable that the Lesbian Mothers Association appeared in Taiwan in 2005 and began to publish its monthly online newsletter, *Lama Post*, in February 2006. In the first issue of *Lama Post*, there was a translation of the article "Making Babies the Gay Way" (Cooper, 2006), which mentioned that a woman can inject a donor's sperm herself. Moreover, the topic of the January 2007 issue was "Lesbian DIY Pregnancy—How Lesbians Become Pregnant by SI" (Che, 2007). The Lesbian Mothers Association addressed multiple ways of empowering lesbians, equipping them with the knowledge to use ARTs and to consider lesbian parenting.

Many respondents, such as Ting-Ting, recalled that their first introduction to the practice was through the *Lama Post* newsletter:

> When I searched online in 2009 with the key words "lesbian ... have babies", I found the website of "Lama Post", and at first, I was surprised by this information ... because it seems so easy. But I didn't have luck with it. I tried [SI] three times, and I failed three times, too.

Despite such failures of SI trials, there were still vibrant discussions about how to improve this technique on the *Lama Post* online forum. For example, this response appeared in a newsletter article:

> My partner and I used a shot instead of a dropper. I don't know if a dropper is better than a shot because we tried several times but still did not succeed. We will give it another try. We also hope that fellow

lesbians with the same experience will share it with us. Maybe there's a model or something for us to follow, so that it's no difficult task for lesbians to bear children. Thank you!

(Allen, 2007)

From this response, it is obvious that *Lama Post* is not just a one-sided source of information but is a place where many lesbians gather to discuss, improve, and modify the SI technology. Lesbian users create their own interpretive flexibility on SI by sharing the same meaning and improving the technique together through the Lesbian Mothers Association and online forums.

While some lesbians failed to get pregnant, they tried to combine different tactics to enhance the probability of conceiving. Rita, a 35-year-old professional and active member who founded the Lesbian Mothers Association, had been involved in the feminist movement since high school. She had a strong belief about the empowerment and demedicalization aspects of SI and rejected a doctor's suggestion about sperm washing because she wanted to know whether the most "natural" method of SI could succeed:

I didn't do the sperm wash for the first trial, and I don't want to use IUI [intrauterine insemination] or IVF [in vitro fertilization] because I want to try the most natural way. But it just failed. So after that, I thought I should not stand too strongly for the natural way; if any other possible way can enhance the probability of getting pregnant, I would like to try. So at the third trial, I tried to combine different tactics; after I tested the follicle maturity by examination, I can get the HCG injection, and then I can do the SI by myself.

Rita's strategy for conceiving corresponds to one of the features of queering reproduction: hybrid technology practices. Her case demonstrates how lesbian users consciously combine high-tech (such as the HCG injection [human chorionic gonadotropin, a gonad-stimulating polypeptide hormone normally secreted by the placenta during pregnancy]) and low-tech (such as SI) methods. However, despite Rita's adoption of multiple tactics to enhance the probability of success, she still was not able to conceive by these methods. In addition to the uncertainty of the practice itself, the other barrier to SI is the lack of suitable resources for sperm and donors. As Rita complained:

I asked two gay [men] for sperm donation … and one of them even suggested I could get pregnant twice and share one child with him. It is totally impossible! The surrogacy and sperm cannot be a "fair" trade between the gay [man] and me. … As for heterosexual men, the single ones are afraid their future wife/girlfriend will not agree to it, and the

married ones said it is impossible to get approval from their wives ...
Many lesbians even call TLFRA [Taiwan LGBT Family Rights Advo-
cacy] to ask for suitable donors because it is hard for them to find it.

In Taiwan, there is no commercialized sperm bank market yet. Assisted
reproduction among infertile couples is reported by the performing doctors
and administered by the Department of Health. Under such circumstances,
most Taiwan lesbians not only face difficulties in finding donors among their
acquaintances but also lack the ability to apply for donated sperm through the
official medical system. To respond to the many requests for sperm donors,
TLFRA even issued an official statement to declare its position: though the
association is highly supportive of lesbians' ART use and parenting, it cannot
mediate donated sperm under the existing laws and regulations (Statement
from TLFRA, 2012).

Despite the fact that health and reproductive rights were not dominant
issues in the Taiwan feminist movement, the Lesbian Mothers Association
created a new network and agency for lesbian users of SI. However, due to
the lack of suitable sperm donors or gynecological problems, no respondent in
this research conceived successfully through SI. These cases demonstrate the
different development of SI in regions outside Western countries as well as
the possible limits and deficits of attempting to create "demedicalization" and
"lesbian empowerment" through SI practices.

Cross-Border Reproductive Treatments Phase (Beginning Approximately
2012): The Co-IVF Practices of Lesbian Couples
The first case of cross-border reproductive treatment[3] publicized in the
Taiwan media was a gay couple's pursuit of surrogacy in China in 2001. With
regard to lesbians, besides the network of the Lesbian Mothers Association,
there are increasing numbers of social and personal networks circulating
detailed information about how to travel abroad to access ARTs. The most
important feature of this period is that lesbian mothers share their cross-
border reproductive treatment experiences on public online forums, bulletin
board systems, and blogs, allowing these discussions and experiences to cross
personal circles and be disseminated to the lesbian community at large and
general public.

Penny, a 33-year-old femme, is the first lesbian who shared her experiences with cross-border reproductive treatment on a public bulletin board
system. In 2012 she shared her first post on the PTT (批踢踢) bulletin board
system, the largest bulletin board system in Taiwan. There, she told her story
of heading to Thailand for co-IVF procedures with her partner. After that,
she continued to post on related topics, all of which triggered heated discussion. In addition, Penny has been interviewed by newspapers, other public

media, and even mainstream parenting magazines for the general public (Yi, 2013). Such intense media exposure has highly enhanced the visibility of lesbian mothers in Taiwan, thereby broadening the imagined possibilities for reproduction and parenting in the lesbian community. For example, the articles in *Girlfriend* in the 1990s usually portrayed the inability to have a child as the most unbearable issue for a lesbian couple (Wen, 1997). However, with the development of more diversified lesbian reproduction possibilities, the attitude toward reproduction also changed. For example, one lesbian expressed her reflections on her blog after reading Penny's story:

> No matter what kind of sexual orientation one is, most people want to have their own children. For heterosexual people, most of them assume they will have children by intercourse and get pregnant. However, for a gay person, it seems more possible choices, such as adoption, donor insemination, stepchildren, or surrogacy, are all possible ways to have a child.
>
> (DMV, 2014)

This comment clearly demonstrates the change of attitude toward parenting in the lesbian community: from "the most unbearable" to "more possible choices." This change also corresponds to Rose's (2007) observation about biomedicalization: new reproductive technologies bring new choices and possibilities and even new possible formations of kinship and family.

One factor in this transformation is the prevalence of the Internet (especially the blogs and the bulletin board systems), which makes knowledge for pursuing ARTs abroad more accessible and easy to circulate. Two of my respondents, Hua-Hua and Kay, a lesbian couple with high economic status, made a detailed table for comparing information about pursuing ARTs in different countries. Additionally, they recalled that they had a translator who had poor Mandarin ability, but when they noticed that there was a better translator in the hospital, they asked for a business card because they wanted to "benefit other lesbians who want to go for ARTs in the future."

The Internet also allows people with similar interests to meet more easily and quickly. Hua-Hua and Penny met each other on the Internet and exchanged information about pursuing ARTs abroad. Hua-Hua even planned to go to Thailand with Penny and undergo ARTs together. As Penny recalled:

> Originally, Hua-Hua even wanted to go to Thailand with me so that we could get IVF together. However, I told her, I will go to try first, and if the doctors can practice it successfully and then you can go to see the same doctor, it would be better for you. I think more lesbian families

can enhance the visibility [and] also form greater pressure for the legislators to amend the law to protect our families.

In addition to Penny and Hua-Hua, there are many other lesbian mothers
who actively share and exchange their information and experiences on the
Internet. These cases demonstrate the multiple resources and networks
formed by lesbian actors, and their intense interactions facilitate the choice to
travel abroad for ARTs. Both Penny and Hua-Hua mentioned that Lemon's
blog, which portrayed an adventure to Canada for IVF treatment, was the
first blog they found when searching the Internet. Lemon is the nickname for
a lesbian from Taiwan who pioneered the pursuit of ART service abroad. She
and her partner had two babies in Canada through IVF. They documented
their experience in detail on their blog. Many respondents mentioned
Lemon's blog in their interviews.

Ban and Alley, a stable couple who have been together for more than 10
years, also found Lemon's blog when they wanted to obtain ARTs. They
responded to the blog with many detailed questions and finally followed
Lemon's suggestion to get IVF treatment in Canada. When they pursued
their own treatment, they started their own blog and tried to record every step
clearly for future lesbian users. As Ban recalled:

> Lemon told me she had already introduced more than seven couples to
> Canada for IVF treatment. Also, one couple was just at Canada at that
> time, that couple gave us a very detailed guide for all of the procedures,
> even including the detailed map to the clinic. ... We recorded every
> single step on our blog, what medicine should I take, and what injec-
> tions should I do, every detailed thing. ... It is just because I benefited a
> lot from many other people, so I wanted to hand on these experiences
> to future possible users, too. ... I am not very good at English, so I ben-
> efited a lot from their experience and information. ... I think my blog is
> a really solid guide; follow all the steps, you almost can have a baby
> [smiling proudly].

Ban vividly portrayed the process of seeking resources from the online lesbian
ART users community, and this comment also demonstrates how community
strength can help individual lesbians overcome the barriers of language (such
as English) to gain access to ARTs.

Furthermore, pursuing ARTs abroad also provides more diverse ARTs
techniques for lesbian procreation. An increasing number of lesbians are consciously adopting ROPA, a technique in which one woman provides the eggs
and the other woman carries the embryo in her womb, to have their babies.
Ting-Ting's case vividly demonstrates this change: she used her partner's

brother's sperm to practice IUI in Taiwan by presenting a fake marriage certificate in 2007. In 2014, she and Mai-Ken went to Thailand for their second child, and this time they used Mai-Ken's egg and Ting-Ting's uterus. Ting-Ting commented that the regulations had become stricter than before, so it was not easy to enter the medical system after 2007. Ban and Alley had a similar observation: they also tried to ask a doctor to practice ARTs for them in Taiwan in 2009. But according to Ban, when Alley asked for help as a single woman, they found that "doctors are very unwilling to do the illegal thing on the risk of having their license revoked."

In the interviews conducted for this research, three couples had used ROPA for procreation, Ting-Ting and Mai-Ken, Hua-Hua and Kay, and Penny and her partner. As Hua-Hua contends, they consciously skipped the SI but went to Thailand for ROPA because:

> we really want to have our baby "together"! We want our child to have both our genes. ... But because it is impossible to combine our genes (or eggs), we choose ROPA consciously because it is the only way both of us can be part of it.

A group of radical feminists who opposed ARTs formed FINRRAGE (Feminist International Network of Resistance to Reproductive and Genetic Engineering) in 1984. They viewed ARTs as a manifestation of patriarchal domination and exploitation of women's bodies. They also worried that ARTs interrupted the consistency of genetic, gestational, and social motherhood, thereby threatening the naturally reproducing unitary maternal subject and her experiences (Farquhar, 1996). As Mai-Ken recalled:

> Due to Ting-Ting's gynecological problems, she always felt unwell after she got many injections. To conduct the egg retrieval surgery, I got many injections for the surgery, and the injection let me ovulate thirty-five eggs, so my belly was totally swelling. It was the first time I felt I could understand and share her pain. I feel it is a real kind of participation.

This comment demonstrates that the labor division is not only in sharing the emotional bond of having children; it can also be an embodied experience of sharing the pain. ROPA serves as a tool for sharing biological motherhood, sharing pain, and providing a feeling of cooperation and combination. As more Taiwan lesbians consciously choose this ART method, it has been praised as an ideal way to have a child together.

Of the couples interviewed in this study, Zoe and Kuan-Kuan, had the widest age gap (Zoe was 47, while Kuan-Kuan was 30 years old). They originally wanted to use ROPA with Zoe's egg and Kuan-Kuan's uterus. However, Zoe's egg was considered "too old" by the doctor. Consequently they used IUI with Kuan-Kuan's egg and uterus. When discussing this choice, Kuan still felt it was a great pity to not have "Zoe's child."

Finally, for legal reasons, some participants contended that allowing a child to have her partner's genes is a good way to ensure both partners' parental rights. Under Taiwan's regulations, only the birth mother can be granted official parental rights for the child. Penny, as a birth mother, consciously chose ROPA to protect her partner's rights: "If I have an accident one day ... at least my partner is the child's genetic mother." Taken together, the pursuits of cross-border reproductive treatments not only weaken the state-bound health regulations but also embody a new transnational biomedical mobility.[4]

Conclusion

This chapter provided a much-needed exploration of how Taiwanese lesbians negotiate their exclusion by legislation and social prejudice from and gain access to ARTs. While most of the literature on lesbian procreation focuses overwhelmingly on experiences in the United States and some European countries, this study is the first to examine lesbians' appropriation of ARTs in Taiwan. Classified by different historical periods, community resources, and types of lesbian appropriations of ARTs, this research generally divides Taiwanese lesbians' ART practices into three phases.

First, due to the lack of parenting imagination and the limited discourses and resources for reproduction in the lesbian community, passing and "smuggling" oneself into the existing medical system were early possible methods of gaining access to ARTs. In this period, lesbians consciously hid social information to "pass" as heterosexual single women in order to become qualified, though still illegal, users of ARTs. Before the passage of the Artificial Reproduction Act in 2007, the guidelines to regulate ART practices in Taiwan gave doctors considerable latitude to decide who were qualified ART users.

Second, the emerging Lesbian Mothers Association consciously used multiple channels to disseminate knowledge about SI. However, the lack of a long history of a feminist health movement as well as appropriate sperm sources in Taiwan were crucial barriers to the practice and prevalence of SI in Taiwan.

Third, lesbian mothers began to share their cross-border reproductive treatment experiences on public online forums, bulletin boards, and blogs, allowing these discussions and experiences to cross personal circles and be disseminated to the whole lesbian community and even to the public. In this phase, ROPA became the new paradigm for procreation in the lesbian community. This technique not only allowed both partners to participate in the process of procreation but also provided an assurance of future parental rights for the genetic mother, since only the birth mother can be the official legal parent in Taiwan.

This chapter suggests taking one important contextual factor into consideration when examining lesbians' appropriation of ARTs: the strictness of legislation and regulation. Before the passage of the Artificial Reproduction Act in 2007 a possible gray area existed that could be manipulated by medical professionals. Of the women interviewed for this study, three made their way into the medical system to use ARTs, and all three of these cases occurred before 2007. Other respondents also claimed to be single women who wanted to have a child by ARTs in 2009, but their requests were declined by the doctor. It may be that the passage of the legislation and stricter regulations have hindered doctors from helping these lesbian users.[5]

While the SI and cross-border reproductive treatments are better documented in recent procreation literature, this research is the first to examine how lesbians consciously hide social information to achieve "passing" to be admitted to the existing medical system for ARTs. This research also demonstrates how lesbians in Taiwan negotiate and navigate in the existing medical system to fulfill their procreative desire. Altogether, "queering" reproduction means that lesbian actors not only embody new biomedical modalities by appropriating ARTs but also create new family formations that can provide normative images for the wider society.

Notes

1 Any lesbian, bisexual, transgender, or gender-queer people or single heterosexual women who consciously do not want to conceive through heterosexual intercourse face similar situations: they must circumvent the legal regulation or adopt creative ways to get the access to ARTs. Only married heterosexual couples are allowed to use ARTs in Taiwan. However, all of the respondents in this chapter are recruited from the Taiwan Lesbian Mothers Association. They identify themselves as lesbians and therefore the scope of this chapter is on the experiences of self-identified lesbians.

2 In the end, single women's reproductive rights were deleted from the final version of the statement, due to the approval rating for single women to access ARTs which was 20.6%. The Physicians Association argued the approval rating was "too low."

3 Due to the strictness of the legal regulations or the lack of ART resources, more and more ART users seek reproductive treatments abroad. This phenomenon is called cross-border reproductive treatment. At the same time, some governments notice this situation and adopt strict regulations prohibiting cross-border reproductive treatment. For example, Turkey became the first country to legislate against the cross-border travel of its citizens seeking third-party reproductive assistance in March 2010 (Gürtin, 2011).

4 According to Beck (2012), transnational biomedical mobility indicates the state is no longer a unit of governing or analysis. Transnational biomedical mobility not only applies to pursuits of ARTs beyond national borders, but also weakens national bioethical or legal regulations. As more and more state authorities notice this situation,

bans on cross-border reproductive treatment occur. For example, Turkey became the first country to legislate against the cross-border travel of its citizens seeking third-party reproductive assistance in March 2010 (Gürtin, 2011).

5   The first version of this chapter was finished in 2014. However, since May 22, 2014, Thailand has been under the rule of a military organization called the National Council for Peace and Order (NCPO). This military government enacts stricter control in every aspect of society, including surrogacy pregnancy and other kinds of ARTs. Since July 30, 2015, the National Legislative Assembly of Thailand enacted the Assisted Reproductive Technology Act, which requires at least one of the applicants to be a Thai citizen. In a cross-nationality marriage, they must be legally married for no less than three years. Consequently, with the surrogacy bans now in place in Thailand, some of respondents for this research reported they went to Cambodia to pursue ART services. Simultaneously, Taiwan became the first country in Asia to legalize same-sex marriage and after a Constitutional Court ruling, same-sex marriage became legal on May 24, 2017. However, Taiwanese lesbians still are not allowed to use ART services in Taiwan (Haas, 2017).

References

Agigian, A. (2004). *Baby Steps: How Lesbian Alternative Insemination is Changing the World.* Middletown, CT: Wesleyan University Press.

Allen, A. (2007). Comments of lesbian DIY pregnancy: How lesbians become pregnant by SI [online]. *Lama Post.* January. Available: http://blog.yam.com/la_ma_news/article/7864914#comments.

Beck, S. (2012). Biomedical mobilities: Transnational lab-benches and other space-effects. In M. Knecht, M. Klotz, & S. Beck (eds.), *Reproductive Technologies as Global Form: Ethnographies of Knowledge, Practices, and Transnational Encounters* (pp. 357–374). Frankfurt/New York: Campus.

Che, A. (2007). Lesbian DIY pregnancy: How lesbians become pregnant by SI [online]. *Lama Post.* January. Available: http://blog.yam.com/la_ma_news/article/7864914.

Cheng, M. L. (1997). *Lesbian circle: Taiwan lesbian's gender, family, and community life.* Taipei: Fembook Press.

Clarke, A. E., Shim, J. K., Mamo, L., Fosket, J., & Fishman, J. R. (2003). Biomedicalisation: Technoscientific transformations of health, illness, and U.S. biomedicine. *American Sociological Review, 68,* 161–194.

Cooper (2006). Making babies the gay way [translated by Lupy Lee] [online]. *Lama Post.* June. Available: http://blog.yam.com/la_ma_news/article/5971367.

Corea, G. (1986). The mother machine: Reproductive technologies from artificial insemination to artificial wombs. *MCN: The American Journal of Maternal/Child Nursing, 11,* 5, 357–363.

Crowe, C. (1990). Whose mind over whose matter? Women, *in vitro* fertilisation and the development of scientific knowledge. In M. McNeil, I. Varcoe, & S. Yearley (Eds.), *The New Reproductive Technologies* (pp. 27–57). London: Palgrave Macmillan.

Daniels, C. R., & Golden, J. (2004). Procreative compounds: Popular eugenics, artificial insemination and the rise of the American sperm banking industry. *Journal of Social History, 38,* 1, 5–27.

DMV. (2014). Conceived by artificial insemination [online]. Available: http://jrfamily.pixnet.net/blog/post/93756374.

Donovan, C. (2000). Who needs a father? Negotiating biological fatherhood in British lesbian families using self-insemination. *Sexualities, 3,* 2, 149–164.

Ethics Committee of the American Fertility Society. (1994). Ethical considerations of assisted reproductive technologies, *Fertility and Sterility*, *61*, 13S–34S.

Farquhar, D. (1996). *The other machine: Discourse and reproductive technologies*. Hove, UK: Psychology Press.

Firestone, S. (1970). *The dialectic of sex: The case for feminist revolution*. New York: Morrow.

Garfield, A. (2001). We want a child. *Girlfriend*, *34*, 46.

Gian, J. S. (1997). *Bring out the lesbians: Taiwan lesbian discourses and movements (1990–1996)*. Master's Thesis. Department of Sociology, National Taiwan University.

Goffman, E. (1963). *Stigma: Notes on the management of spoiled identity*. New York: Simon & Schuster.

Grzanka, P. R. (2008). From turkey basters to the fertility clinic: Lesbian reproductive practices in biomedicalization. *Symbolic Interaction*, *31*, 3, 345–348.

Gürtin, Z. B. (2011). Banning reproductive travel: Turkey's ART legislation and third-party assisted reproduction. *Reproductive Biomedicine Online*, *23*, 5, 555–564.

Haas, B. (2017, May 24). Taiwan's top court rules in favor of same-sex marriage. *Guardian*.

Haimes, E., & Weiner, K. (2000). "Everybody's got a dad…" Issues for lesbian families in the management of donor insemination. *Sociology of Health and Illness*, *22*, 4, 477–499.

Herrera, F. (2009). Tradition and transgression: Lesbian motherhood in Chile. *Sexuality Research and Social Policy*, *6*, 2, 35–51.

Hornstein, F. (1984). Children by donor insemination: A new choice for lesbians. In R. Arditti, R. D. Klein, & Shelley Minden (eds.), *Test-tube women: What future for motherhood?* (pp. 86–93). London: Pandora Press.

Horton, C. (2016, November 18). Taiwan may be first in Asia to legalize same-sex marriage. *New York Times*.

Inhorn, M. C. (2012). Reproductive exile in global Dubai: South Asian stories. *Cultural Politics, an International Journal*, *8*, 2, 283–306.

Jones, H. W., Cooke, I., Kempers, R., Brinsden, P., & Saunders, D. (2010). *International Federation of Fertility Societies Surveillance 2010* [online]. International Federation of Fertility Societies. Available: http://c.ymcdn.com/sites/www.iffs-reproduction.org/resource/resmgr/newsletters/iffs_surveillance_2010.pdf.

Klein, R. D. (1984). Doing it ourselves: Self insemination. In R. Arditti, R. D. Klein, & S. Minden (Eds.), *Test-tube women: What future for motherhood?* (pp. 382–390) London: Pandora Press.

Mamo, L. (2007). *Queering reproduction: Achieving pregnancy in the age of technoscience*. Durham, NC: Duke University Press.

Marina, S., Marina, D., Marina, F., Fosas, N., Galiana, N., & Jove, I. (2010). Sharing motherhood: Biological lesbian co-mothers, a new IVF indication. *Human Reproduction*, *25*, 4, 938–941.

Morgan, D., & Lee, R. G. (1991). *Blackstone's guide to the Human Fertilization and Embryology Act*. London: Blackstone Press.

Nygren, K., Hirshikesh, P., Le Roux, P., & Sullivan, E. (2013). *International Federation of Fertility Societies Surveillance 2013* [online]. International Federation of Fertility Societies. Available: www.iffs-reproduction.org/resource/resmgr/iffs_surveillance_09-19-13.pdf.

Oakley, A. (1984). *The captured womb: A history of the medical care of pregnant women*. Oxford: Blackwell.

O'Donnell, Mary, Pollock, K., Leoffler, V., & Saunders, Z. (1979). *Lesbian health matters! A resource book about lesbian health matters*. Santa Cruz, CA: Santa Cruz Women's Health Collective.

Patterson, C. J. (1992). Children of lesbian and gay parents. *Child Development*, *63*, 5, 1025–1042.

Pinch, T. J., & Bijker, W. E. (1984). The social construction of facts and artefacts: Or how the sociology of science and the sociology of technology might benefit each other. *Social Studies of Science, 14*, 3, 399–441.

Raboy, B. (1993). Secrecy and openness in donor insemination: A new paradigm. *Politics and the Life Sciences: The Journal of the Association for Politics and the Life Sciences, 12*, 2, 191–192.

Rose, N. (2007). *The politics of life itself: Biomedicine, power, and subjectivity in the twenty-first century*. Princeton, NJ: Princeton University Press.

Rothman, B. K. (1984). *Giving birth: Alternatives in childbirth*. London: Penguin Books.

Rothman, B. K. (2000). *Recreating motherhood*. New Brunswick, NJ: Rutgers University Press.

Rowland, R. (1987). Technology and motherhood: Reproductive choice reconsidered. *Signs: Journal of Women in Culture and Society, 12*, 3, 512–528.

Ruzek, S. (1978). *The women's health movement: Feminist alternatives to medical control*. New York: Praeger.

Saffron, L. (1994). *Challenging conceptions: Pregnancy and parenting beyond the traditional family*. London: Cassell.

Shieh, G. S. (2003). *A sociography of Ping-Lin, Taiwan: Wage, governmentality, and total social categories*. Nangang: Institute of Sociology, Academia Sinica.

Wen, W. (1997). Alternative family: Soothing our little thing. *Girlfriend, 17*, 32.

Weston, K. (1997). *Families we choose: Lesbians, gays, kinship*. New York: Columbia University Press.

Wikler, D., & Wikler, N. J. (1991). Turkey-baster babies: The demedicalization of artificial insemination. *Milbank Quarterly*, 5–40.

World Bank. (2011). *Removing barriers to economic exclusion: Measuring gender parity in 141 economies*. Washington, DC: World Bank.

Wu, C. L. (2002). The new reproductive technologies and gender politics in Taiwan, 1950–2000. *Taiwan: A Radical Quarterly in Social Studies, 45*, 1–67.

Wu, C. L. (2011). Managing multiple masculinities in donor insemination: Doctors configuring infertile men and sperm donors in Taiwan. *Sociology of Health and Illness, 33*, 1, 96–113.

Wu, C. L. (2012). Excluding unmarried women: Assisted reproductive technology governance and access politics in Taiwan. Paper presented at the International Conference on "The Making of 'Asia': Health and Gender," University of Hong Kong, March 9–10.

Yi, Y. S. (2013, April 9). Diversified families: Rainbow flags, love, and same-sex marriage [online]. *BabyHome*. Available: http://info.babyhome.com.tw/info/women/matrimony/article/7638.

6

ABORTION RIGHTS AND HUMAN RIGHTS IN MEXICO

JENNIFER NELSON

El aborto debe ser libre y gratuito para que esté al alcance de todas las mujeres. [Abortion should be accessible and free in order to be within reach for all women.]

(Editorial, *Fem*, 1 (2) January-February 1977, p. 2)

Introduction

The second edition of the journal *Fem*, the issue in which this editorial appeared, focused on illegal abortion in Mexico. To illustrate the particular dangers confronted by Mexican women seeking to illegally terminate an unwanted pregnancy, an article in the issue featured four vignettes narrated by a nurse who worked in a clinic in a poor neighborhood on the outskirts of Mexico City. In each vignette she describes a woman who came to her after she attempted a self-induced abortion—in one case using potassium permanganate which could be bought over the counter—or went to an underground abortion provider—another woman paid a lay midwife to introduce a cannula into her uterus. The stories emphasize the risks Mexican women faced when they aborted illegally, particularly poor women who often sought terminations due to economic circumstances that would only be made worse by another child ("El aborto en una colonia proletaria" 1997, 7–9). Mexican feminists recognized that many women, particularly in rural parts of the country, felt abortion was wrong, yet terminated a pregnancy when they could not support another child. Abortions were most common among single mothers with few resources to support a family (Molina 1977).

I begin this chapter in the 1970s with the emergence of modern Mexican feminism because Mexican feminists were dramatically outspoken in their challenges to the penalization of abortion in their country. I then shift to the 1980s and 1990s as non-governmental organizations (NGOs) and the United Nations became more prominent in bolstering feminist campaigns for the legalization of abortion. Mexican feminists increasingly drew on international claims for reproductive autonomy for women forged at United Nations meetings in the 1990s. They centered their demands on a discourse that brought together claims for democracy, secularism, and human rights (Maier 2015).[1] While they met with some successes, their mobilization of this discourse did not achieve their goal of legal abortion access for all Mexican women.

The purpose of this chapter is to demonstrate that demands for abortion rights have consistently been central to Mexican feminism since the 1970s. Yet, 1970s feminist hopes that a democratic shift away from one-party rule in Mexico would lead to the legalization of abortion nationwide were not realized. Feminists in the 1990s, recognizing that an emphasis on democratic secularism alone had not been effective in pressing the government to legalize abortion nationwide, additionally employed a discourse of human rights linked to reproductive rights forged at the 1994 United Nations conferences on Population and Development (ICPD) in Cairo and the 1995 World Conference on Women in Beijing (Ewig 2006, 638). This argument had its own limitations, including appropriation of human rights language by right-to-life activists who argued that human life began with conception so that embryos and fetuses must also be protected under human rights law. Mexican feminists in the 1990s and 2000s also drew on a language of "liberty of conscience" circulated by Catholic women who supported legal abortion.

Abortion has been common in Mexico despite its illegality. As an illegal practice, accurate estimations of the incidence of abortion are impossible, but even the most conservative calculations based on hospital reports of incomplete abortions estimate between 250,000 and 750,000 abortions each year (Nahmad 1997).[2] If a woman did not experience a complication and attend a hospital, her abortion would not be counted, so these numbers are likely low (Ortiz-Ortega 2001). By other measures, researchers estimated that the abortion rate in Mexico was 33 abortions per 1,000 women in 2006; by contrast the abortion rate in North America between 2010 and 2014 was 17 per 1,000 women and in Western and Northern Europe it was 18 per 1,000 women (Becker and Olavarrieta 2013). According to the Alan Guttmacher Institute, illegal abortion is associated with higher abortion rates (2016).

Abortion complications due to illegal procedures have also been a problem in Mexico. In 1977 Clara Elena Molina, feminist law professor and member of the Mexican delegation to the 1975 World Conference of the International Women's Year, estimated that hemorrhage caused by illegal abortion was a leading cause of death among Mexican women (Molina 1977). In 2001 Católicas por el Derecho a Decidir (CDD) reported that 800,000 clandestine abortions occurred each year; these resulted in more than 1,500 deaths a year, making abortion the fourth leading cause of death among all Mexican women ("We Are Women" 2001). High rates of mortality due to abortion complications have made abortion a national public health concern which has fostered alliances between feminists who defined abortion as essential to their fight for sex equality and those concerned with improved public health.

Debates over the role of religion in politics have also fueled the movement both for and against legal abortion in Mexico. This is unsurprising, as scholars of the relationship between the Catholic Church and Mexican state have noted, Catholic values have often legitimized politics in Mexico (Camp 1997, 5). Roderic Ai Camp argues further that "religion, Christianity, Catholicism, and the Catholic Church are held in high esteem by the vast majority of Mexicans, and that these beliefs give the Church the potential to perform an important role in society in secular affairs" (12). At the same time, the Catholic Church is not a homogeneous or unified hierarchical entity in Mexico (or elsewhere). Local churches tend to impact local communities (13).

While the Mexican state is officially secular, there has been growing pressure to relax anticlerical laws dating to the 1917 Constitution that restricted Catholic participation in the public (Reich 1997, 85), particularly in light of the growing influence of the PAN (Partido Acción Nacional) opposition party (Fallow 2003).[3] As the PAN has increased its democratic representation in some Mexican states, Catholic beliefs about fetal personhood have gained ground and weakened attempts to establish legal abortion. Beliefs in fetal personhood have also prevented women from accessing *legal* abortions in cases of rape or health concerns, and caused women to be incarcerated for performing abortions on themselves.[4] Mexican feminists have argued that although state secularism was enshrined at the end of the revolution, state laws that make abortion illegal and that establish conception as the moment life begins are evidence that secularism is being challenged even as the Mexican political landscape becomes more democratic with the strengthening of opposition parties. With this recognition, many contemporary feminists have begun to question 1970s feminist presumptions that increased democracy would usher in legal abortion.

State-Sponsored Population and Fertility Control
In the early 1970s President Luis Echeverría, responded to United States-led fears associated with rapid population growth often referred to as a "population explosion"—and the assumption that positive economic development needed to be tied to a reduction in population. In a reversal of its previous pronatalist position, the government began to promote birth control use by legalizing contraceptives in 1973 and promoting the birth control pill through popular media such as serial television programming aimed at women, or

telenovelas, in which characters limited their fertility (Laveaga 2007). At the same time, and amidst Echeverría's bid for the United Nation's International Women's Conference to be held in Mexico City (Olcott 2017, 55), the state also established a constitutional right to contraception (this is important because it has been used by feminists to make claims for legal abortion) with a rhetorical commitment to individual contraceptive choice, although articulated in terms that would preserve the conventional family (Lamas 1997). Article 4 of the constitution declares,

> Men and women are equal before the law. This equality will protect the organization and development of the family. Each individual has the right to determine the number and the spacing of his/her children in a free, responsible, and informed manner.
>
> ("We are Women" 2001, 24)

Demographic goals, however, were often prioritized by the state (Ortiz-Ortega 1996, 194–198).[5]

In 1976, in concert with its new emphasis on reducing population growth, the government attempted to address illegal abortion as a public health problem that contributed to high rates of maternal mortality. The state organization Consejo Nacional de Población (CONAPO) created the Grupo Interdisciplinario para el Estudio del Aborto en México (GIEA), bringing together 62 experts—doctors, legal experts, psychologists, demographers, economists, philosophers, and anthropologists—who concluded that the abortion law should be rescinded, and abortion should be legal and available on demand. They rested their argument on the World Health Organization (WHO) definition of health, stating that health was not merely the absence of disease, but also included mental and social well-being. They argued that nobody—not the church or the state—should compel a woman to continue an unwanted pregnancy. They emphasized that health promotion was fundamental to both the individual and the community (Lamas 1997, 11).

GIEA rested their analysis on medical and economic claims; few women had access to safe illegal abortion, which led to high rates of mortality among women who were already mothers and had more children than they could adequately care for. The ability to limit family size would decrease both maternal and infant mortality. The committee also asserted that legal abortion could have the result of decreasing repeat abortions because women would have more information about contraception and sexuality. Finally, abortion was an inexpensive procedure, but the cost of treating abortion complications due to unsafe illegal procedures was a costly burden carried by public hospitals. Dr. Cándano, in an interview with Marta Lamas, pointed out that very little training was required to perform a safe abortion early in a pregnancy even in medical facilities in remote areas of the country (Ortiz-Ortega 1996, 153–154; Lamas 1977, 11). Neither the Echeverría nor the Portillo administrations followed the recommendation (Ortiz-Ortega and Barquet 2010, 115; Garcia Molina 2004, 1). Despite its support for birth control and population reduction, to appease the Catholic Church, the state retained the criminal abortion law (Ortiz-Ortega and Barquet 2010, 154).

Feminist Interventions in the 1970s

Feminists of the "second wave"[6] movement in Mexico, many of whom traced their political roots to the student movement of the 1960s, were both relatively economically privileged and educated. They focused on abortion rights among other issues including "stricter penalties for violence against women, support for rape victims, and connecting the personal and the political" (Stephen 2006, 251). In 1972, at one of the first feminist workshops, activists named abortion a fundamental element in achieving "el derecho de las mujeres a elegir [the right to choose]" (Ortiz-Ortega 1999, 228). Some feminists broadened their arguments for legal abortion to recognize abortion as one part of a comprehensive public health program most needed by women without economic resources (Ortiz-Ortega 1999, 232–233). Drawing on feminist criticism of international population control associated with dire warnings of a "population explosion," Mexican feminists like Ruby Betancourt, an economist, warned that coercive contraception promotion linked to colonial development efforts violated women's right to decide their family size (which included choosing to have children) (Betancourt 1977, 34). Feminists argued that abortion needed to be both legal and free, taking into consideration the lack of economic resources among most Mexican women. To this end, many feminists argued that abortion should be supported by the public health services available in state hospitals (Grau 1977, 36–37). They also emphasized that legal abortion needed to be accompanied by changes to ideas about sexuality, particularly about sexual pleasure as an end in itself for single women (Rozenfaig 1977, 19–21).

Other activism among Mexican women during this period included involvement in liberation theology, union organizing, the promotion of land ownership among peasant and indigenous women, and demands for improved housing and access to services among urban poor women (Lamas et al. 1998, 333). Indeed, the Mexican feminist movement, like the burgeoning women's movement internationally, was heterogeneous with myriad fault lines that included geographical location, political ideology, class, ethnic identification, language, and sexuality. Adriana Ortiz-Ortega and Mercedes Barquet argue that the movement brought attention to "matters of personal and bodily integrity, health, and reproduction, which provoked legal and institutional change" (Ortiz-Ortega and Barquet 2010, 115).

In the early years, the feminist campaign focused on "maternidad voluntaria," a term coined by Mujeres en Accion Solidaria (MAS). Founded in 1971 as one of the earliest feminist organizations in Mexico City, MAS largely comprised students, intellectuals, and women connected to the political left. At their first Conference on Abortion Legalization held in 1972, they proposed abortion be decriminalized, but with no political influence their proposal remained largely unrecognized (Jaiven 1985, 80–81).

The Movimiento Nacional de Mujeres (MNM), was founded in 1972 by women associated with the media. It was more hierarchical than MAS as they modeled themselves on the National Organization for Women in the United States (Jaiven 1985, 100–101). MNM organized a series of conferences on abortion beginning in 1974. The MNM also decided that it was important to negotiate with the state about abortion policy (a position not held by all Mexican feminists) in order to achieve their goal of abortion law reform. To this end they met with Rodolfo González Guevara (without the backing of other feminist organizations), President of the Cámara de Diputados, to propose the legalization of abortion as articulated at the first Conference on Abortion Legalization. Their proposal, however, received no official backing or response from any government official (Grupo Cinco 1991, 7–8).

In a document produced in September 1976, the MNM argued that abortion needed to be legal for several reasons: first of all, illegal abortion was common and dangerous. They also argued that it was expensive for state hospitals to treat women who came to them hemorrhaging from clandestine abortion. Furthermore, the poorest Mexican women suffered the most from abortion illegality without access to safe procedures by trained medical professionals. They also pointed out that the abortion law upheld a double sexual standard with women disproportionately risking their health and their lives for sexual pleasure. Finally, they advocated that information on male sterilization should be disseminated since it was one of the most reliable methods of contraception and would, thus, reduce the need for abortion ("El movimiento nacional de mujeres frente al aborto" 1977, 71–72).

Feminism in Transition: Post-1970s Abortion Rights Activism
Feminists continued their campaign for legal abortion in the late 1970s and into the 1980s. In 1979 feminists from Coalición Mujeres Feminista (CMF) and another coalition of left feminists—from the Partido Comunista Mexicana and the Partido Revolucionario de los Trabajadores—calling themselves Frente Nacional de Lucha por Los Derechos de las Mujeres (FNALIDM), organized in support of the proposal first brought to González Guevara by the feminist group MNM. To make public their support, they staged a rally outside the Cámara de Diputados in Mexico

City and they declared May 10 (Mothers' Day in Mexico) the "Dia de la Maternidad Libre y Voluntaria." To honor women who had died from illegal abortions, the feminists dressed as women in mourning, wearing crowns of the dead, and carrying the tools women used to provoke self-abortions (Jaiven 1985, 135–136). On December 29 they presented the proposed law to the Coalición de Izquierda, an independent left coalition that included the newly legal Mexican Communist Party. The Communist Party officially presented the bill as their own, excluding feminists from the political process. The PAN countered the bill with a proposal for a constitutional amendment that would establish political rights from the moment of conception (Ortiz-Ortega 1996, 173–177; Molina 1977, 2). In 1980, two Partido Revolucionario Institucional (PRI) *diputadas*, María Luisa Oteyza and Adriana Parra Portillo, signaled their support for legal abortion in a letter to President Lopez Portillo that stated "abortion, as a last resort, is a solution that all women have a right to, and requires the attention of medical personnel who are both recognized and capable ... The penalization of abortion violates the spirit of the Constitution" (Molina 1977, 2). In 1980 and 1981, feminists from FNALIDM held conferences on abortion and repeated their demonstration on Mothers' Day to honor women who died from abortion. For the march in 1980, they dragged cloth dolls through the streets of the city to signify that women should not be defined by motherhood (Grupo Cinco 1991, 10). None of these efforts resulted in changes to the abortion law. In fact they may have had even less of an impact during the particularly conservative years of the Portillo *sexenio* from 1976 to 1982 (Rodríguez 2003, 104).

After a 1985 earthquake devastated Mexico City, and during the economic crisis of the 1980s, Mexican women did not prioritize abortion legalization although some feminists continued the campaign. Many other women mobilized in grassroots groups to address problems associated with the disaster and with acquiring basic necessities in the face of poverty. According to Elizabeth Maier, low-income women organized for "basic material needs, including government welfare benefits, affordable housing, health care, and child care services" (Maier 2012, 158). Lamas and others refer to cross-class organizing among women during the 1980s in response to Mexico's economic challenges (Lamas et al. 1998, 336).

Secular Democracy

The feminists who continued the fight for legal abortion in the 1980s began to refine the argument that article 4 of the federal constitution gave Mexican women the right (as citizens) to control their fertility in a secular state. This occurred in a context of increasing demand for democratic rights from the political left and the right. Ortiz-Ortega argues that feminists developed an inclusive notion of abortion rights as citizen's rights: by the end of the eighties, feminists argued that "the right to legal and safe abortion" was more than an issue of public health or social justice. It became an issue of democratic representation ... women ... were citizens who claimed their rights to abortion as a right to citizenship.

She explained further that they also linked abortion to social and economic demands that would make voluntary control over reproduction a concrete reality; a recognition that legal abortion did not guarantee access to abortion (Ortiz-Ortega 1996, 207–208).

Lamas and other Mexican feminists argued that increasing democracy in the context of a secular political system was central to achieving feminist goals, including legal abortion. In her book *Política y Reproducción*, Lamas called for political alliances—not among the established parties who had either opposed abortion legalization (PAN) or avoided it (PRI and PRD [Partido Revolucionario Democrático])—that would unite progressives in the struggle for democracy and against a fundamentalist religious state (2001, 38–39). Lamas argued that the population of Mexico held much more liberal and tolerant ideas about abortion and reproductive rights than the political parties in power or the Catholic Church (40).

Recent examples of the Church's influence on the abortion question are many, revealing why Mexican feminists have often been frustrated by the state's nominal secularism. For instance, in 1990 the legislature of the state of Chiapas[7] began a process of liberalizing the exceptions for legal abortion, including making family planning (or contraceptive failure) a legal reason a woman could access an abortion within the first 90 days of pregnancy. The governor of Chiapas supported the law saying, the law "does not compel a woman to have an abortion" (Grupo Cinco 1991, 13). The legislature reversed itself, however, due to pressure from the Catholic Church (Kulczycki 2007, 58). In 1999, during efforts to reform the abortion law in Mexico City the Pope spoke against abortion, declaring, "May no Mexican dare to harm the precious and sacred gift of life in the maternal womb" (Lamas and Bissell 2000, 11). In another instance, Catholic organizations, as well as the Catholic director of Mexicali General Hospital in the state of Baja California, prevented a legal abortion by a 13-year-old girl (Paulina) who had become pregnant as the result of a rape (13–14). Where the conservative PAN holds legislative power, fetal personhood amendments have been introduced to modify state (19 at this writing) constitutions, decreasing women's access to abortion even in cases where a pregnancy is the result of a rape or threatens her life. Lamas estimates that as many as 300 women have been jailed as a result of these laws (Lamas 1997, 62; Maier 2012, 157). Maier reports that

679 women were accused of causing an abortion by hospital employees or medical professionals between 2009 and 2011 (Maier 2015, 18).

In the 1990s feminists increasingly influenced the international nonprofit population establishment which had adopted arguments forged at the United Nations Conferences in Cairo and Beijing promoting women's health and access to reproductive control based on claims to human rights over purely demographic goals (Smyth 1998; Ortiz-Ortega 1999, 239). As Rosalind Petchesky explains, "Feminist groups in the 1990s had a major impact ... in shifting dominant discourses about reproduction, population and sexuality in a direction that puts the ends of women's health and empowerment above that of reducing population growth" (2003, 247–248). In 1991 Lamas and other feminists, including Lucero González, María Consuelo Mejia, Patricia Mercado, and Sara Sefchovich, responded to the increasing power of the PAN (and continued power of the Catholic Church) by creating Grupo de Información en Reproducción Elegida (GIRE), a nonprofit organization linked to the Population Council based in New York City.

According to Lamas, members of GIRE also wanted to more directly connect reproductive self-determination to the movement for democracy. She wrote, "The central issue became: who decides and according to what precepts are decisions made in a diverse society with democratic aspirations?" (Lamas 1997, 61). Surveys done by GIRE in 1992 and 1993 demonstrated that a majority (78%) of Mexicans believed a woman and her partner should decide whether or not to carry a pregnancy to term (Lamas 2009). Further emphasizing the links between the movements for democracy and reproductive rights, Lamas and co-author Sharon Bissell wrote, "reproductive rights are intrinsically democratic rights: they stem from freedom, particularly sexual freedom, and require a common ground, i.e. equal access." They added, however, that there is also a social justice argument for reproductive rights that rests on "equal access to good quality health services, reductions in maternal and infant mortality and in unwanted adolescent pregnancy, and therefore the need to provide safe and legal abortion in the health services" (Lamas and Bissell 2000, 21). On April 24, 2007, feminists achieved their most important legislative win when the Asamblea Legislativa del Distrito Federal (Mexico City) decriminalized abortion for the first 12 weeks of gestation, reduced sentences for women convicted of abortion after 12 weeks, and established implantation as the beginning of pregnancy (Van Dijk et al. 2007, 395). The Supreme Court upheld the Mexico City law in 2008. Abortions in Mexico City are free to all women when provided in Ministry of Health institutions. Mexican feminists achieved this legislative victory over the course of nearly three decades of organizing, yet it still leaves the vast majority of Mexican women without easy legal abortion access (GIRE 2008).

Contemporary Feminist Activism: Abortion and Human Rights

During the summer of 2015 I interviewed various members of allied NGOs—
GIRE, CDD, and Equidad de Genero: Ciudadanía, Trabajo, y Familia (also
allied with IPAS and the Population Council)—all based in Mexico City, but
active throughout Mexico to expand women's access to reproductive control.
For purposes of brevity in the last section of this chapter I will only consider
the work of GIRE—their utilization of legal and human rights frameworks
and their emphasis on broad access to reproductive rights—and CDD efforts
to link Catholic feminist arguments for legal abortion access to human rights
and democracy claims and arguments for religious liberty of conscience. I will
leave the work of Equidad de Genero: Ciudadanía, Trabajo, y Familia to
another essay. All of these organizations collaborate with each other to form
the backbone of the present-day reproductive rights movement in Mexico.

As I noted earlier, GIRE was founded by Lamas and other Mexican feminists in 1991 to defend and promote women's rights "within a human rights
[legal] framework" (GIRE 2013, 12). In this period feminists began to draw
on a "human rights framework" to affirm women's right to abortion. In an
interview with Ortiz-Ortega for the Population Council, Mexican feminist
Marie Claire Acosta claimed, "We believe that illegal abortion is against
women's human rights because it exposes women to forms of risk and abuse
that would come to an end if abortion was made legal" (Ortiz-Ortega 1996,
229). Rebecca J. Cook and Bernard M. Dickens emphasize that a human
rights frame has increasingly been claimed by feminists internationally
because "[i]n many countries of the world, women's alternative to unsafe
abortion is not safe pregnancy and childbirth, but predictable complications
during pregnancy resulting in maternal death or disability" (2006, 557).

The emphasis on human rights among feminists in Mexico has been particularly significant since 2011 when Mexico reformed its constitution to
"incorporate human rights standards included in international treaties to
which Mexico is part into the Mexican Constitution" (GIRE 2013, 14; Maier
2015, 19). Mexico is a signatory to the Convention on the Elimination of All
Forms of Discrimination against Women (CEDAW) monitored by the
CEDAW committee which argues that "abortion should be permitted and
accessible at least in cases of pregnancy resulting from rape, fetal anomalies
incompatible with life, and when the woman's life or health is at risk."
CEDAW also "characterizes the refusal of medical procedures that only
women require, such as abortion, as sex discrimination" (Cook and Dickens
2006, 560). Furthermore, GIRE organizers argue that reproductive rights,
including access to abortion, were already enshrined in the Mexican constitution "based on the right to life; the right to health, including reproductive
health; the right to physical integrity; the right to privacy; the right to
freedom from discrimination and the right to reproductive autonomy." When

Mexican states pass laws that protect fetal personhood or fail to grant abortions to women to protect life, protect health, in the case of rape, or in the case of fetal anomaly, GIRE members argue they violate the Mexican constitution (GIRE 2013, 16).

According to Regina Támes, Executive Director of GIRE, both pro-legal abortion and anti-legal abortion activists have been drawing on human rights discourses to support their case with anti-abortion forces arguing that human rights should apply to fertilized eggs, embryos, and fetuses. Interestingly, this has led to some areas of agreement among groups that are on opposite sides of the abortion debate. For example, Támes explained that pro-women's health groups in Mexico (who do not necessarily support legal abortion) have begun to emphasize the idea that life begins at conception to gain access to maternal protections (such as access to quality health care) in order to fight high rates of maternal mortality (Támes July 2015, interview with author). This strategy brings attention to some of the criticisms feminist theorists have made of human rights claims that rest on an individualistic legal framework that tends to marginalize "social, economic, and cultural rights" (Yuval Davis 2006, 290).

Early in its existence, GIRE recognized that women have variable access to the means to control their fertility and forged a broadly inclusive set of demands around reproductive rights. Its promotional literature states, "In our country all women do not have the same access to reproductive rights. Social class, sexual orientation, and ethnicity can affect access to these rights. Without a common base of equality, there cannot be reproductive liberty." It also recognized that to establish reproductive autonomy for all women, the movement would have to broaden its scope beyond abortion legalization to focus on reproductive health, although legal abortion was still fundamentally important. Services it listed that needed to be available to all women included,

> economically accessible and high quality medical services; equally accessible high quality prenatal care; programs to reduce maternal and infant mortality; sexuality education at all grade levels; reduction of pregnancy among adolescents; safe, effective, and affordable contraception; legal abortion; and voluntary sterilization.

Social class was identified as a pivotal factor affecting access to health care. GIRE explained,

> Inequalities and injustice in terms of access to reproductive health are manifested in the deficient functioning of our public health system. Because of this, whatever discussion about democracy is pure

demagoguery without the development of social alternatives so that there is not a chasm between the reproductive control available to rich and poor women.

("Editorial: ¿Qué es GIRE?" 1994, 1)

Another influential group in the campaign for legal abortion in Mexico is CDD. Catholic positions on abortion and birth control among Mexicans have not been uniform, nor do they consistently conform to the official position of the Vatican. CDD has been at the forefront of representing the views of pro-choice and feminist Catholics in Mexico, with an emphasis on the connection between the right to determine personal fertility, human rights, social justice, and secular democracy. Its emphasis on secular democracy and human rights resonates with the rest of the Mexican feminist movement for abortion; its difference from other feminist perspectives, however, hinges on its acknowledgement of religion as a fundamental aspect of many Mexican women's moral belief systems. Its slogan since its founding in 1994 has been: "Mary was consulted by God before becoming a mother. Choice is everyone's right. Free motherhood, voluntary motherhood" ("Católicas por el Derecho a Decidir" 2014, 13).[8] The emphasis on "voluntary motherhood" can be traced to the 1970s feminist movement, but the invocation of Mary as a model for Mexican women's right to choose was not a "second wave" feminist abortion rights strategy. The organization works to disconnect sex from an association with sin and to foster a belief that women have a right to embrace destinies that might include more than motherhood ("We are Women" 2001, 24).

The organization came into being in 1994, during a period of increasing emphasis on human rights and democratic reform in Mexico. Just two years before the founding of CDD, President Carlos Salinas de Gortari (1988–1994) and the Mexican Congress relaxed restrictions on the public participation of the Catholic Church (imposed by the 1917 constitution) and reestablished diplomatic relations with the Vatican. These actions came in response to what most viewed as Salinas's fraudulent electoral victory in 1988 and mounting pressure from the PAN to repeal the anticlerical restrictions of the Mexican constitution of 1917. The year 1994 also saw the Zapatista uprising in response to the North American Free Trade Agreement which canceled Article 27 of the constitution protecting Indigenous land from sale. Finally, 1994 was also the year of the United Nations International Conference on Population and Development in Cairo which affirmed the link between women's empowerment, development, and population limitation ("We are Women" 2001, 24; Nikolay 1994).

CDD founders viewed all of the events listed above as connected to their struggle for reproductive choice for Catholic women with a particular emphasis on access to safe and legal abortion as a human right. They explained,

In this year [1994], so significant and difficult for national political life, we continue to be an organization of believers who from an ethical, Catholic, feminist, democratic, and secular perspective assume the defense of the human rights of women and youth, in particular sexual and reproductive rights, including access to safe and legal abortion.

("Católicas por el Derecho a Decidir" 2014, 40–41)

CDD sought to transform the culture so that women's moral authority over their reproductive bodies and their sexuality would be respected. They continued, "In the years [since their founding], we have sought to articulate and strengthen sexual and reproductive rights as part of the human rights agenda and connect these rights to social justice, democracy and the secular state" (40–41).

Despite its common invocation of a human rights discourse similar to that employed by GIRE, at the center of its theological argument for legal abortion, and in marked contrast with arguments made since the 1970s by secular Mexican feminists fighting for legal abortion, CDD emphasizes the tradition of liberty of conscience in the Catholic religion. This argument allows CDD members to embrace human rights and secular democracy, without rejecting religion. They argue that all humans have the ability to make moral decisions and the Church does not impose morality (or legislation) on believers. Elena Poniatowska Amor (2009), the journalist and abortion rights defender explained,

> Católicas base their defense [of abortion] on the principal of the catholic tradition of liberty of conscience, a basis of human dignity, that has been defended by Popes and by Church documents, because all humans are created in the image and likeness of God with choice and liberty to dissent and decide.

In 2003 CDD held a demonstration in El Zócalo [central square] in Mexico City honoring the women who died of abortion. Some of the protesters dressed as bishops who the organization argued turned their backs on women infected by HIV. Others sang, "Joy is not a sin. Risking your life and that of your partner is. Love the other as yourself, use a condom." They pointed out in their protest that Mexican women who abort are mostly poor, Catholic, and already mothers. They are usually supported in their decision by their partner and family and sometimes by their priest who understands that they cannot support another child. Thus, they argued, the official teachings of the Church that abortion is a sin in all circumstances do not align with the beliefs of many Mexican citizens ("Católicas por el Derecho a Decidir" 2014, 73).

In 2010 they launched a campaign to educate Catholic women about the rules for excommunication in relation to abortion; not all women who abort would be excommunicated from the Church. This campaign underlined the importance of recognizing the moral authority of women to make decisions about their life within the dictates of their conscience. Women responded to the campaign very positively sending messages to CDD indicating their relief that they had had an abortion in circumstances that do not warrant excommunication ("Católicas por el Derecho a Decidir" 2014, 73).

International Debates
In a world linked by economic, political, and popular media networks, it should come as no surprise that the abortion debate in Mexico, on both the feminist pro-legal abortion and anti-abortion side, has been an international one with political positions influenced by international NGOs, international conferences, treaties, and United Nations resolutions, and, of course, the theological/political arguments of the Catholic Church. The non-profit Catholic-affiliated organization Pro-Vida, founded in 1978 with support from the Church, has gained backing from US anti-abortion groups and US Catholics; on the pro-legal abortion side, the International Projects Assistance Services (IPAS), a US-based NGO, was founded to train abortion providers internationally, including in countries where abortion is illegal. Providers are trained to care for women suffering from complications caused by clandestine abortions. The Population Council and the Ford Foundation both provide research on abortion in international contexts, including to NGOs working in Mexico (Kulczycki 2007, 61).

Of course, all of these "transnational linkages" have particular local effects (Grewal and Kaplan 2006, 13). As discussed in the previous section, Mexican feminists in groups such as GIRE have tried to bring international legal norms and human rights agreements to bear on national politics, but this has been a contested process wherein anti-abortion supporters have also invoked human rights claims to support the notion that life must be protected before birth (Laville 2012, 222–230).[9] Mexican feminists have been working to take advantage of the Mexican government's endorsement of the United Nations resolutions from the 1994 International Conference on Population and Development in Cairo at which reproductive rights were defined as "human rights which are inalienable and inseparable from basic rights such as the right to food, shelter, health, security, livelihood, education and political empowerment," (as quoted in Reilly 2009, 638; Ewig 2006)[10] and also from the Fourth World Conference on Women held in Beijing in 1995, which asked governments to "consider reviewing laws that provide punitive measures against women who have had illegal abortions" (Van Dijk et al. 2007, 395; Lamas and Bissell 2000, 63). The Mexican federal government is bound to uphold all international treaties it signs as national law, which has encouraged

Mexican feminists to strengthen their own human rights discourses (Lamas and Bissell 2000, 63). Yet, as Petchesky argues, "Even when governments sign on to commitments ... there is still no effective machinery of global governance to enforce" the agreements (2003, 266).

Thus, the Mexican government has made international commitments to guarantee women's human rights, which Mexican feminists have tried to maneuver into material changes in women's status and access to resources, including reproductive health care and political power (Maier 2012, 162). Yet, how do feminists ensure that states comply with these agreements? According to Maier, the Supreme Court of Mexico ruled that fetal personhood laws violate Mexican women's human rights: she explained, "the majority opinion contends that absolute defense of the fetus's right to life denies women the right to autonomy, dignity, and control over their bodies and their lives, thus viewing the laws as a violation of women's human rights." Although the opinion was seven to four against the personhood laws, it takes a super-majority of eight justices (out of 11) to overturn a state law, so at this point the fetal personhood laws are still in effect despite their contradiction with federal law and international agreements (162). Feminists continue to pressure the Mexican government to recognize reproductive determination by women as a fundamental human right.

Conclusion: Transnational Alliances

To conclude, as a historian of the United States, I want to provide a few thoughts on the US context in light of the history of feminist abortion rights activism in Mexico. Most important in US history was the establishment of legal abortion by the Supreme Court in *Roe v. Wade* in 1973 and then the almost immediate attack on abortion access by a fundamentalist Christian anti-legal abortion movement from the 1970s onward. In my previous work on reproductive politics, I have pointed out that targeted abortion clinic protests and violence by anti-abortion organizations have been less effective than legislative attempts to restrict access to abortion. Particularly effective have been laws that can be characterized as "protecting" women's health. These laws are promoted as beneficial to women and religiously neutral. Fortunately, in the summer of 2016, the Supreme Court found a 2013 Texas law of this sort to be unconstitutional.

Yet, there is every reason to believe that the anti-legal abortion movement will continue to successfully press conservative state legislatures to pass laws restricting abortion; it is impossible to predict the resilience of these laws with the changing composition of the Supreme Court. Glen Halva-Neubauer and Sara Zeigler argue convincingly that the anti-abortion movement has evolved its rhetoric to appear to be protecting "women's interests" when they continue to promote fetal personhood from a perspective rooted in Christian fundamentalism (2010, 101–123). This strategy has succeeded in making abortion less accessible in the United States (Greenhouse 2016, 1, 4–5).

Thus, in both Mexico and the United States, the dual strategy of promoting fetal personhood and restricting women's access to abortion (even legal abortion) are parallel. US feminists need to be cognizant that the religious fundamentalism that has been wielded so effectively in Texas and other states to restrict abortion is a transnational discourse. Feminists in Latin America are already aware of the transnational reach of the Catholic Church, and, increasingly, of fundamentalist Christians (Grewal and Kaplan 2006, 24).

I believe we need to strengthen our transnational feminist discourse. Feminists in Mexico and the United States have been influential on each other; a human rights discourse around reproductive autonomy is a common factor to both movements, growing out of the series of United Nations World Conferences. In these types of international forums, feminists have communicated across borders they increasingly focus on legal abortion as a fundamental international human right. In both national contexts, there is also increasing emphasis on forging a broad reproductive justice framework that focuses on rights to health care, but also is attentive to linked demands associated with income inequality and racial injustice.

We also need to be careful to understand the heterogeneity of women's reproductive needs and demands in different local contexts. For this reason, I believe a broad reproductive justice lens would be most politically powerful as we make alliances across borders. Feminist groups organized by women of color, such as Sister Song, are already doing this sort of organizing within the United States, as are the feminist NGOs in Mexico I discussed here. I think these efforts could be expanded, particularly in the United States where a narrow focus on abortion legality exists among feminists and a tendency to see US politics in isolation.

Notes

1   Elizabeth Maier (2015) argues that debates over abortion encompass contemporary transnational cultural debates much larger than the topic of legal abortion itself. These include the relationship between personhood and rights, the definition of citizenship, the meaning of human rights, the family, and the relationship between the state and religion.

2   The frequency and practice of abortion vary depending on location (rural or urban) and also by ethnic group. Mexican feminists were aware of these differences in the 1970s (Nahmad, 1977).

3   See Fallow (2003) for a comprehensive history of the relationship between the state and the Catholic Church.

4   According to GIRE (Grupo de Información en Reproducción Elegida), 127 women were sentenced for the crime of abortion in 19 states between April 1, 2007 and July 31, 2012. Women are being incarcerated in other Latin American countries as well, particularly those countries like El Salvador that have a total ban on abortion. International organizations, including the Center for Reproductive Rights in New

York, are organizing to release these women from prison. Author's interview with Paula Avila-Guillen, September 29, 2015.

5 Ortiz-Ortega (1996) notes that financing for state family planning programs came from the following: "the United Nations Fund for Population Assistance (UNFPA), International Planned Parenthood Federation (IPPF), The Population Council, Columbia University, Pathfinder Fund, The Program for the Introduction and Adaptation of Contraceptive Technology (PIACT, International), and Development Associates," indicating a close relationship between the Mexican state and the international movement for population control.

6 The "second wave" is a term that roughly applies to women's rights activism of the 1970s. However, the periodization of the "second wave" has been contested in the United States by historians (including myself) who argue that the restriction of the movement to the 1970s leaves out women of color activism, much of which flourished in the 1980s. The "wave" metaphor does not apply very well to the Mexican context, although I use it here for the sake of brevity. In Mexico, feminist activism of the 1970s primarily emerged from student movements and left organizations in the urban context of Mexico City and around the 1975 International Women's Year Conference held in Mexico City. Feminist political engagement by Mexican Indigenous and working class women followed the earthquake in Mexico City in 1985 and also Indigenous women were part of the Zapatista movement in Chiapas in the 1990s.

7 Feminists (Indigenous and non-Indigenous) in Chiapas, collaborating with the Mexican government and NGOs, continued to organize to strengthen access to reproductive health after the 1990 effort failed to decriminalize abortion. Although the details go beyond the bounds of this chapter, I plan to write about Chiapas in more detail for the larger project that this chapter is a part. In particular, it is notable that women members of the Zapatista Army (Ejército Zapatista de Liberación Nacional—EZLN) put the right to decide the number of children they would have and care for at the top of their list of revolutionary laws. Feminists in Chiapas also emphasized that reproductive health should be part of a larger campaign for human rights and democracy. See Enciso and Caligaris 1994.

8 *María fue consultada para ser madre de Dios. Elegir es derecho de todas. Maternidad libre, maternidad voluntaria.*

9 Other scholars working on feminist movements and international human rights have explored the relationship between international "norms" set by United Nations agreements and national laws (Laville 2012). See Lynn Morgan's (2015) discussion of competing human rights claims between anti-legal abortion and pro-legal abortion groups.

10 Ewig (2006) also discusses feminist criticism of Cairo, arguing that the population establishment appropriated feminist reproductive rights language to foster a non-feminist agenda focused on population limitation and manipulation.

References

Alan Guttmacher Institute. 2016. "Induced Abortions Worldwide." www.guttmacher.org/fact-sheet/induced-abortion-worldwide [Accessed December 1, 2016].

Amor, Elena Poniatowska. 2009. "15 Años Defendiendo la Autoridad Moral de Mujeres y Jóvenes." *La Jornada*, 157, August 6. www.jornada.unam.mx/2009/08/06/ls-catolicas.html [Accessed December 24, 2016].

Becker, David, and Claudia Diaz Olavarrieta. 2013. "Decriminalization of Abortion in Mexico City: The Effects on Women's Reproductive Rights." *American Journal of Public Health* 103(4): 590–593.

Betancourt, Ruby. 1977. "La Mujer y el Crecimiento Demográfico." *Fem* 1(2): 34.

Camp, Roderic Ai. 1997. *Crossing Swords: Politics and Religion in Mexico.* Oxford: Oxford University Press.

"Católicas por el Derecho a Decidir: 20 Años en México." 2014. Coyoacan, Mexico: Católicas por el Derecho a Decidir, 13.

Cook, Rebecca J., and Bernard M. Dickens. 2006. "Human Rights Dynamics of Abortion Law." In *Women's Rights: A Human Rights Quarterly Reader*, edited by Bert B. Lockwood. Baltimore, MD: Johns Hopkins University Press.

"Editorial: ¿Qué es GIRE?" 1994. *GIRE: Boletín Trimestral Sobre Reproducción Elegida* 1(Abril): 1.

"El Aborto en una Colonia Proletaria." 1977. *Fem* 1(2): 7–9.

"El Movimiento Nacional de Mujeres Frente al Aborto." 1977. *Fem* 1(2): 71–72.

Enciso, Graciela Freyermuth, and María Garza Caligaris. 1994. "Comités de Salud Reproductiva en Chiapas: Una Experiencia de Participacion Ciudadadana." *Debate Feminista* 9(Marzo): 6.

Ewig, Christina. 2006. "Hijacking Global Feminism: Feminists, the Catholic Church, and the Family Planning Debacle in Peru." *Feminist Studies* 32(3): 633–670.

Fallow, Ben. 2003. *Religion and State Formation in Postrevolutionary Mexico.* Durham, NC and London: Duke University Press.

Garcia Molina, Aleyda. 2004. "Derecho a la Vida, Derecho a la Muerte." *Fem* 250(Enero): 1.

GIRE. 2008. *Topics for Discussion: The Process of Decriminalizing Abortion in Mexico City.* Mexico, DF: GIRE.

GIRE. 2013. "Omission and Indifference: Reproductive Rights in Mexico." Mexico, DF: GIRE, 12.

Grau, Elena. 1977. "Por un Aborto Gratuito." *Fem* 1(2): 36–37.

Greenhouse, Linda. 2016. "The Facts about Abortion Rights." *New York Times: Sunday Review*, February 28: 1, 4–5.

Grewal, Inderpal, and Karen Kaplan. 2006. "Introduction: Transnational Feminist Practices and Questions of Postmodernity." In *Scattered Hegemonies: Postmodernity and Transnational Feminist Practices*, edited by Inderpal Grewal and Karen Kaplan, 13. 5th edition. Minneapolis and London: University of Minnesota Press.

Grupo Cinco. 1991. *Sobre el Aborto (una antologia).* Grupo Cinco, Ciudad de Mexico.

Halva-Neubauer, Glen A., and Sara L. Zeigler. 2010. "Promoting Fetal Personhood: The Rhetorical and Legislative Strategies of the Pro-Life Movement after *Planned Parenthood v. Casey.*" *Feminist Formations* 22(2): 101–123.

Haussman, Melissa. 2005. *Abortion Politics in North America.* Boulder, CO: Lynne Rienner Publishers.

Jaiven, Ana Lau. 1985. *La nueva ola del feminismo en México.* México, DF: Grupo Editorial Planeta.

Kulczycki, Andrzej. 2007. "The Abortion Debate in Mexico: Realities and Stalled Policy Reform." *Bulletin of Latin American Research* 26(1): 50–68.

Lamas, Marta. 1977. "Manuel Mateo Cándano: Un Problema de Salud Público." *Fem* 1(2): 11.

Lamas, Marta. 1997. "The Feminist Movement and the Development of Political Discourse on Voluntary Motherhood in Mexico." *Reproductive Health Matters* 5(10): 58–67.

Lamas, Marta. 2001. *Política y Reproducción: Aborto: La Frontera del Derecho a Decidir.* México, DF: Plaza & Janés.

Lamas, Marta. 2009. "La despenalización del aborto en México," *Nueva Sociedad* 220(Marzo-Abril): 260.

Lamas, Marta, and Sharon Bissell. 2000. "Abortion and Politics in Mexico: 'Context Is All.'" *Reproductive Health Matters* 8(16): 11.

Lamas, Marta, Alicia Martínez, María Luisa Tarrés, and Esperanza Tuñon. 1998. "Building Bridges: The Growth of Popular Feminism in Mexico." In *The Challenge of Local Feminisms: Women's Movements in Global Perspective*, edited by Amrita Basu, 328. Boulder, CO: Westview Press.

Laveaga, Gabriela Soto. 2007. "'Let's Become Fewer': Soap Operas, Contraception, and Nationalizing the Mexican Family in an Overpopulated World." *Sexuality Research and Social Policy* 4(3): 19–33.

Laville, Helen. 2012. "'Stay Involved': Transnational Feminist Advocacy and Women's Human Rights." *Journal of Women's History* 24(4): 222–230.

Maier, Elizabeth. 2012. "Documenting Mexico's Culture War." *Latin American Perspectives* 39(6): 155–164.

Maier, Elizabeth. 2015. "La disputa sobre el aborto en México: Discursos contrastados de personificación, derechos, la familia y el Estado." *Revista Gerencia y Políticas de Salud* 14(29): 10–24.

Molina, Clara Elena. 1977. "Aspectos sociales del aborto." *Fem* 1(2): 45–47.

Morgan, Lynn. 2015. "Reproductive Rights or Reproductive Justice? Lessons from Argentina." *Health and Human Rights* 17(1): 136–147.

Nahmad, Elena Azaola Salomon. 1977. "El Aborto en Zonas Rurales e Indígenes." *Fem* 1(2): 28–32.

Nikolay, Renate. 1994. "Cairo Conference Invokes the Empowerment of Women." *Human Rights Brief*. www.wcl.american.edu/hrbrief/v2i1/cairo21.htm [Accessed March 2, 2017].

Olcott, Jocelyn. 2017. *International Women's Year: The Greatest Consciousness-Raising Event in History*. New York and London: Oxford University Press.

Ortiz-Ortega, Adriana Nohemi. 1996. *The Feminist Demand for Legal Abortion*. PhD thesis, Yale University.

Ortiz-Ortega, Adriana. 1999. "El Papel de los Derechos Reproductivos en la Construcción de Ciudadanía para las Mujeres." In *Derechos Reproductivos de las Mujeres: Un Debate Sobre Justicia Social en Mexico*, edited by Adriana Ortiz-Ortega. Mexico: Edamex.

Ortiz-Ortega, Adriana. 2001. *Si los Hombres se Embarazaran, ¿El Aborto Seria Legal?* México: Edamex and the Population Council.

Ortiz-Ortega, Adriana, and Mercedes Barquet. 2010. "Gendering Transition to Democracy in Mexico." *Latin American Research Review*, Special Issue (2010): 108–137.

Petchesky, Rosalind Pollack. 2003. *Global Prescriptions: Gendering Health and Human Rights*. New York: Zed Books.

Reich, Peter L. 1997. "The Mexican Catholic Church and Constitutional Change since 1929." *Historian* 60(1): 77–86.

Reilly, Niamh. 2009. *Women's Human Rights*. Malden, MA: Polity Press.

Rodríguez, Victoria E. 2003. *Women in Contemporary Mexican Politics*. Austen, TX: University of Texas Press.

Roe v. Wade, 410 US 113 (1973).

Rozenfaig, Diana. 1977. "El Psicoanálisis Y El Aborto." *Fem* 1(2): 19–21.

Smyth, Inez. 1998. "Gender Analysis of Family Planning: Beyond the 'Feminist vs. Population Control' Debate." In *Feminist Visions of Development: Gender, Analysis, and Policy*, edited by Cecile Jackson and Ruth Pearson. New York: Routledge.

Stephen, Lynn. 2006. "Rural Women's Grassroots Activism, 1980–2000: Reframing the Nation from Below." In *Sex in Revolution: Gender, Politics, and Power in Modern Mexico*, edited by Jocelynn Olcott, Mary Kay Vaughan, and Gabriela Cano. Durham, NC: Duke University Press.

Van Dijk, Marieke G., Diana Lara, and Sandra G. Garcia. 2007. "Opinions of Decision-makers on the Liberalization of Abortion Laws in Mexico." *Salud Pública de México* 49(6): 394–400.

"We are Women, We are Catholic, and We are in the Struggle: Catholics for the Right to Decide in Mexico." 2001. *Conscience* 22(3): 24.

Yuval Davis, Nira. 2006. "Human/Women's Rights and Feminist Transversal Politics." In *Global Feminism: Transnational Women's Activism, Organizing, and Human Rights*, edited by Myra Marx Ferree and Aili Mari Tripp. New York: New York University Press.

III
MIGRATION AND ACCESS
TO CARE

7

ACCESS TO MATERNITY CARE FOR UNDOCUMENTED MIGRANT WOMEN IN EUROPE

RAYAH FELDMAN

Introduction

The dramatic increase in migration in the European Union (EU) in recent years, both within and from outside the EU, has become a central political and social policy concern of our time. Foreign born residents constitute approximately 10 per cent of the total population in the 15 oldest EU member states (EU15) which joined the EU before 2004 (Biffl, 2012, p. 19). The EU15 comprised Austria, Belgium, Denmark, Finland, France, Germany, Greece, Ireland, Italy, Luxembourg, Netherlands, Portugal, Spain, Sweden, United Kingdom (UK). Approximately 0.5 to 1 per cent of the total population in the EU, consisting of between 1.9 and 3.8 million migrants, is irregular or undocumented. Ninety per cent of undocumented migrants live in the EU15 member states (Biffl, 2012, p. 21).

The term 'migrants', as used in this chapter, refers to people who have crossed borders to live in another country. 'Migrant' and 'immigrant' are often used interchangeably, though migration can also refer to internal movement within a country. "'Irregular migrants' typically refer to the stock of migrants in a country who are not entitled to reside there, either because they have never had a legal residence permit or because they have overstayed their time-limited permit" (Vollmer, 2011). 'Irregular', often referred to as 'undocumented' migrants include a wide range of people without secure immigration status, including asylum applicants whose claim has been refused, people who have overstayed their residence permit, and those who have never had one. In this chapter we describe migrants with insecure immigration status as 'undocumented'. Undocumented migrants are among the most excluded and vulnerable people in European countries, usually having no right to work or to claim benefits. They therefore mainly live at the margins of society. Undocumented migrant women are especially vulnerable. They are often destitute as a result of domestic violence or relationship breakdown. Many are asylum seekers whose applications have been refused, but who still fear returning to their country of origin. Some have children born in the host country. Many women who have experienced violence or abuse are unaware of rights which may stem from their situation. Indeed, such women are often afraid to report abuse in case they will face arrest or deportation (LeVoy & Geddie, 2009).

Migration has become a key electoral issue in many countries and governmental responses to anti-immigrant sentiment have included ever stricter restrictions on who may enter or stay legally. Hostility to immigration is thought to have been a main reason for the majority vote to leave the EU in a 2016 referendum in the UK on British membership of the EU, also known as Brexit (Bulman, 2017; Sampson, 2017).

Even before the European 'refugee crisis', since 2015, most EU15 member states had already developed growing distinctions between the rights of citizens and various types of migrants, responding to, but also fueling anti-immigrant views (Engbersen & Broeders, 2009; Bommes & Geddes, 2000; van der Leun, 2006). Rights of access to national health-care schemes have become important markers of differentiation between citizens, residents, and migrants. Legislation to restrict rights of some migrants is widely used by governments to exercise control over migration inside the border. In doing so they both respond to and increase invidious distinctions between different types of migrants, and between migrants and the 'host' population. Undocumented migrants, as the least protected among migrant categories, often live and work in precarious and insecure circumstances and have fewer rights to health and welfare benefits than almost any other migrant group (LeVoy, 2008; Triandafyllidou, 2009). This has particular significance for undocumented migrant women, who face the added health-care needs involved in maternity care.

Undocumented Migrant Women and Maternity Care

Pregnancy and childbirth are widely regarded in most cultures and within national international legal and human rights frameworks as involving a special status and requiring priority in care (see discussion of human rights instruments below). Maternity care has been a long-term concern of the World Health Organization (WHO) both to reduce maternal mortality and to support women's health generally (AbouZahr, 2003; WHO, 2016). Policies on maternity care therefore provide a useful baseline for comparing whether and how national governments seek to address health and welfare generally and among specific groups within their populations. Barriers to maternity care for undocumented migrant women may thus be seen not just as problems for pregnant women, but also as indicators of how well other, less valued health needs of undocumented people are likely to be met.

This chapter summarizes official policies on access to cost-free or very low-cost maternity care available to undocumented migrant women in 14 of the EU15 member states and considers how other social and institutional obstacles also restrict undocumented women's access to safe maternity care. Data was gathered from secondary sources mainly available in English though some sources were translated from the original languages where necessary. Accuracy of information was checked as far as possible with locally knowledgeable experts. The study made no attempt to link national policies with data on pregnancy outcomes. However, the data highlights how far provision for maternity care falls short in those EU countries which host the vast majority of undocumented migrants.

Undocumented Migrants' Rights to Health

Although the right to health is recognised in both European and United Nations conventions as a human right, in practice this gives little protection to undocumented migrants. General human rights law provides only a limited basis for the provision of health care for undocumented migrants. The United Nations Declaration on the human rights of individuals who are not nationals of the country in which they live restricts the application of social rights to migrants living *lawfully* in a state (United Nations, 1985, Article 8). Similarly, the Charter of Fundamental Rights of the European Union subjects the right to benefit from health care to "conditions established by national laws and practices" (European Agency for Fundamental Rights (FRA), 2015, p. 9).

Several legally binding instruments, including both the Convention on the Rights of the Child (CRC) and the Convention on the Elimination of All Forms of Discrimination against Women (CEDAW), oblige states to provide appropriate antenatal and postnatal health care for women (United Nations, 1989, 1999). CEDAW specifically requires states to "ensure to women appropriate services in connection with pregnancy, confinement and the postnatal period, granting free services where necessary, as well as adequate nutrition during pregnancy and lactation" (United Nations, 1999, Article 12).

However, these international conventions are not routinely enshrined in national laws and their provisions not easily enforceable. States that sign up to them are only required to report to the relevant UN Committee every few years, and although the Committee will make recommendations on where a state must improve, individuals have no right to complain directly to the Committee or to a court that their rights under the Convention have not been provided. Hence, there is considerable variation in provision between countries. In Europe, undocumented migrants' guaranteed legal access to health care is limited to emergency health care, deriving from the right to life and the prohibition of inhuman treatment under the European Convention on Human Rights (FRA, 2011). This results in childbirth itself being very widely recognised as an emergency and hence normally eligible for free treatment. By contrast, as is shown later, antenatal and postnatal care, not being emergency treatments, are often denied to undocumented women unless they are able to pay.

Pregnancy Risks of Undocumented Migrant Women

There is substantial evidence that migrant women have worse pregnancy outcomes than those of women in host populations despite difficulties of comparisons between studies using different classifications of people according to immigration status or ethnicity (Bollini, Pampallona, Wanner, & Kupelnick, 2009; Gibson-Helm et al., 2014; Minsart, Englebert, & Buekens, 2012; Gissler et al., 2009; Essen, Hanson, Östergren, Lindquist, & Gudmundsson, 2000). The variability in relationships between pregnancy outcomes, patterns of migration, and the definitions of reference groups for comparison observed in systematic reviews, limits the conclusions that may be drawn from such studies (Urquia et al., 2010; Gagnon, Zimbeck, Zeitlin, & The ROAM Collaboration, 2009). However, it does not undermine the claim that migrant populations are likely to face specific risk factors to maternal health, particularly those with underlying medical conditions or who are living in insecure or unsafe conditions. Undocumented migrant women are particularly likely to face complex social risk factors including especially domestic abuse, precarious housing, or sexual exploitation as they have no access to legitimate sources of income (Feldman, 2017; Safety4Sisters, 2016).

Some studies have found that national policies of migrant 'integration', measured by ease and rates of naturalisation are associated with improved pregnancy outcomes (Bollini et al., 2009; Minsart et al., 2012). These studies highlight the positive effects of integrative policies or experiences of societal integration in reducing social exclusion, thus reducing the stress and discrimination migrant mothers face. Unfortunately, they make only passing reference to the improvements in access to maternity care which naturalization or a more positive integration policy might enable, and very little reference to the social and economic circumstances of the most vulnerable group of migrants, those who have irregular immigration status.

In spite of the limitations of studies which focus primarily on migration, other studies addressing social deprivation show an unambiguous connection between factors such as low income, unemployment, poor housing, and poor health, including poorer pregnancy outcomes (Marmot Review, 2010;

Whitehead, Callaghan, Johnson, & Williams, 2009; Braveman et al., 2010; Kapaya et al., 2015). Whatever the problems of definition in studies of migrants' health outcomes, the fact that undocumented migrants are universally among the poorest and most socially excluded groups in society, justifies paying attention to their health and health needs.

There is also a good deal of evidence that as well as socio-economic disadvantage, migrants in general and undocumented people in particular, face powerful social and legal barriers which restrict their access to health care in nearly all countries (Platform for International Cooperation on Undocumented Migrants (PICUM), 2007; HUMA Network, 2009; FRA, 2011; Roland, Simonnot, & Vanbiervliet, 2013). These include practical barriers, which, to varying degrees, often limit access to the services to which undocumented migrants are entitled. For example, administrative barriers, incorrect refusals of care due to lack of awareness or discrimination, lack of knowledge about rights and how to access care on the part of migrants, and fear or risk of detection through service use are major barriers to access.

Policies for Undocumented Migrants' Access to Maternity Care

Policies towards maternity care provision for undocumented migrant women in 14 of the EU15 countries, all of which have substantial immigrant populations, are summarised in Table 7.1. The table shows that where there is established provision for undocumented migrants, whether comprehensive or limited, maternity care is always included, and also, in most cases, family planning and abortion services. However, maternity services are normally not available in countries where there is only emergency health provision for undocumented migrants. Between these two approaches, there may also be ambiguities and contradictions where receiving any health care, including maternity care, can expose undocumented migrant women to risks of deportation or other immigration sanctions, as in Germany and the UK.

Administrative and Political Barriers to Care

As shown in Table 7.1, there is a right to free maternity care for all women in France, Sweden, Belgium, Netherlands, Spain, Italy, and Portugal. This should mean that most undocumented women migrants in those states have easy access to maternity services. However, administrative barriers often make it difficult for women to access care even where it is, in principle, available (Chauvin, Simonnot, Douay, & Vanbiervliet, 2014; PICUM, 2007; Chauvin et al., 2013; Karl-Trummer, Novak-Zezula, & Metzler, 2010; Woodward, Howard, & Wolffers, 2014). This can be the result of confusion about eligibility, complex regulations, or linked reporting to immigration authorities.

Doctors of the World, or Médecins du Monde, an international health charity which provides health care and advocacy to excluded populations in

Table 7.1 Policies for Maternity Care Provision for Undocumented Migrants in 14 European Countries[1]

Type of Health Provision for Undocumented Migrants (UDMs)	Country	General Provision for UDMs	Maternity Care for UDMs	Funding and Administration for UDM Provision	Limitations	Additional Sources
Comprehensive provision	France	• AME (*Aide Médicale d'Etat – state medical aid*) provides full medical care for UDMs with limited resources for residents >3 months. • Free at point of service. • Where residence >3 months cannot be proved, entitlement exists for care deemed urgent. • Universal public health provision for HIV, sexually transmitted infections, and tuberculosis (TB), without identification documents.	• Included as part of AME and emergency care. Includes abortion. • Family planning requires no identification documents.	• AME funded by the state. • Special state funds for non-AME emergency care.	• AME granted for 1 year. Application involves proof of address, income, etc. • For non-AME emergency care hospitals must confirm patient eligibility.	France DHOS/DSS/DGAS, 2005

| Limited provision | Sweden | • Since 2012 UDM adults have same rights as asylum seekers.
• Access to health care that cannot be postponed on payment of €6 visit fee.
• Municipalities have power to provide further services. | • Includes maternal health care, abortion care, and counseling for contraceptives. | • State funded. | • Automatic qualification but limited provision.
• Controversy/confusion over meaning of 'care that cannot be postponed.'
• Lack of uniform administrative procedure.
• Lack of awareness of the reform and undocumented migrants' rights. | PICUM, 2013 |

continued

Table 7.1 Continued

Type of Health Provision for Undocumented Migrants (UDMs)	Country	General Provision for UDMs	Maternity Care for UDMs	Funding and Administration for UDM Provision	Limitations	Additional Sources
	Belgium	• 'Urgent medical care' under AMU (*Aide Médicale Urgente – urgent medical aid*) for UDMs. • Access to essential health-care services (both preventive and curative).	• Includes all maternity care. • Can include abortion.	• AMU provided by local municipal welfare centre Centre Public d'Action Sociale (CPAS). • Must be certified by investigation of address, lack of resources, and medical need. • Providers reimbursed by CPAS. Federal government reimburses CPAS. • Some autonomy to CPAS regarding non-reimbursable medical needs e.g., infant milk, painkillers, etc.	• Evidence of difficulties getting necessary certification for AMU. • The card is provided for specific treatments or for limited periods. • Complex registration procedure. • Administrative costs to service providers and to CPAS.	Druyts, 2006

Netherlands	• UDMs have no right to insurance but entitled to receive medically necessary care as indicted by clinician. • UDMs have access to 'directly accessible' services including General Practioners (GPs), midwives, dentists, and emergency care from any provider.	• Includes care for pregnancy and childbirth.	• Providers get reimbursed 80% costs for these services but 100% costs for pregnancy and childbirth. • Costs borne by state but administered by health insurance companies. • To obtain reimbursement providers must prove patients' inability to pay.	• Limited number of contracted providers for 'not directly accessible services' (mainly hospitals). Other providers cannot be reimbursed. • Ignorance as to which providers are contracted. • UDMs and providers lack information about reimbursement.	Schoevers, Loeffen, van den Muijsenbergh, & Lagro-Janssen, 2010

continued

Table 7.1 Continued

Type of Health Provision for Undocumented Migrants (UDMs)	Country	General Provision for UDMs	Maternity Care for UDMs	Funding and Administration for UDM Provision	Limitations	Additional Sources
	Spain	• UDMs without residence permit living in Spain >3 months entitled to care for emergencies, serious disease, or accidents only. • All care for pregnant women and for children also provided. • Other care requires payment of €710 per year for ages <65 and €1864 for >65 to obtain basic health insurance package. • Autonomous communities have power to provide further services.	• Includes pregnancy and childbirth services which is the same as for authorised residents.	• General taxation.	• Change from National Health Service universal access system in 2012. • Discretionary power to health professionals about what should be considered 'emergency care.' • Health-care providers poorly informed about the rules. • Discrimination against pregnant women in practice. • Cost of state health insurance beyond the means of UDMs.	Benítez, 2013; Royo-Bordonada, Diez-Cornell, & Llorente, 2013

| Italy | • UDMs get STP (*Straniero Temporaneamente Presente* – temporary residing foreigner) code 6 months, renewable.
• Access to 'urgent' care same as regular residents.
• Access to 'essential' primary and secondary care.
• Includes entitlement to preventive care and care for public health reasons.
• Regions have power to provide further services. | • Includes prenatal and maternity care.
• Abortion free to women with health card.
• Women and their husbands (not unmarried partners) are entitled to a residence permit 'for health care' during pregnancy and up to 6 months after the child's birth. | • General health system financed by taxation.
• UDM health-care cost covered by local health service and reimbursed by state. | • Regional autonomy gives wide variability in provision according to local political control.
• Migrants cannot register with GPs. This may create a barrier to accessing secondary care as normally a referral is needed from primary care. | Pedone, 2012; PICUM, 2010 |

continued

Table 7.1 Continued

Type of Health Provision for Undocumented Migrants (UDMs)	Country	General Provision for UDMs	Maternity Care for UDMs	Funding and Administration for UDM Provision	Limitations	Additional Sources
	Portugal	• UDMs resident over 90 days can obtain temporary registration. This gives access to free medical care for a public health 'basket of services' to those unable to pay. • UDMs with less than 90 days' residence – access to emergency care only but may not be withheld on financial grounds.	• Free maternity care including antenatal and postnatal care. • Pregnant women exempt from user fees until 8 weeks postnatal. • Free dental care for pregnant women. • Free family planning. • Abortion in approved health-care establishment.	• National Health Service (NHS) funded by general taxation.	• Recurring administrative barriers to access. • Lack of professionals' awareness of UDM entitlements. • Ambiguous legislation re UDMs' entitlements. • UDMs avoid registration because of fears of being reported to authorities.	Fonseca, Silva, Esteves, & McGarrigle, 2009; PICUM, 2015

| Contradictory policies (sanctions undermine benefits of formal provision) | Germany | • UDMs have right to access care for 'serious illness or acute pain' if they obtain *Krankenschein* (sickness certificate) in advance from social welfare offices except for emergency care.
• Social welfare offices have legal duty to report undocumented migrants to the Foreigners Office. | • Free maternity care and family planning – pregnant women exempted from cost sharing (in theory).
• *Duldung* (exemption from deportation) granted 6 weeks antenatal to 8 weeks postnatal. Covers antenatal care and delivery. | • Reimbursement for some providers from tax-funded social welfare office.
• In practice, often provided by doctors foregoing fees.
• Some voluntary organisations and regional authorities provide health services to UDMs. | • Entitlement is undermined by the reporting requirement of Social Welfare offices which in practice deters UDMs from accessing health care.
• The *Duldung* also involves reporting to the Foreigners Office. | German Institute for Human Rights, 2007; Schrover, 2008 |
| | UK | • UDMs chargeable at 150% of cost for secondary care.
• GP registration at discretion of GPs.
• Exemptions for selected infectious diseases and emergency care (only within the emergency department).
• Immediately necessary care must be delivered but is chargeable after completion of care. | • All maternity care is viewed as *immediately necessary* so must be provided but is chargeable.
• Family planning is exempt from charging.
• Abortion is chargeable. | • Fees must be recouped from chargeable patients by hospital trusts unless they decide they are not recoverable.
• Hospital must notify the Home Office of patients with debts over £500. | • Debts over £500 are liable to penalties in further visa applications, regularisation, etc. This can deter women from seeking maternity care.
• Requirement to recover fees from individuals is disincentive to provide care to destitute UDMs. | Department of Health, 2015; Maternity Action, 2016a |

continued

Table 7.1 Continued

Type of Health Provision for Undocumented Migrants (UDMs)	Country	General Provision for UDMs	Maternity Care for UDMs	Funding and Administration for UDM Provision	Limitations	Additional Sources
No provision for general health care	Austria	• All non-insured including UDMs have no entitlement to access health services except emergency care. This is subject to charging. • Universal care to people with TB. • HIV tests are free but not treatment.	• Emergency care includes childbirth but not general maternity care.	• Some voluntary organisations provide care to UDMs supported through federal and local grants and voluntary work by medical professionals. • Fees must be recouped from chargeable patients or covered by hospitals' own budgets.	• Unpaid health-care bills continue to be payable after regularisation of immigration status. • Health care virtually dependent on non-state providers. • Lack of awareness of alternative providers can result in very late presentation.	Karl-Trummer, Metzler, & Novak-Zezula, 2009

Denmark	• UDMs have access to free emergency care.	• Emergency care includes childbirth but not general maternity care.	• Limited provision from informal networks of health-care providers but these are not coordinated.	• UDMs may request health care from Immigration Service but Immigration Service legally obliged to report UDMs to police. • Some decentralisation creates regional variation in access.	Hansen, 2005
Greece	• Limited emergency care for life threatening conditions only. • Free access to primary health care in few local authority settings and provided by NGOs.	• Uninsured pregnant women must pay for antenatal care, delivery, and lab tests. • No removal of UDMs during pregnancy or for 6 months after giving birth.	• Some access based on goodwill of individual doctors. • Limited NGO provision for UDMs.	• Emergency treatment often unavailable because of austerity crisis.	Chauvin, Parizot, & Simonnot, 2009; Economou, 2010

continued

Table 7.1 Continued

Type of Health Provision for Undocumented Migrants (UDMs)	Country	General Provision for UDMs	Maternity Care for UDMs	Funding and Administration for UDM Provision	Limitations	Additional Sources
	Ireland	• Hospital coverage universal for anyone 'ordinarily resident' (resident for at least 1 year). • UDMs only eligible for urgent medical treatment at reduced or no charge at provider's discretion. • Chargeable full fee for any other service.	• Prenatal and postnatal care not freely available to UDMs. • Childbirth considered emergency.	• No provision.	• Confusion as to what constitutes urgent medical treatment. • Fear of authorities constitutes barrier to accessing emergency care.	Pillinger, 2008

| Finland | • UDMs have access to emergency care only (subject to charging).
 • Public provision dependent on health staff's willingness to respond to need and flexibility in dealing with costs. | • Some public health nurses provide maternity care to undocumented migrants with the permission of the head physician.
 • Free family planning and abortion. | • No special provision except care at the discretion of providers in which case costs will be borne by state, municipality, or social insurance organisation. | • Lack of clarity of UDMs' rights to health care. | Hofverberg, 2014 |

Note

1 Data in this table was drawn from the following sources referred to in the main text: Chauvin, Simonnot, & Vanbiervliet. (2013); Cuadra, (2010); HUMA Network (2009); Platform for International Cooperation on Undocumented Migrants (PICUM) (2007); Macherey, Simonnot, & Vanbiervliet (2015). Other country specific sources are indicated in the table.

both developed and developing countries, provided an example of such barriers. They reported the case of a woman who was refused a termination of pregnancy in Sweden unless she paid several hundred euro, in spite of a new law on health care which allows undocumented women the right to obstetric care and pregnancy termination. Doctors of the World found that none of the hospital receptionists were aware of the change in the law (Chauvin et al., 2014, p. 12).

The FRA notes that it is essential both that health staff and treatment centres be aware of undocumented migrants' entitlements, and that authorities at different levels in the state take responsibility to ensure that migrants can benefit in practice from the provision of public health services (FRA, 2011, p. 22). Often, however, the default position is to refuse care, requiring the intercession of charities and lawyers to enable undocumented migrants to access health care to which they are entitled.

Other widespread administrative barriers involve requirements for migrants to provide proof of address which is often not possible when people are subletting, 'sofa-surfing', staying with friends, living in shelters, or are street homeless (FRA, 2011, p. 19). In France, which has the most comprehensive provision for irregular migrants, many still fail to obtain state medical assistance (AME) because they do not have the right documents such as passports or utility bills to prove that they have been three months resident in France (FRA, 2011, p. 19). In Belgium, despite a programme of medical assistance to undocumented migrants, which includes maternity care, the process for certification is cumbersome and locally variable, even when the state child and family organisation provides assistance (HUMA Network, 2009).

Frequently the local incentives for imposing administrative barriers are financial as providers want to be assured that they will be reimbursed. Reimbursement procedures can be very cumbersome, constituting a disincentive to provide treatment. For example, in the Netherlands the provider must invoice the patient and send them a payment reminder, as well as investigate their ability to pay before the costs of 'medically necessary care' can be recouped. This situation is complicated by a lack of clarity over what constitutes 'necessary care' (Cuadra, 2010, p. 11). But underlying such procedures are the political decisions to exclude undocumented migrants from mainstream care, and to insist on complex gatekeeping measures before the residual care to which they are entitled becomes available.

Health Care as Border Control

At least as powerful as administrative barriers are the risks to undocumented migrants of becoming known to the authorities and being removed or legally sanctioned as a result of receiving medical care. For example, in Germany undocumented migrants must obtain a *Krankenschein* (sickness certificate) in order to receive medical treatment. Such certificates are only available from Social Welfare Centres which have a legal duty to inform regional authorities about the whereabouts of undocumented migrants, except in the case of emergency care (HUMA Network, 2010, p. 21). Undocumented pregnant women can obtain a *Duldung* (Toleration) exemption which allows them to access antenatal and postnatal care, and care in labour. The *Duldung* lasts from six weeks before the expected date of delivery to eight weeks postnatally (12 weeks in the case of twins or premature birth) (Scott, 2004, p. 15).

Although the *Duldung* grants limited access to maternity care for undocumented migrant women, it is not a residence permit, and when it expires, women, who may previously have been unknown to the authorities, may be at greater risk of being removed. As a result many women interviewed in one study were too scared to obtain a *Duldung* because they feared that the authorities would look for them once it had expired. It is also noteworthy that the *Duldung* only enables women to obtain care from the third trimester of pregnancy in spite of the fact that such women are always considered to have high risk pregnancies (Castañeda, 2008).

In the UK too, hospitals are required to report to the Home Office any overseas patient who has failed to pay a bill for treatment of £500 or more within two months (Department of Health, 2016). This can make it impossible for undocumented pregnant women to regularise their immigration status in the future. There are growing numbers of reports of women who have avoided antenatal care and even a hospital delivery to avoid this sanction (Aston, 2014; Feldman, 2017).

Where medical care invites the automatic risk of immigration sanctions, avoiding such a risk is likely to trump the need or desire of vulnerable women to book early and sustain regular maternity care. Inevitably this will also prevent these women receiving related support for problems such as mental health, domestic violence, or child protection. It also creates a punitive climate within the health-care system against patients unable to pay. Doctors of the World reported cases in Greece and Belgium where hospitals refused to issue a birth certificate to babies of women who could not pay for the cost of giving birth (Chauvin et al., 2014, p. 13).

Facilitating Full Maternity Care for Undocumented Migrants

There has been a range of initiatives in Europe to try to compensate for, or to help overcome, some of the barriers to access to health care for undocumented migrants. Few have been restricted to maternity care, but much of the work has been concerned with pregnant women. In situations where there is a legal obligation to pay for care or where entitlements have been very restrictively interpreted by local authorities, such initiatives have often been the sole source of treatment. Doctors of the World operates health programmes in more than 12 European countries for people who find it difficult or impossible to access standard health care. Its regular reports based on the use of its services provide valuable documentation of the extent of migrant women's exclusion from maternity care in many European countries (Chauvin & Simonnot, 2012; Chauvin et al., 2013; Chauvin et al., 2014; Simonnot et al., 2016).

In some countries, clinics for undocumented migrants and other marginalised groups have been established by regional charities, sometimes in collaboration with public authorities. Such clinics provide dedicated services to these groups which are not always available in public health facilities. Several provide special clinics for pregnant women. For example, in Milan, a migrant women's cooperative, *Crinali*, works in partnership with the public health sector to provide medical support to pregnant migrant women, whatever their immigration status. The *Crinali* clinic assists women to obtain a Temporary Resident Foreigner (STP) code and offers in-house gynaecological and obstetric services to women registered with it (FRA, 2011, p. 25; La Cooperativa Crinali, 2015).

Another Italian non-governmental organisation (NGO), NAGA, uses volunteer clinicians to provide free basic health care to refugees and temporary migrants, including undocumented migrants. NAGA has established a special women's service dealing with reproductive health and maternity (PICUM, 2007, p. 57; NAGA, 2016). In Frankfurt, a not-for-profit women's project, *Maisha*, set up a health clinic for African women, men, and families in 2001 in collaboration with the Frankfurt Public Health Department and other municipal departments. Since 2009 the clinic has provided free and anonymous health consultations to migrants from all over the world who are unable to access regular health care in Germany. Up to 75 per cent of its service users are women (Maisha, 2012).

In Britain, Doctors of the World runs drop-in clinics offering primary health care and advocacy for vulnerable people, including a clinic for women and children which provides advice for pregnant women (Doctors of the World, 2016). A national charity, Maternity Action, runs a training and advice service on vulnerable migrant women's entitlement to maternity care for midwives and voluntary sector organisations working with migrant women who are pregnant or new mothers (Maternity Action, 2017). It also runs a direct advice service for women and their families about access to maternity care (Maternity Action, 2016b). These services highlight the rights of all women to full maternity services whatever their administrative status, and whether or not they may be chargeable. In some areas specialist clinical pathways enabling links with local voluntary organisations have been developed in acknowledgement of the wide range of potential social and medical needs of migrant women (Feldman, 2012, p. 54; Sharpe, 2010,

p. 39). In common with many other services for migrants, few such initiatives have been formally evaluated but ongoing and growing demand for them indicates a continuing need.

Conclusion

This overview of access to maternity care for undocumented women in Europe shows that maternity services are not exempt from monetary charges in over half the countries reviewed, and that access to cost-free care can be linked to immigration controls in some countries. Barriers to maternity care put the health of vulnerable women and babies at risk by preventing services addressing pressing medical and social needs.

In many countries the complexity of rules about entitlement and the linkages between health-care access and immigration enforcement act as barriers to access much more widely than is often realised and delegitimises the use of health services by all migrants and minority groups. Excluding some migrants on account of their immigration status also risks excluding foreigners and ethnic minorities whatever their eligibility, especially if they do not speak the language or do not understand the requirements of the health-care system (Chauvin et al., 2014, p. 5).

In all countries there is a need for a responsible authority to ensure that rights to health care for migrants in irregular situations are protected rather than policed. This could involve providing support for NGOs assisting with registration and access, but also needs a full separation or *firewall* between health services and immigration enforcement (PICUM, 2014, p. 21) so that the use of health services by migrants is not presumed to be an 'abuse', and migrants are not deterred from seeking necessary health care.

References

AbouZahr, C. (2003). Safe Motherhood: A brief history of the global movement 1947–2002. *British Medical Bulletin, 67*, 13–25. doi: 10.1093/bmb/ldg014.

Aston, J. (2014, March 20). Heavily pregnant immigrant carrying dead child wouldn't seek help as she was afraid she'd have to pay NHS under "health tourism" rules. *Independent*. Retrieved from www.independent.co.uk/news/uk/home-news/heavily-pregnant-immigrant-carrying-dead-child-wouldnt-seek-help-as-she-was-afraid-shed-have-to-pay-9205591.html.

Benítez, I. (2013, May 24). Health care for immigrants crumbling in Spain. *Inter Press Service*. Retrieved from www.ipsnews.net/2013/05/health-care-for-immigrants-crumbling-in-spain/.

Biffl, G. (2012). Migration in Europe and undocumented migrants. In G. Biffl and F. Altenburg (eds.), *Migration and health in nowhereland* (pp. 19–24). Bad Vöslau: Omnium.

Bollini, P., Pampallona, S., Wanner, P., & Kupelnick, B. (2009). Pregnancy outcome of migrant women and integration policy: A systematic review of the international literature. *Social Science and Medicine, 68*(3), 452–461. doi: 10.1016/j.socscimed.2008. 10.018.

Bommes, M., & Geddes, A. (eds). (2000). *Immigration and welfare: Challenging the borders of the welfare state*. London: Routledge.

Braveman, P., Marchi, K., Egerter, S., Kim, M., Metzler, S., Stancil, T., & Libet, M. (2010). Poverty, near-poverty, and hardship around the time of pregnancy. *Maternal and Child Health Journal, 14*(1), 20–35. doi: 10.1007/s10995-008-0427-0.

Bulman, M. (2017, June 28). Brexit: People voted to leave EU because they feared immigration, major survey finds. *Independent.* Retrieved from www.independent.co.uk/news/uk/home-news/brexit-latest-news-leave-eu-immigration-main-reason-european-union-survey-a7811651.html.

Castañeda, H. (2008). Illegal migration, gender and health care: Perspectives from Germany and the United States. In M. Schrover, J. van der Leun, L. Lucassen, & C. Quispel (eds), *Illegal migration and gender in a global and historical perspective* (pp. 171–188). Amsterdam: Amsterdam University Press.

Chauvin, P., Parizot, I., & Simonnot, N. (2009). *Access to healthcare for undocumented migrants in 11 European countries.* Médecins du Monde. Retrieved from www.epim.info/wp-content/uploads/2011/02/Access-to-healthcare-for-Undocumented-Migrants-in-11-EU-countries-2009.pdf.

Chauvin, P., & Simonnot, N. (2012). *Access to health care for vulnerable groups in the European Union in 2012.* Médecins du Monde. Retrieved from www.doktersvandewereld.be/sites/www.doktersvandewereld.be/files/publicatie/attachments/eu_vulnerable_groups_2012_mdm.pdf.

Chauvin, P., Simonnot, N., Douay, C., & Vanbiervliet, F. (2014). *Access to healthcare for the most vulnerable in a Europe in social crisis.* Médecins du Monde. Retrieved from http://b.3cdn.net/droftheworld/ddba157be802b8a13e_l1m6bup6k.pdf.

Chauvin, P., Simonnot, N., & Vanbiervliet, F. (2013). *Access to health care in Europe in times of crisis and rising xenophobia: An overview of the situation of people excluded from healthcare systems.* Doctors of the World. Retrieved from www.uems.eu/news-and-events/news/news-more/access-to-healthcare-in-europe-in-times-of-crisis-and-rising-xenophobia.

Cuadra, C. (2010). *Policies on health care for undocumented migrants in EU27: Country report—the Netherlands.* Malmo: Malmö University. Retrieved from http://c-hm.com/wp-content/uploads/2015/08/country_report_The_Netherlands.pdf.

Department of Health. (2015). *Guidance on implementing the overseas visitor hospital charging regulations.* London: Department of Health. Retrieved from www.gov.uk/government/uploads/system/uploads/attachment_data/file/418634/Implementing_overseas_charging_regulations_2015.pdf.

Department of Health. (2016). *Overseas chargeable patients NHS debt and immigration rules: Guidance on administration and data sharing.* London: Department of Health. Retrieved from https://groups.ic.nhs.uk/TheInformationGovernanceKnowledgebase/The%20Information%20Governance%20Knowledgebase/Overseas%20chargeable%20patients%202016.pdf.

DHOS/DSS/DGAS (Direction de l'Hospitalisation et d'Organisation des Soins, Direction de la Securité Sociale & Direction Général del'Action Sociale). (2005). *Circulaire no 141 du 16 mars.* Retrieved from www.sante.gouv.fr/IMG/pdf/Circulaire_no141_du_16_mars_2005.pdf.

Doctors of the World. (2016). *Our UK clinics.* Retrieved from www.doctorsoftheworld.org.uk/our-clinics.

Druyts, E. (ed.). (2006). *Aide Médicale Urgente pour personnes en séjour illégal: Manuel pour des collaborateurs de CPAS et prestataires de soins.* Brussels: Medimmigrant. Retrieved from www.medimmigrant.be/uploads/Publicaties/Handleiding/DMH%20voor%20MZ

WV%20handleiding%20voor%20OCMWmedewerkers%20en%20zorgverstrekkers%20
basispakket%20FR.pdf.

Economou, C. (2010). Greece: Health system review. *Health Systems in Transition, 12*(7), 1–180.

Engbersen, G., & Broeders, D. (2009). The state versus the alien: Immigration control and strategies of irregular immigrants. *West European Politics, 32*(5), 867–885. doi: 10.1080/01402380903064713.

Essen, B., Hanson, B., Östergren, P., Lindquist, P., & Gudmundsson, S. (2000). Increased perinatal mortality among sub-Saharan immigrants in a city-population in Sweden. *Acta Obstetricia et Gynecologica Scandinavica, 79*(9), 737–743. doi: 10.1034/j.1600-0412.2000.079009737.x.

European Agency for Fundamental Rights (FRA). (2011). *Migrants in an irregular situation: Access to healthcare in 10 European Union member states.* Luxembourg: Publications Office of the European Union.

European Agency for Fundamental Rights (FRA). (2015). *Cost of exclusion from healthcare: The case of migrants in an irregular situation.* Luxembourg: Publications Office of the European Union.

Feldman, R. (2012). *Guidance for commissioning health services for vulnerable migrant women.* Maternity Action and Women's Health and Equality Consortium. Retrieved from www.maternityaction.org.uk/wp-content/uploads/2013/09/guidancecommissioning healthservvulnmigrantwomen2012.pdf.

Feldman, R. (2017). *The impact on health inequalities of charging migrant women for NHS maternity care: A scoping study.* Maternity Action and Women's Health and Equality Consortium. Retrieved from www.maternityaction.org.uk/wp-content/uploads/Charging ReportMarch2017FINALcompressed.pdf.

Fonseca, M., Silva, S., Esteves, A., & McGarrigle, J. (2009). *Portuguese state of the art report.* Lisbon: Mighealthnet. Retrieved from www.ceg.ul.pt/migrare/Mighealthnet SOAR_eng.pdf.

Gagnon, A., Zimbeck, M., Zeitlin, J., & The ROAM Collaboration. (2009). Migration to western industrialised countries and perinatal health: A systematic review. *Social Science and Medicine, 69*(6), 934–946. doi: 10.1016/j.socscimed.2009.06.027.

German Institute for Human Rights. (ed.). (2007). *Frauen, Männer und Kinder ohne Papiere in Deutschland: Ihr Recht auf Gesundheit* (summary in English). Berlin: German Institute for Human Rights. Retrieved from www.institut-fuer-menschenrechte.de/fileadmin/user_upload/PDF-Dateien/Ergebnispapiere_Zusammenfassungen_Hintergrundpapiere/executive_summary_undocumented_migrants_in_germany.pdf.

Gibson-Helm, M., Teede, H., Block, A., Knight, M., East, C., Wallace, E., & Boyle, J. (2014). Maternal health and pregnancy outcomes among women of refugee background from African countries: A retrospective, observational study in Australia. *BMC Pregnancy and Childbirth, 14*, 1–11. doi: 10.1186/s12884-014-0392-0.

Gissler, M., Alexander, S., Macfarlane, A., Small, R., Stray-Pedersen, B., Zeitlin, J., Zimbeck, M., & Gagnon, A. (2009). Stillbirths and infant deaths among migrants in industrialized countries. *Acta Obstetricia et Gynecologica, 88*(2), 134–148. doi: 10.1080/00016340802603805.

Hansen, A. (2005). *Access to health care for undocumented immigrants in California (USA) and Denmark: Rights and practice.* Copenhagen: University of Copenhagen. Retrieved from http://samf.ku.dk/pkv/faerdige_projektopgaver/140/140_samlet_pdf_til_web.pdf.

Hofverberg, E. (2014, March 25). Finland: Universal health care for undocumented immigrants. *Global Legal Monitor.* Retrieved from www.loc.gov/lawweb/servlet/lloc_news?disp3_l205403907_text.

HUMA Network. (2009). *Access to health care for undocumented migrants and asylum seekers in 10 EU countries: Law and practice, Brussels, European programme for integration and migration.* Retrieved from www.episouth.org/doc/r_documents/Rapport_huma-network.pdf.

HUMA Network. (2010). *Are undocumented migrants and asylum seekers entitled to access health care in the EU?* Retrieved from www.epim.info/wp-content/uploads/2011/02/HUMA-Publication-Comparative-Overview-16-Countries-2010.pdf.

Kapaya, H., Mercer, E., Boffey, F., Jones, G., Mitchell, C., & Anumba, D. (2015). Deprivation and poor psychosocial support are key determinants of late antenatal presentation and poor fetal outcomes: A combined retrospective and prospective study. *BMC Pregnancy and Childbirth, 15*, 309. doi: 10.1186/s12884-015-0753-3.

Karl-Trummer, U., Metzler, B., & Novak-Zezula, S. (2009). *Health care for undocumented migrants in the EU: Concepts and cases.* Brussels: International Organisation for Migration. Retrieved from www.migrant-health-europe.org/files/Health%20Care%20for%20 Undocumented%20Migrants_Background%20Paper6.pdf.

Karl-Trummer, U., Novak-Zezula, S., & Metzler, B. (2010). Access to health care for undocumented migrants in the EU: A first landscape of NowHereland. *Eurohealth, 16*(1), 13–16. Retrieved from www.lse.ac.uk/LSEHealthAndSocialCare/pdf/euro health/VOL16No1/Karl_Trummer.pdf.

La Cooperativa Crinali. (2015). *Operatrici Socio-Sanitarie.* Retrieved from www.crinali.org/teams/operatrici/.

LeVoy, M. (2008). Which challenges and policy responses concerning the social rights of undocumented migrants? *Newsletter of the European Anti-poverty Network, 127.* Retrieved from www.eapn.eu/wp-content/uploads/2008/10/nn%20127_en.pdf.

LeVoy, M., & Geddie, E. (2009). Irregular migration: Challenges, limits and remedies. *Refugee Survey Quarterly, 28*(4), 87–113 doi: 10.1093/rsq/hdq010.

Macherey, A-L., Simonnot, N., & Vanbiervliet, F. (2015). *Legal report on access to healthcare in 12 countries.* Médecins du Monde International Network. Retrieved from https://mdmeuroblog.files.wordpress.com/2014/05/mdm-legal-report-on-access-to-healthcare-in-12-countries-3rd-june-20151.pdf.

Maisha. (2012). *Internationale Humanitäre Sprechstunden.* Retrieved from www.maisha.org/was-wir-tun.html.

Marmot Review. (2010). *Fair society, healthy lives: Strategic review of health inequalities in England post 2010.* Retrieved from www.instituteofhealthequity.org/resources-reports/fair-society-healthy-lives-the-marmot-review/fair-society-healthy-lives-the-marmot-review-full-report.pdf.

Maternity Action. (2016a). *Entitlement to free NHS maternity care for women from abroad England only.* Retrieved from www.maternityaction.org.uk/wp-content/uploads/(2015)/07/NHS-maternity-care-England-(2016).pdf.

Maternity Action. (2016b). *Maternity care access advice service.* Retrieved from www.maternityaction.org.uk/advice-2/maternity-care-access-advice-service/.

Maternity Action. (2017). *Migrant women's rights service.* Retrieved from www.maternityaction.org.uk/advice-2/migrant-womens-rights-service/?doing_wp_cron=1495707860.5706520080566406250000.

Minsart, A., Englert, Y., & Buekens, P. (2012). Naturalization of immigrants and perinatal mortality. *European Journal of Public Health, 23*(2), 269–274. doi: 10.1093/eurpub/cks032.

NAGA. (2016). *Women's space.* Retrieved from www.naga.it/index.php/spazio-donne.html.

Pedone, A. (2012). Guide to residence permit for pregnancy. *Studio Legale Website.* www.antonellapedone.com/guide/permesso-di-soggiorno-per-gravidanza.

Pillinger, J. (2008). *HSE national intercultural health strategy consultation report*. Dublin: Health Service Executive. Retrieved from www.lenus.ie/hse/bitstream/10147/45775/1/9101.pdf.

Platform for International Cooperation on Undocumented Migrants (PICUM). (2007). *Access to health care for undocumented migrants in Europe*. Retrieved from http://picum.org/picum.org/uploads/file_/Access_to_Health_Care_for_Undocumented_Migrants.pdf.

Platform for International Cooperation on Undocumented Migrants (PICUM). (2010). *Undocumented migrants' health needs and strategies to access health care in 17 EU countries: Country report Italy*. Brussels: PICUM.

Platform for International Cooperation on Undocumented Migrants (PICUM). (2013, July 12). Sweden: A new reform will grant access to health care for undocumented migrants. *PICUM Bulletin*. Retrieved from http://picum.org/nl/nieuws/bulletins/41469/#news_41417.

Platform for International Cooperation on Undocumented Migrants (PICUM). (2014). *Access to health care for undocumented migrants in Europe: The key role of local and regional authorities*. Brussels: PICUM. Retrieved from http://picum.org/picum.org/uploads/publication/PolicyBrief_Local%20and%20Regional%20Authorities_AccessHealthCare_UndocumentedMigrants_Oct.(2014).pdf.

Platform for International Cooperation on Undocumented Migrants (PICUM). (2015). *Protecting undocumented children: Promising policies and practices from governments*. Brussels: PICUM. Retrieved from http://picum.org/picum.org/uploads/publication/Protecting%20undocumented%20children-Promising%20policies%20and%20practices%20from%20governments.pdf.

Roland, F., Simonnot, N., & Vanbiervliet, F. (2013). *Access to healthcare for vulnerable populations: Update of legislation in 10 European countries*. Doctors of the World International Network. Retrieved from http://mdmeuroblog.files.wordpress.com/2014/01/legal-update-full-v06042013.pdf.

Royo-Bordonada, M., Díez-Cornell, M., & María Llorente, J. (2013). Health-care access for migrants in Europe: The case of Spain. *Lancet, 382*(9890), 393–394. doi: http://dx.doi.org/10.1016/S0140-67361361667-0.

Safety4Sisters. (2016). *Migrant women's rights to safety pilot project*. Retrieved from www.southallblacksisters.org.uk/wp-content/uploads/2016/11/Safety4Sisters-North-West-Report.pdf.

Sampson, T. (2017). Brexit: The economics of international disintegration. *Journal of Economic Perspectives, 31*(4), 163–184. doi: https://doi.org/10.1257/jep. 31.4.163.

Schrover, M. (2008). *Illegal migration and gender in a global and historical perspective*. Amsterdam: Amsterdam University Press.

Schoevers, M., Loeffen, M., van den Muijsenbergh, M., & Lagro-Janssen, A. (2010). Health care utilisation and problems in accessing health care of female undocumented immigrants in the Netherlands. *International Journal of Public Health, 55*(5), 421–428. doi: 10.1007/s00038-010-0151-6.

Scott, P. (2004). Undocumented migrants in Germany and Britain: The human "rights" and "wrongs" regarding access to health care. *Electronic Journal of Sociology*. Retrieved from www.sociology.org/content/2004/tier2/scott.html.

Sharpe, H. (2010). *Migrant friendly maternity services: Toolkit for improving local service provision*. Birmingham, Department of Health and West Midlands Strategic Migration Partnership. Retrieved from www.wmemployers.org.uk/media/upload/Library/Migration%20Documents/Publications/Toolkit%20for%20improving%20maternity%20services%20for%20migrant%20women%20v4.pdf.

Simonnot, N., Rodriguez, A., Nuernberg, M., Fille, F., Aranda-Fernández, P., & Chauvin, P. (2016). *Access to healthcare for people facing multiple vulnerabilities in health in 31 cities in 12 countries: Report on social and medical data gathered in 2015 in 11 European countries and Turkey.* Paris: Doctors of the World International Network. Retrieved from https://mdmeuroblog.files.wordpress.com/(2016)/11/observatory-report(2016)_en-mdm-international.pdf.

Triandafyllidou, A. (2009). *CLANDESTINO project, final report.* Retrieved from http://cordis.europa.eu/documents/documentlibrary/126625701EN6.pdf.

United Nations. (1985). *General Assembly, Resolution 40/144. Declaration on the human rights of individuals who are not nationals of the country in which they live.* Retrieved from www.un.org/documents/ga/res/40/a40r144.htm.

United Nations. (1989). *Convention on the Rights of the Child Article 24d.* Retrieved from www.ohchr.org/EN/ProfessionalInterest/Pages/CRC.aspx.

United Nations. (1999). *Convention on the Elimination of All Forms of Discrimination against Women CEDAW Article 12:2.* Retrieved from www.un.org/womenwatch/daw/cedaw/text/econvention.htm#article12.

Urquia, M., Glazier, R., Blondel, B., Zeitlin, J., Gissler, M., Macfarlane, A., Ng, E., Heaman, M., Stray-Pedersen, B., & Gagnon, A. (2010). International migration and adverse birth outcomes: Role of ethnicity, region of origin and destination. *Journal of Epidemiology and Community Health, 64*(3), 243–251. doi: 10.1136/jech.2008.083535.

van der Leun, J. (2006). Excluding illegal migrants in the Netherlands: Between national policies and local implementation. *West European Politics, 29*(2), 310–326. doi: 10.1080/01402380500512650.

Vollmer, B. (2011). *Irregular migration in the UK: Definitions, pathways and scale.* Migration Observatory Briefing, COMPAS, University of Oxford, UK. Retrieved from www.migrationobservatory.ox.ac.uk/wp-content/uploads/2016/04/Briefing-Irregular_Migration.pdf.

Whitehead, N., Callaghan, W., Johnson, C., & Williams, L. (2009). Racial, ethnic, and economic disparities in the prevalence of pregnancy complications. *Maternal and Child Health Journal, 13*(2), 198–205. doi: 10.1007/s10995-008-0344-2.

Woodward, A., Howard, N., & Wolffers, I. (2014). Health and access to care for undocumented migrants living in the European Union: A scoping review. *Health Policy and Planning, 29*(7), 818–830. doi: 10.1093/heapol/czt061.

World Health Organization (WHO). (2016). *WHO recommendations on antenatal care for a positive pregnancy experience.* Geneva: World Health Organization. Retrieved from www.who.int/reproductivehealth/publications/maternal_perinatal_health/anc-positive-pregnancy-experience/en/.

8

¿ME VES?

How Bay Area Health Agencies Address the Mental Health Needs of Migrant Women of Color During Pregnancy, Birth, and Postpartum Experiences
Morgan Melendres Mentz[1]

Introduction

The process of pregnancy, labor, and postpartum recovery can be both a powerful and transformative experience as well as a time of increased depression and anxiety. For many women, especially those who have endured sexual assault and domestic violence at some point in their lifetime, their experience can include symptoms of severe depression. Therefore, it is important for reproductive healthcare providers serving populations at greater risk of depression related to domestic and sexual trauma to provide added outreach, education, and support. The Health Resources and Services Administration (HRSA) under the U.S. Department of Health and Human Services defines depressive symptoms experienced during and after pregnancy as Perinatal Depression. Perinatal Depression is a condition that has "a broad range of physical and emotional struggle[s]," where women experience, "sadness, fear, anxiety, and difficulty making decisions" (HRSA 2006). Identifying populations at risk for Perinatal Depression, the HRSA notes that this condition indiscriminately affects numerous women across all variables of race, class, age, and educational proficiency (HRSA 2006). However, the HRSA highlights common causes of Perinatal Depression such as sleep deprivation, hormone fluctuation, family history of depression, past physical and psychological trauma, and other reasons that are unique to each woman affected by the condition (HRSA 2006). It has been established that trauma experienced from sexual assault and physical violence increases one's risk of depression and other mental health complications during and after pregnancy (Melville et al. 2010).

Recent related studies report that as high as 80% of Latinas immigrating to the United States experience rape and other forms of assault during their migration journey (Goldberg 2014). According to Amnesty International, the prevalent use of sexual violence against migrant women and girls is often committed by local gangs, fellow migrants, family members, and even government employees at checkpoints and detention centers through their passage to the United States (Amnesty International 2010). Amnesty International documents how, despite the prevalent exploitation and brutality that migrant women face, they often receive little to no psychological support or care to treat any mental health conditions associated with traumas they have encountered as part of their migration experience (Amnesty International 2010). Unfortunately, reaching the border and finding residence in the United States does not necessarily mean the end of physical abuse or violence nor does it ensure access to adequate mental and physical healthcare. Thus, for the 80% of migrant Latinas that experience sexual and physical violence, developing depressive symptoms during and after pregnancy becomes a substantial risk.

For survivors of domestic violence, which is the leading threat of injury to women in the United States, accessing reproductive and mental healthcare services can be burdensome and complicated due to barriers of class, ethnicity, and immigration status (Owen 2006, 13–36). This is in part because of fear that seeking support and care may negatively impact one's immigration process, access to public services, and risk their safety within their home and familial relationships (Owen 2006, 13–36). Laurie Owen notes that the mass of immigrants acquiring visas for U.S. entry are done so through "family-based immigration categories," and for 77% of migrant women experiencing domestic abuse, the path to citizenship often relies on their abuser. This set of circumstances can make it extremely difficult if not impossible to seek out help and support for mental healthcare and other services as reliance on their abusers isolates women migrants from financial, legal, and public resources (Owen 2006, 13–36). In addition, current immigration law bars women within abusive situations from petitioning for citizenship on their own behalf for themselves or their children (Owen 2006, 17). While the Violence Against Women Act (VAWA) of 1994 offered some protections for immigrant victims of domestic violence by suspending deportation and offering an alternative path to citizenship based on special circumstances, the VAWA of 2000 subjects this protection to the authority of the Attorney General (Owen 2006, 17).

Regarding reproductive health matters, providing care and outreach to migrant Latinas has its own distinct struggles for healthcare workers, as explained by Parmet, Sainsbury-Wong, and Prabhu (2017). For example, health industry workers are confronted with challenges such as language barriers, inaccessibility to health insurance for their patients, and the inability of workers to address the effects of trauma experienced by patients in their home countries and the retraumatization they experience during the immigration process (Parmet et al. 2017, 55–59). Fuentes-Afflick and Hessol (2009) add to the discussion by highlighting the struggles of migrant women, who comprise nearly 27% of California's total population; a significant portion of which are undocumented. Fuentes-Afflick and Hessol (2009) hypothesize that California's Latina migrants are less likely to use health services than their citizen counterparts, revealing a direct correlation between citizenship status and access to healthcare that disproportionately impacts undocumented Latinas negatively (1275–1280). Using a multivariable logistic regression analysis, they found that undocumented Latinas were less likely to be insured, have a primary healthcare provider, or seek out preventative care such as regular cancer screenings (1275–1280). These findings address the need for alternative public service organizations to provide support to vulnerable populations who face disproportionate barriers in accessing comprehensive reproductive healthcare.

Challenges in accessing public health services for migrant Latinas are also impacted by the political climate influencing policy and social programs for migrant communities in general. In *Disposable Domestics* (2016), Grace Chang carefully delineates how the militarization of the U.S. southern border and anti-immigration propaganda directly threaten and impact the lives of migrant Latinas. Chang (2016) draws attention to the state violence targeting migrant women of color and their families under the Bush and Obama administrations' policies of incarceration, community raids, and the separation of families. These practices continue as the amplification of racialized targeting of all Latinx immigrants in the era of Trump (32–33). Chang poignantly critiques policies like the Development, Relief, and Education for Alien Minors (DREAM) Act and Deferred Action for Childhood Arrivals (DACA) which create a narrative of deserved citizenship based on children's "innocence" in illegal migration while criminalizing millions of undocumented parents that risked and sacrificed much of their lives to settle within and contribute to the United States. This criminalization, as Chang argues, perpetuates stereotypes of migrant women, Latinas in particular, as abusers of the welfare system and public programs through policy language, labeling them "as resource depleters" with their "high fertility rates," making their bodies a political threat to society (32–33). Such villainizing tropes continue to persist even in spite of research showing no evidence that undocumented women's reproductive activity has any influence on the availability of public resources for all (32–33).

Focusing on overlapping barriers to health, Lara-Cinisomo et al. (2014) conducted group interviews amongst migrant Latina mothers to study risk for depression during their perinatal experiences. They found that nearly 35% of participants experienced depressive symptoms as a result of their social location, which were compounded by their doctors' dismissal of those symptoms both during and after pregnancy (232). Lara-Cinisomo et al. identify issues of language, economic status, and cultural barriers as obstacles that block migrant Latinas from accessing the support they require. Their work draws attention to the inadequacy of healthcare providers to validate the intersectional experience of patients (233). Addressing such obstacles puts pressure on reproductive healthcare agencies serving large populations of communities of color to provide adequate information and outreach to populations at higher risk for conditions like Perinatal Depression, including diagnosis and treatment.

It is critical for organizations serving large populations of migrant Latinas to be comprehensive in addressing the intersectionality of their reproductive health experiences. Migrant Latinas that face higher rates of sexual assault, domestic abuse, and trauma require reproductive healthcare that validates their increased risk for experiencing depression during and after pregnancy (Goldberg 2014). However, public discussion, as noted previously, tends to focus on healthcare for migrant Latinas based on their deservingness or ability to access care instead of recognizing it as a basic human right.

At present, little scholarship has been done investigating the intersectional experience of migrant Latinas and their relationship to Perinatal Depression. Kendall-Tackett (2013) asserts this fact by differentiating variables between women of all ethnic backgrounds experiencing gender based violence, finds a lack of data on women of color who are especially vulnerable to increased rates of physical abuse, and critiques how women of color remain widely neglected in academic research on these topics (207–212). Kendall-Tackett's study also reveals how migrant women experiencing trauma are affected by cultural relativity, such as one's cultural beliefs about mental illness as being shameful. This ideology can further bar them from acquiring proper diagnosis and treatment as a result of cultural stigmatization (207–212). Such barriers involving mental health compounded with societal and economic constraints increase the importance of creating better resources and outreach by healthcare organizations.

Within the context outlined above, this study investigates how Planned Parenthood clinics in Santa Clara County, California include, speak to, and offer solutions for patients experiencing Perinatal Depression vis-á-vis their online presence. The Planned Parenthood clinics in this geographic region serve large immigrant populations and are uniquely positioned at the epicenter of Silicon Valley's booming technology industry whose wealth has impacted the improvement and increased development of new medical centers and services in the region. The intersection between these unique metropolitan and socioeconomic factors adds to the dynamic of increased economic hardship (in terms of an exorbitant rise in cost of living due to gentrification from the technology industry) in accessing healthcare for many migrant Latinas (Brekke 2015).

According to the Bay Area Census based on data collected from 2006–2010, Santa Clara County recorded the non-citizen population at 319,995 comprising an estimated 18.4% of the county's total population. However, it is important to note that this number potentially is much larger as it does not include those who did not participate in the census based on their immigration status (American Community Survey 2006–2010). Adding to this, the Pew Research Center notes how San Jose, one of the largest cities in Santa Clara County, alone is home to 120,000 undocumented immigrants making it 18 in the top 20 cities in the United States with the highest concentrations of undocumented migrants (Passel and D'Vera Cohn 2017). However, beyond the repetitive debates on immigrant healthcare previously critiqued, little conversation has focused on exposing how the medical industry itself is currently serving working class immigrant populations in preventative care and treatment for specific conditions like Perinatal Depression. To highlight the need for intersectional analysis, this chapter asks "¿Me Ves?," as an homage to local Bay Area women of color feminist movement "Do You See Me?," and to encourage readers to view the healthcare needs of migrant Latinas through a more complex lens that validates their heterogeneous experiences.

Methods

Looking at online resources focuses attention on the importance and power the internet has to effectively reach populations facing social, physical, and even political obstacles in accessing information pertinent to their health. According to Parra-Cardona and DeAndrea (2014) up to a third of people seek information on mental health services online. They hypothesize the search for mental health support online signifies the unmet needs of mental health services within Latinx communities (281). They also state that Latinos "are less likely ... to access formal mental health services" due to language barriers, literacy, and socioeconomic issues of cost (283). The anonymity of online services for stigmatized conditions like depression also creates a virtual safe space for providing support. Although accessing health resources outside on-site clinics through online services can be made harder by what Parra-Cordona and DeAndrea call a digital divide (282) the improvement of technological advances like smart phones with internet access makes online health outreach more accessible for those who do not have access to traditional laptops and computers for internet browsing. This is an important point considering the growing use of information technology and implementation of software by healthcare providers to personalize patient care.

Using content analysis, I examined the websites of the six Santa Clara County Planned Parenthood clinics and the national Planned Parenthood website to assess how they visually and discursively address the healthcare needs of migrant Latinas in terms of mental healthcare awareness in the larger context of reproductive healthcare provision. I considered the imagery, text, and layout of their online presence using semiotic analysis as a means of parsing out the intended meaning and function of these informational signifiers (Sturken and Cartwright 2001). Identifying visual and linguistic signs helps to deconstruct certain codes that inform and shape how observers view and come to know the world around them. Also, semiotics addresses the malleability signs are subject to dependent upon the relationship between the observer and what they are viewing (10–12). Understanding online clinical content in this way allows for an intersectional lens to be used in identifying how similar content can be understood, dismissed, or become inaccessible based on the population viewing the material. For example, understanding the stigmatization of mental illness for certain communities is important for healthcare providers to consider when disseminating information on mental health. Online spaces are particularly important for analysis, since seeking information online offers an opportunity for patients to gain critical information about stigmatized conditions like Perinatal Depression and locate support services anonymously and without cultural judgement, shame, or taboo. Thus, online content becomes a critical resource for understanding what is being communicated to vulnerable populations seeking healthcare support online. By exploring this topic, this chapter aims to increase dialogue around patient access to healthcare information that validates the intersectional experiences of migrant Latinas within reproductive healthcare.

This study begins with an analysis of the national Planned Parenthood main website, which provides online search for site users to find general information about Planned Parenthood services and find clinic locations near them. I then looked at the various Santa Clara County clinic sites and assessed how each of them defined and outlined reproductive healthcare services. Looking at the local Planned Parenthood websites for Santa Clara County's East Side Health Center, San Jose Health Center, Blossom Hill Health Center, Mar Monte Community Clinic, Mountain View Health Center, and the Gilroy Health Center, I examined how each clinic's webpage attempts to communicate to migrant Latina populations through Spanish language services, ethnic representation in online imagery, and written content that is understandable to visitors of varying educational levels.

By deconstructing how these various sites articulate their services, this work systematically analyzed the extent to which each clinic meets the heterogeneous healthcare needs of the community by offering information on preventative and support measures for Perinatal Depression. While I recognize the existence of numerous other healthcare providers in Santa Clara County, Planned Parenthood, as the nation's largest and most widely known reproductive healthcare provider administering much needed services to the most marginalized populations, was critical for study.

Findings

Comprehensive reproductive healthcare should not only be a basic right in a general sense but specified to the needs of each patient. For populations at higher risk of developing Perinatal Depression, it is critical that healthcare facilities provide effective outreach and information about these conditions. For many who use the internet to locate and retrieve healthcare, it is important that clinics have detailed resources for users to easily access the information they require in order to make educated healthcare decisions.

When looking up a Planned Parenthood location online, one can visit the national PlannedParenthood.org main page and immediately see at the top of the page a banner picture of a pregnant Black physician in a white lab coat talking to a young woman, seemingly of Asian descent, sitting on a patient bed (Planned Parenthood Federation of America, Inc. [Planned Parenthood] 2017h). This image gives an impression of friendliness and safety as both women in the photo amicably smile at one another. The physician displays relaxed body language with her hands tucked gently in her pockets while grinning at her patient. The young woman sitting on the medical bed appears to be listening intently with her head slightly tilted away from the viewer displaying a half smile. The centering of two women of color, with the Black doctor wearing a colorful hot pink, lime green, and mustard yellow patterned dress beneath her doctor's cloak and donning her natural hair in twists, alongside the young Asian-American woman with long brown hair dressed in casual blue jeans and a loose-fitting satin pink sleeveless blouse, promotes an image of Planned Parenthood as safe space of inclusion and visibility for women of color.

At the top right corner of the website the option for Spanish translation is available making all Planned Parenthood content online accessible to Spanish speakers who may not be proficient in English. Further down on the Planned Parenthood main website page, a pale grey tool bar drops down providing four link options with dark slate grey text and icons of "Learn" paired with a book, "Get Care" with a heart, "Get Involved" with a megaphone, and

"Donate" with a star (Planned Parenthood 2017h). Then just beneath the image header, bold black lettering in large text shouts "Care. No Matter What." reassuring the visitor of the organization's efforts to serve their health-care needs regardless of circumstance or social location. Following this, text in smaller thin font states, "Find a health center online or call 1-800-230-PLAN," alongside a convenient search box placed directly below for site visitors to input their city and state or zip code to get a list of health center locations near them. The rest of the main website offers other options such as a link to its Take Action page; short descriptions of the different services it offers such as birth control, abortion, STD services, and emergency contraceptives; and links to recent articles highlighting different Planned Parenthood topics. The main site page also has a chat feature offering the option to click a link to chat online or text to "PPNOW or 774636" with a Planned Parenthood representative to answer the patient's health related questions via a mobile device. This creates a virtual safe space where online visitors can seek sensitive healthcare information anonymously and provides increased access for those without personal computers or home internet.

For more detailed information on getting care from the main organization page, the site user is directed to a "Get Care" page displaying a photo of a seemingly Latina nurse wearing fuchsia scrubs and smiling at a patient with black hair looking away from the viewer while taking her blood pressure (Planned Parenthood 2017h). Similar to the main organization page, the "Get Care" banner photo centers women of color both as providers and receivers of reproductive healthcare services pertinent to them. Also, this page briefly describes Planned Parenthood's status as a leading provider of affordable healthcare and the biggest provider of sexual education in the country with a history of over 100 years of "research in reproductive care." The content on Planned Parenthood's "Get Care" page creates a narrative of trust in the organization's ability to provide holistic and comprehensive reproductive healthcare services. This language provides a sense of reassurance to visitors who may be wary of seeking help for stigmatized conditions, like Perinatal Depression.

The "Get Care" page has the same search box for finding a clinic location as the main page, as well as the same links to access care via their online and mobile texting chat service, current topics page, and other online services. Planned Parenthood's positionality on accessible healthcare is stated under the heading "Affordable Access" near the center of the webpage. The statement, "everyone deserves equal access to the entire range of sexual and reproductive healthcare services," sets a tone of inclusivity of all patients no matter their economic means or citizenship status. In sum, the "Get Care" page offers a general portrait of accessible care to a diversity of people living in the United States. Adversely, however, the language used when referring to patient type as well as services offered, is general and does not directly specify or speak to vulnerable underrepresented populations and their heterogeneous experiences.

For visitors looking for a health center located near them, they need only type in the desired location in the search box and the visitor is redirected to a search result page listing all the centers located nearest the city or zip code they entered, sorted from nearest to farthest location. The list includes the names of each health center, its distance, address, phone number, a link to directions, a link to health insurance information, and two large blue buttons to either make an appointment online or to see more information. Booking an appointment online is a short three-step process of clicking "Select Visit Reason" causing a drop-down menu to appear with service options, selecting the desired service from the drop-down menu, and then selecting an appointment day and time from a weekly calendar that shows the available days and times (Planned Parenthood 2017b). Once selected, a pop-up page opens to request the user to confirm their appointment. Options from the drop-down list include abortion, annual exam, birth control, morning after pill, pregnancy test, STDs, UTI, and other. All of these options are open for online appointment booking, except for "other" in which the calendar box disappears and is replaced with a message informing the user to call Planned Parenthood directly. Mental health conditions related to reproductive health like Perinatal Depression are not listed in the drop-down menu.

If a visitor wishes to research each Santa Clara County location to get a list of the different types of services each clinic offers, they can select the "More Info" button for each location. Semiotic analyses of Santa Clara County Planned Parenthood website content proved to be uniform with little variance in conformity across the websites of each Santa Clara clinic site. On each page, the title of the clinic is located towards the top of the page with a link to the local Planned Parenthood network that operates the clinic (Planned Parenthood 2017i). For the Santa Clara County locations, the Planned Parenthood Mar Monte network operates all previously listed South Bay locations. Immediately below, in a thin font, is a note to visitors that reads, "We accept many insurance plans. If you don't have insurance, affordable coverage options may be available," with a link below to see what type of insurance and payment options are available (2017i). Following this, the contact for the center is listed including the address, link to directions, a small map, the clinic phone and fax number, language services, and information on how to book an appointment.

For each clinic, language services vary by either in-person translation services or via the phone with a remote translator. The Blossom Hill, Gilroy, and East Side Health Center websites state they offer onsite English and Spanish language services in addition to other language translation services onsite via telephone (Planned Parenthood 2017a, 2017c, 2017d). The Mountain View Health Center website states that it offers onsite English and Spanish with Tagalog, Mandarin, and other language translations over the phone (Planned Parenthood 2017g). The Mar Monte Community Clinic offers English and Spanish onsite services with Russian, German, French, and Punjabi translation over the phone (Planned Parenthood 2017e). Lastly, the San Jose Health Center site states that it offers onsite English and Spanish services with Vietnamese, Chinese (dialect not specified), and Tagalog interpretation services over the phone (Planned Parenthood 2017i).

Beneath the language descriptions on each clinic page a service listing is also provided to inform the site visitor of what types of services each location offers with corresponding links for providing further detail. Services include abortion, birth control, men's health, pregnancy testing and services, morning after-pill, STD testing and treatment, vaccines, HIV testing, general healthcare, and women's healthcare (Planned Parenthood 2017i). Each Santa Clara County Planned Parenthood health center offers the services listed above, except for the Mar Monte and Blossom Hill locations, which do not have abortion services but offer abortion referral instead (Planned Parenthood 2017a). Information for all services online are extensive with each having their own information page with a bulleted list of the different types of options the service can include in addition to full detailed descriptions for each bullet title directly beneath the list.

Semiotic analysis of language used in the detailed description of various services fully explains important information concisely and with brevity, making understanding each service clear for readers with varying levels of education. For example, the more complex services involving surgery, such as abortion services, are cohesively described in one short paragraph but simplistically breaks down with precision the timeline of the procedure, what is required of the patient to provide, what to expect, follow-up outcomes and information on added medication treatment requirements for patients wishing to make their procedure more comfortable (Planned Parenthood 2017j). A short explanation of payment options for patients is also made available along with contact information and opportunity for payment assistance for low-income patients.

However, while issues of healthcare accessibility in terms of class are addressed, barriers due to race and ethnicity are not. This is problematic for locations serving large populations of low-income women of color. Particularly, it is imperative for clinics serving working class migrant Latinas to break through the aforementioned barriers that isolate this specific group by making themselves aware of the intersectional needs of their patients (Lara-Cinisomo et al. 238). In other words, the specific barriers their patients face including barriers arising from their patients' personal worldviews, beliefs, and social knowledge of mental health must be addressed so that healthcare providers can include cultural and individual preferences in treatment plans (238). With no visible or explicit reassurance that Planned Parenthood locations are safe and accessible spaces for reproductive related mental healthcare, the clinics ignore the intersectional reality of patients who may not seek medical help because of social and political fear due to their immigration status.

Lara-Cinisomo et al. explain how the real fear of detention by federal authorities creates a significant barrier for migrant Latinas wanting to seek help for Perinatal Depression related to sexual and domestic violence (236). With the increased political scrutiny and targeting of transnational Latinx communities under the current Trump administration, safety concerns for vulnerable populations are heightened. In such a hostile political landscape, leading healthcare providers like Planned Parenthood must take responsibility for providing comprehensive online resources and outreach to support unique and specific community needs. Patients experiencing depressive symptoms or other mental health concerns during or after pregnancy may not seek care from these Planned Parenthood Mar Monte sites as they do not address such conditions anywhere within the descriptions of care provided on each clinic website.

With the visibility of Planned Parenthood as the nation's leading provider of women's reproductive healthcare, it is problematic that such an important medical risk during the perinatal process would have no mention anywhere within the services it offers. The only mention of reproductive care services for survivors of trauma and sexual assault is a short bullet listed under the "Morning After Pill" page stating, "rape crisis counseling referrals" (Planned Parenthood 2017f). Clearly this service is in place to care for those who have experienced trauma through referral to affiliate organizations more able to provide the necessary mental health needs for such patients. For many who are at risk of Perinatal Depression due to previously experienced trauma, rape counseling for a current pregnancy or for emergency contraceptive might not be adequate. Referring back to Kendall-Tackett (2013), not all reactions to trauma are immediate, but can be delayed and even multigenerational through the passage of trauma symptoms between generations (208). Thus, if rape crisis counseling referrals are important enough to be included under emergency contraceptive services on the Planned Parenthood website, then why not mental health referral to be included under general health, women's health, or even pregnancy services, as it is a prevalent concern in women's reproductive health?

This is not to say that patients already receiving prenatal or postnatal care at these Planned Parenthood locations are not also receiving services for mental health concerns. My critique focuses on the online content for visitors wishing to seek help via the internet first, to assess if these clinics will be able to address their reproductive mental healthcare concerns before going in for services. With little information about counseling services and no mention of depressive symptoms during and after pregnancy, the Planned Parenthood national and regional websites ignore those at higher risk for such conditions. Women who may be looking for resources and help online anonymously can be deterred from seeking help at these clinics as they do not see their symptoms as relevant or visible within the general scope of reproductive healthcare as delineated on these Planned Parenthood websites.

The lack of visibility and discussion of these important topics related to women's reproductive healthcare by a large and well recognized women's health organization like Planned Parenthood, risks promoting a culture of silence that perpetuates shame and further stigmatization for migrant Latinas experiencing Perinatal Depression. As Marita Sturken and Lisa Cartwright (2001) point out in their analysis of visual culture, prevalent imagery no matter how benign, holds significant power in impacting how society perceives, shapes, and defines cultural norms (10–12). Therefore, visibility of and dialogue around pertinent issues regarding women's reproductive healthcare is important in creating social norms and acceptance of such medical issues. The exclusion of perinatal mental health conditions in Planned Parenthood clinic service descriptions positions the condition of Perinatal Depression as marginal. For populations attempting to first seek online information to help them decide whether they can safely and privately access the mental health services they need, this situation can discourage them from accessing care. For migrant Latinas with limited access to financial resources or other supportive networks to help them in identifying, managing, and treating depressive symptoms during and after pregnancy, places like Planned Parenthood might be the only lifeline they have for help, which is why visibility of this issue on clinic websites is imperative.

Furthermore, because health insurance and cost of services can prevent immigrant communities from accessing basic care, Planned Parenthood's ability to communicate health coverage options for transnational clients is crucial (Parmet et al. 2017, 55). Planned Parenthood's website provides help in finding coverage by providing information on how to sign up on the open market or how to sign up for free or cost reduced insurance for low income patients that qualify for public programs like Medicaid (2017i). For information on qualifying for public programs like Medicare and Children's Health Insurance Program (CHIP) clients are directed from the main Planned Parenthood website to different sites like HealthCare.gov, which offers site translation in Spanish, or Medicaid.gov, which does not offer Spanish or any other language services on its online platform (U.S. Centers for Medicare & Medicaid Services 2017). For users seeking information regarding insurance coverage and payment for low-income families, an online calculator that estimates the potential financial help one might receive from Medicaid or CHIP is also made available on the Planned Parenthood website (U.S. Centers for Medicare & Medicaid Services 2017). However, other than these specified public resources, Planned Parenthood does not list any alternative options for those in need of financial assistance but who do not qualify for public resources due to immigration status.

For undocumented migrant Latinas, finding public aid on the federal Medicaid websites can be difficult. Furthermore, Medicaid.org, which Planned Parenthood redirects patients to, does not have Spanish translations available on its website, creating a language barrier for those seeking to gain financial assistance (U.S. Centers for Medicare & Medicaid Services 2017). For those who can comprehensively understand the information given in English, the Medicaid website does provide information in the form of official letters in PDF format that are available for reading online. These letters delineate how non-citizen immigrants can access services, but the language in the letter is complex, legalistic, and not easily accessible for readers of varying education levels (Department of Health and Human Resources 2009). Furthermore, the only alternative to the convoluted public service options mentioned on the Planned Parenthood website is located under "Payment Information" which vaguely states, "If you are uninsured, you may qualify for ... a lower fee scale" (Planned Parenthood 2017i). For those who do not qualify for state-funded healthcare programs, this sliding scale option is the only other alternative resource listed on the website.

To reiterate, because Planned Parenthood is the largest national provider of women's reproductive healthcare, it is of great importance for the organization to consider the intersectional mental and physical reproductive healthcare needs of its most vulnerable clients. Planned Parenthood plays an important role in providing healthcare to our nation's most marginalized communities who rely on this vital organization for necessary and life-saving services. As Alice Pettway notes, the ongoing debates in our country around women's health and backlash to reproductive rights that has targeted Planned Parenthood for defunding only highlights how vital and important the services they offer are (2017, 16–18). However, laws governing reproductive rights, like the newly proposed Equal Access to Abortion Coverage in Health Insurance Act also known as the EACH Woman Act, often ignore the inclusion of migrant women of color and their rights to comprehensive reproductive healthcare services (16–18). Therefore, organizations serving populations at higher risk of conditions like Perinatal Depression based on their intersectional experiences must recognize the uniqueness of these communities and provide them with the proper information, care, and treatment services specific to their heterogeneous needs.

Conclusion

The issues around access to treatment for women with Perinatal Depression are as complex as they are diverse. Populations of women who are at higher risk of experiencing Perinatal Depression as a result of sexual assault or abuse require safety nets and added measures to address their unique healthcare needs. Populations such as migrant Latinas, especially those who are undocumented, face various barriers to access comprehensive healthcare information pertinent to their intersectional experiences and depend upon extra support and assistance by the healthcare organizations serving them. In looking at Planned Parenthood as the leading reproductive healthcare provider in the country, it is extremely problematic that information and service descriptions offered by the organization have no mention of Perinatal Depression as a reproductive health issue.

Lack of visibility, educational information, and resources for help with Perinatal Depression can leave those who are especially at risk and affected by the condition to feel extremely isolated; and can prevent them from seeking the supportive care that they very much need and deserve. Populations like migrant Latinas, who face added challenges such as community stigmatization of mental health and sexual assault, require added care and outreach from healthcare providers to holistically recognize and validate their intersectional experiences. The lack of visibility of Perinatal Depression as a reproductive health condition on the Planned Parenthood website is exceedingly problematic and must be addressed.

By exposing these inadequacies and concerns, the intent of this chapter was to raise awareness and normalize the conversation around mental health as a part of comprehensive reproductive healthcare. Like the title of this chapter asks, "¿Me Ves?" (Do you see me?), this exploratory study makes visible the challenges migrant Latinas face in accessing holistic reproductive healthcare. This chapter aimed to amplify the call for reproductive healthcare providers to acknowledge the intersectional experiences that shape the unique healthcare needs of migrant Latinas and provide better outreach and treatment. Only by recognizing and making visible these issues, can we begin to build stronger networks of support for transnational women of color and their unique reproductive healthcare needs.

Note

1   The author would like to acknowledge contributions to this chapter made by Monica M. Smith.

References

American Community Survey. 2006–2010. "Santa Clara County." Bay Area Census. Accessed May 31, 2017. www.bayareacensus.ca.gov/counties/SantaClaraCounty.htm.

Amnesty International. 2010. "Invisible Wounds: Crime Victims Speak." *Amnesty International Secretariat* (2010): 1–46.

Brekke, Dan. 2015. "A Map of Gentrification in the Bay Area." *KQED News*. August 28. Accessed May 31, 2017. https://ww2.kqed.org/news/2015/08/27/uc-berkeley-bay-area-gentrification-displacement-map/.

Chang, Grace. 2016. *Disposable Domestics: Immigrant Women Workers in the Global Economy.* Chicago, IL: Haymarket Books.

Department of Health and Human Resources. 2009. "Center for Medicaid and State Operations Letter to Health Official." Baltimore, MD, May.

Fuentes-Afflick, Elena, and Nancy A. Hessol. 2009. "Immigration Status and Use of Health Services among Latina Women in the San Francisco Bay Area." *Journal of Women's Health 8*(18): 1275–1280.

Goldberg, Eleanor. 2014. "80% of Central American Women, Girls are Raped Crossing into the U.S." *Huffington Post.* September 12. Accessed May 31, 2017. www.huffingtonpost.com/2014/09/12/central-america-migrants-rape_n_5806972.html.

Health Resources and Services Administration (HRSA), U.S. Department of Health and Human Service. 2006. "Depression During and After Pregnancy: A Resource for Women, Their Family, and Friends." *PsycEXTRA Dataset*. November, 1–22. Accessed May 2017. doi:10.1037/e504422010-018.

Kendall-Tackett, Kathleen A. 2013. *Handbook of Women Stress and Trauma.* Hoboken, NJ: Taylor & Francis.

Lara-Cinisomo, Sandraluz, Katherine L. Wisner, Rachel M. Burns, and Diego Chaves-Gnecco. 2014. "Perinatal Depression Treatment Preferences Among Latina Mothers." *Qualitative Health Research 24*(2): 232–241.

Melville, Jennifer L., Amelia Gavin, Yuqing Guo, Ming-Yu Fan, and Wayne J. Katon. 2010. "Depressive Disorders during Pregnancy: Prevalence and Risk Factors in a Large Urban Sample." *US National Library of Medicine National Institutes of Health 116*(5): 1064–1070. doi:10.1097/aog.0b013e3181f60b0a.

Owen, Lauri J. 2006. "Forced through the Cracks: Deprivation of the Violence Against Women Act's Immigration Relief in San Francisco Bay Area Immigrant Domestic Violence Survivors' Cases." *Berkeley Journal of Gender, Law and Justice 21*: 13–36.

Parmet, Wendy E., Lorianne Sainsbury-Wong, and Maya Prabhu. 2017. "Immigration and Health: Law, Policy, and Ethics." *Journal of Law, Medicine and Ethics, 1st ser., 45*: 55–59.

Parra-Cardona, Jose Ruben, and DeAndrea, David C. 2014. "Latinos' Access to Online and Formal Mental Health Support." *Journal of Behavioral Health Services and Research 43*(2): 281–292.

Passel, Jeffrey S., and D'Vera Cohn. 2017. "20 Metro Areas are Home to Six-in-Ten Unauthorized Immigrants in U.S." Pew Research Center. February 9. Accessed May 31, 2017. www.pewresearch.org/fact-tank/2017/02/09/us-metro-areas-unauthorized-immigrants/.

Pettway, Alice. 2017. "The Fight for Reproductive Right." *Progressive 81*(4): 16–18.

Planned Parenthood Federation of America, Inc. 2017a. "Blossom Hill Center." *Planned Parenthood*. Accessed May 31, 2017. www.plannedparenthood.org/health-center/california/san-jose/95123/blossom-hill-health-center-3230-90130.

Planned Parenthood Federation of America, Inc. 2017b. "Book Online." *Book Online.* Accessed May 31, 2017. https://docasap.com/white-label/key_prac_id/3263/key_map/1/key_level/4/key_type/INLINE/hide_filter/1/hide_header/1/hide_footer/1/hide_other_provider/1/key_partner_code/PPFA/external_src/1/hide_profile/1/hide_insurance/1/hide_location/1/hide_profile_infoset/1/key_language/english?_ga=2.2608 73163.79333967.1496272503-1029693621.1495749073.

Planned Parenthood Federation of America, Inc. 2017c. "Eastside Health Center." *Planned Parenthood.* Accessed May 31, 2017. www.plannedparenthood.org/health-center/california/san-jose/95127/eastside-health-center-2435-90130.

Planned Parenthood Federation of America, Inc. 2017d. "Gilroy Health Center." *Planned Parenthood.* Accessed May 31, 2017. www.plannedparenthood.org/health-center/california/gilroy/95020/gilroy-health-center-2433-90130.

Planned Parenthood Federation of America, Inc. 2017e. "Mar Monte Community Clinic." *Planned Parenthood.* Accessed May 31, 2017. www.plannedparenthood.org/health-center/california/san-jose/95121/mar-monte-community-clinic-2437-90130.

Planned Parenthood Federation of America, Inc. 2017f. "Morning After Pill." *Planned Parenthood.* Accessed May 31, 2017. www.plannedparenthood.org/health-center/california/san-jose/95126/san-jose-health-center-3263-90130/emergency-contraception.

Planned Parenthood Federation of America, Inc. 2017g. "Mountain View Health Center." *Planned Parenthood.* Accessed May 31, 2017. www.plannedparenthood.org/health-center/california/mountain-view/94040/mountain-view-health-center-2310-90130.

Planned Parenthood Federation of America, Inc. 2017h. "Official Site." *Planned Parenthood.* Accessed May 31, 2017. www.plannedparenthood.org/.

Planned Parenthood Federation of America, Inc. 2017i. "San Jose Health Center of San Jose, CA." *Planned Parenthood.* Accessed May 31, 2017. www.plannedparenthood.org/health-center/california/san-jose/95126/san-jose-health-center-3263-90130.

Planned Parenthood Federation of America, Inc. 2017j. "Women's Health." *Planned Parenthood.* Accessed May 31, 2017. www.plannedparenthood.org/health-center/california/san-jose/95126/san-jose-health-center-3263-90130/womens-health.

Sturken, Marita, and Lisa Cartwright. 2001. *Practices of Looking: An Introduction to Visual Culture.* Oxford: Oxford University Press.

U.S. Centers for Medicare & Medicaid Services. 2017. "Get 2017 Health Coverage. Health Insurance Marketplace." *HealthCare.gov.* Accessed June 1, 2017. www.healthcare.gov/.

IV
GLOBALIZATION, REPRODUCTION, AND TRANSNATIONAL POLITICS

9

AS MANY AS I CAN AFFORD

IDEAL FAMILY SIZE IN CONTEMPORARY UGANDA
ERIN M. HEINZ AND LOUISE MARIE ROTH

Introduction

Contemporary Uganda is a case of extreme *reproductive injustice*, with high fertility, high maternal and infant mortality rates, an epidemic of gender-based violence, patriarchal family systems, and high rates of HIV. Most Ugandan women lack negotiating power in their relationships with men, and thus have limited control over their fertility. In this context, Western-funded non-government organizations (NGOs) advocate for girls' education and offer family planning programs so that women can delay childbearing, space their births, and have smaller families. But how do women in contact with these NGOs navigate the tensions between development prescriptions for low fertility and existing cultural practices that restrict women's sexual and reproductive agency and encourage high fertility? What is the ideal family size for women in rural Uganda after exposure to international NGOs that promote low fertility? In this study, we address these questions using data from 33 semi-structured interviews with women in rural Uganda who volunteered to participate as peer-mentors in an international NGO-funded program designed to encourage family planning and women's economic empowerment. We use Ann Swidler's (1986, 2001) toolkit theory of culture-in-action to analyze how the interview respondents described their ideal family size in a context of extreme reproductive injustice.

A Tale of Two Repertoires

Swidler argues that culture provides a toolkit, or *repertoire*, "of symbols, stories, rituals, and worldviews, which people may use in varying configurations to solve different kinds of problems" (Swidler 1986:273). Cultural repertoires are complex, rule-like structures that individuals can use strategically to understand their lives, solve problems, and justify their choices or behavior (Bourdieu 1980; DiMaggio 1997; Sewell 1992; Swidler 1986). The typical toolkit is large and draws from multiple cultural traditions, especially when individuals live unsettled lives. As a result, cultural toolkits often include inconsistent elements that allow individuals to choose strategies that respond effectively to the various situations that they face (DiMaggio 1997; Swidler 1986, 2001). As individuals develop fluency in multiple cultural repertoires, they can use them to interpret different experiences and make sense of sometimes contradictory choices.

In Swidler's toolkit theory, some cultural repertoires are based on tradition or common sense: they are unconscious, taken-for-granted, and often lack coherence. We call a tradition-based repertoire in Uganda "tribal-colonial" because it comes from the dominant Baganda tribal culture, which colonial administrators reinforced under British rule from 1855–1962 (Kyomuhendo and McIntosh 2006). The tribal-colonial repertoire is based on a restrictive gender division of labor and a patriarchal/patrilineal family system, where Ugandan women have no inheritance rights and restricted property rights over their family's land (Kyomuhendo and McIntosh 2006). Ugandan tribal-colonial culture subordinates women by confining girls to domestic roles from an early age, discouraging girls' education, and encouraging early marriage and childbearing. The tribal-colonial repertoire also privileges the collective over the individual, and grants decision-making about family size to men (Chrisler 2014; Kyomuhendo and McIntosh 2006; Norsworthy, Mclaren, and Waterfield 2012; Shaw 2013; Zucker 2014).

At the same time, efforts to integrate into a global economy have introduced neoliberal values like self-expression, individualism, and investments in human capital into low-income countries, attempting to displace traditional worldviews with a rational, overarching "world society" (Meyer 2010). The cultural repertoire that accompanies this world society emphasizes free market policies, individual autonomy, agency, and the importance of investments in human capital (skills, knowledge, and experience with value for the labor market) (Becker, Murphy, and Tamura 1994). Because terms like "modern," "Western," and "neoliberal" can have varied connotations, we call this the "development" repertoire. The development repertoire encourages individuals to invest in their human capital and that of their offspring by developing skills that produce financial or social returns. This repertoire rejects traditional sources of status that impede economic development, like high fertility.

In fact, increasing investments in education and other human capital typically reduce fertility by increasing the cost of leaving the labor force for educated women with marketable skills (Becker et al. 1994; Montgomery and Lloyd 1999). A desire to develop children's human capital also encourages parents to invest more in each child's socialization and education, which encourages them to have fewer offspring. Western-funded NGOs and other international aid agencies aim to expedite the transition to smaller families by promoting girls' secondary education, women's integration into the economy, and effective family planning (Pillai and Wang 1999). As women in Uganda gain fluency with the development repertoire, it informs their attitudes toward fertility.

Ugandans are familiar with the development repertoire because Uganda has attempted to conform to development norms and integrate into a global society since the 1980s, when they began soliciting foreign direct investment to resuscitate a feeble national economy after the destructive reign of Idi Amin (1971–1979) (Obwona 2001). In 1997, the Ugandan government implemented Universal Primary Education (UPE), which removed formal barriers to girls' education (UBOS 2015). In 2000, Uganda also introduced the National Minimum Healthcare Package to provide free primary health-care for all citizens. However, clinics often charge patients for medical supplies and access to free primary education is restricted to those with enough money for transportation, uniforms, and supplies.

Uganda as a Case of Reproductive Injustice
Uganda is a small, largely rural, highly male-dominated country in Eastern Africa with a subsistence economy. In Uganda, there are many barriers to women's ability to make decisions about their reproductive lives, so that Ugandan women suffer from *reproductive injustice*. Based on the work of women's health activists of color in the United States, we use theories about Reproductive Justice (RJ) that emphasize both the right to choose how many children to have and access to the resources that are necessary to parent effect-ively, including food security, economic security, freedom from violence, and environmental justice (Shaw 2013; Chrisler 2012). In developed countries, RJ theory aims to explain how social inequalities limit reproductive choice for low-income women and women of color, who have historically experienced coercive practices like forced sterilization and the separation of parents and children (Luna and Luker 2013; Ross 2006; Gurr 2011). On the international scene, the Convention on the Elimination of All Forms of Discrimination against Women (CEDAW) and the Cairo Conference of 1994 (ICPD) defined reproductive rights as fundamental human rights. Some scholars have also extended RJ theory to include an international perspective on the ways that many women of the world lack reproductive rights, autonomy over

reproductive decisions, and/or reproductive health services (Shaw 2013; Chrisler 2012). RJ theory defines reproductive health and self-determination as inherent human rights that require both legal rights and the resources necessary to achieve those rights (Chrisler 2012; Luna and Luker 2013; Luna 2009).

Contemporary Uganda represents an extreme case of *reproductive injustice*, with high excess fertility (births above the number that women want), high maternal and infant mortality rates, high rates of HIV/AIDs, and extreme levels of gender-based violence. Uganda's maternal mortality rate (368 deaths per 100,000 births) is in the bottom quartile globally, and women in Uganda have a one in 50 chance of dying during childbirth in their lifetime (UBOS and ICF 2017). Gender-based violence is common in Uganda, where one in five women experience sexual violence, and rates are higher in rural areas and among the poorest women (UBOS and ICF 2017). Sexually transmitted diseases like HIV/AIDs are common, with 7.1% of the population HIV-infected and 28,000 children orphaned annually as a result. While 94% of HIV-positive pregnant women receive anti-retroviral treatment to reduce intrapartum transmission, 33% of their babies still contract the disease (UMOH and NADIC 2015).

Uganda has among the highest *excess fertility* rates in the world: the average of 5.4 children per woman is nearly two more than they want (UBOS and ICF 2017). Unintended pregnancy is common because the majority of women does not use modern contraceptives. Among married women, 28% lack the means to stop having children or to space their next birth (UBOS and ICF 2017). The unmet need for contraception is highest among rural, less educated, and poor women (UBOS and ICF 2017). Abortion is also illegal in Uganda, which leads to high rates of unsafe abortion, maternal injury, and death (IWHRC 2013; Knudsen 2006). Family planning programs have aimed to reduce birthrates, but have been unable to address aspects of the Ugandan social context that contribute to high fertility (Knudsen 2006).

To combat high fertility, many international NGOs promote RJ by encouraging secondary education for girls, helping to integrate women into the cash-based economy, and offering services to improve reproductive health, lower excess fertility, and reduce maternal and infant mortality. In this study, we gained access to women in rural Uganda through an NGO whose mission is to empower women and girls, which we will call Women's Development Foundation (WDF). NGOs like WDF view reproductive rights as fundamental human rights and as a keystone of women's rights (Gurr 2011; Luna and Luker 2013; Pillai and Wang 1999; Ross 2006; Shaw 2013). NGOs promote RJ transnationally by attempting to meet the reproductive needs of poor, rural women in developing countries, who may lack knowledge about or access to effective contraception and may have little bargaining power in their relationships (Chrisler 2012). These women cannot obtain abortions legally and also suffer from high levels of gender-based violence.

At the same time, RJ includes the right to choose how many children to have, and the right to sufficient resources to parent effectively (Chrisler 2014; Luna 2009; Luna and Luker 2013; Shaw 2013). Women in developing countries are often suspicious of international efforts to reduce fertility, which have not been altruistic or benign when it comes to permitting them to choose their family size (Hartmann 2016). Historically, some family planning programs have pushed lower fertility without informed consent and have experimented on women in the developing world with long-acting contraceptives, like implants and IUDs, before establishing their safety—sometimes leading to health problems or infertility (Hartmann 2016). It is in this context that we interviewed rural women who had contact with an international NGO and asked them about the challenges facing girls and women in the community and their attitudes toward marriage and childbearing.

Methods and Data

In June 2016, the first author led a small research team to Luwero in central Uganda, in collaboration with WDF to gather data from women in the community on family, gender, local challenges, and resources available to face those challenges. WDF is a small foundation funded by donors in southern California and managed by local Ugandan professionals. On a budget of less than a million dollars a year, WDF delivers a three-day girls' empowerment curriculum in schools of vulnerable communities. The curriculum includes sex education, self-esteem building, and communication skills. WDF's primary goals are to reduce early pregnancy, prevent the spread of HIV/AIDs, and keep girls in school. They also cultivate a community support system by training adult mentors and legal volunteers to provide social and legal resources to girls in the community. The Ugandan employees are women with college degrees and experience in teaching and program evaluation.

The research team collected data using both a survey and semi-structured interviews to learn about women's experiences with WDF, challenges for girls in the community, and women's and girls' beliefs about family and marriage in Uganda. We selected women who participated as volunteers with WDF or worked closely with women and girls in the community as healthcare workers and development professionals. In addition we used referrals to find other respondents in eight villages in Luwero, the central region of Uganda. Luwero is similar to most rural areas in Uganda outside the Northern region, which is unstable and lacks many government and NGO services. The research team conducted interviews in English if women were fluent and otherwise in Luganda, the local language, using a local translator.

This analysis uses 33 semi-structured interviews that lasted from 15 minutes to over one hour. The interview respondents also completed the survey, which collected data on their actual number of children, income source, education level, if they lived on a main road, and their participation with WDF. Women's sources of income included agricultural production, owning a business, or working as a certified professional, medical personnel, teacher, development worker, or religious leader. In the interviews, we asked women about challenges for girls in the community, their motivations for marriage, their ideal family size, and their preferences regarding the gender of their children. Like many qualitative studies, the sample is not representative. Compared to the general population, the sample has slightly more average education (over one-third completed secondary school versus 25% of the general population) and fewer children (4.9 versus 5.4) (UBOS and ICF 2017). It is likely that some younger respondents have not completed their lifetime childbearing.

We categorized women with an ideal of zero to four children as having a small-family ideal and those with an ideal of five or more children as having a large-family ideal. We chose the cutoff of four or fewer for small families because this is below the average number of children (5.4) in Uganda (UBOS and ICF 2017). We also labeled some women's family ideal as "It Depends," if they said that the ideal number of children depended on economic resources or health. We use pseudonyms for the respondents. We found that women's descriptions of their ideal family size and their ideas about gender and marriage reflected both *development* and *tribal-colonial* repertoires. Tribal-colonial repertoires emphasize a strict gender division of labor, obedience to male authority, and the fatalistic progression of life events. Development repertoires include an emphasis on rationality, economic feasibility, resource-intensive childrearing, individual self-expression, and human rights.

Reproductive Injustice in Rural Uganda

The interviews revealed several sources of gender inequality in rural Uganda that contributed to reproductive injustice. First, gender inequality in education and a preference for sons were significant obstacles to women's life choices outside marriage. Victoria, a 38-year-old mother of four who earned income from farming said:

> In Uganda, from my experience, girls are treated as lesser than boys. I know more people are happy to have boys. And as a girl, the biggest challenge is that you'll never have time for self-exploration or to do what you want to do because you have to be a mother ... You're taking care of the rest of the kids, you're doing all these chores, you're taking care of all these people who are older than you, and so you don't have any time for self-exploration to do what you really want to do.

As Victoria suggests, a preference for sons and expectations that girls must serve other family members limited girls' opportunities in this male-dominated society. The Ugandan tribal-colonial culture often confined girls to domestic roles from an early age and forced them to marry young.

Extreme gender inequality and a preference for sons meant that parents often educated their sons and not their daughters. Prossy, a 25-year-old unmarried lawyer with no children, said:

> People still believe that girls shouldn't be sent to school and in most cases you'll see a family that only has enough money to send one person to school. They are much more likely to send a son than a daughter. Also, girls are really looked at as the helpers in the home … The parents don't take the education of women seriously. I come from a family of ten children. Eight girls and two boys. My father is very well-educated, but I am fairly certain that one of the biggest reasons why he sent all of his daughters to school is because, one, there were too many. He would look bad only sending two children to school. And two, when you send your daughters to school you get more bridewealth, so maybe that's something that we should be saying in the communities: send your daughters to school and get more bridewealth.

Here, Prossy suggested that men's interests in their daughters' potential bridewealth should encourage them to invest in girls' education. However, the tribal-colonial practice of paying bridewealth in the form of livestock (cows and goats) to the bride's family was also a significant source of reproductive injustice because it reinforced men's power over women in marriage (Kyomuhendo and McIntosh 2006). Men could use this power to restrict access to contraception, HIV testing, or prenatal check-ups.

In fact, women had very little power in their marital relationships. Family systems in Uganda are patriarchal: men have authority in the family, and women are economically dependent on their male next-of-kin, which can be their husband, father, or brother. Because of the patrilineal family structure, women had limited rights over the fruits of their own labor. Patience, a 55-year-old nun who worked as a hospital administrator and had no children, said:

> Life in Africa, here in Uganda, is still a lot of culture. A woman doesn't have a voice. When you give yourself to marriage earlier, you are still looked at as someone lower than a man. There is no thinking that we can look at things together and see what is best for our family life. A man has to decide. Even if a woman was doing something, earning, it's the man who is responsible. It is the man who is the owner of everything. The woman cannot own children, cannot own animals, you

name it. For example, in agriculture, the woman does eighty percent of the work but only owns twenty percent because whatever comes is to be kept by the man, owned by the man. The man decides. The man can sit the whole day while the woman is working and will come and demand food although he has not been working.

The patriarchal family system gave women little influence in their families, including influence over decisions about family size (Kyomuhendo and McIntosh 2006).

Men sometimes objected to contraception because they believed that it might cause women to have extramarital affairs (Kaye 2006). Men also viewed large families as a source of status and children as an essential source of income and caregiving as they aged, because Uganda offers unreliable and often ineffective state welfare and social security (Norsworthy et al. 2012). This may be one reason that Uganda has the highest desired family size in east Africa (Muhoza, Roekhuis, and Hooimeijer 2014). Men sometimes refused to use contraception and some women who used WDF's family planning services did so against their husbands' wishes. Eshe, a 35-year-old development professional with three children, said:

> The mothers come and start the service without the partner knowing. This shows us that there is no agreement between the pair. They cannot sit down and discuss what they want. Due to the pressure and the environment at home, the lady decides to use family planning, but ... the man is not aware of the family planning that the woman had started three years back.

Women who wanted to restrict their fertility frequently sought contraception without their male partner's consent or cooperation. Patience, the 55-year-old nun and hospital manager, said:

> There has also been in the introduction of artificial birth control which has helped some people, but ... we are seeing a majority where a woman comes to seek for birth control alone, because there's no equal understanding, so she comes in hiding ... And then we have cases where the woman has given birth too much and there is a health risk, and she sighs and says to the doctor, "Please, the tubes must be done." And later, the man sees that the woman is not giving birth anymore and there is pressure and violence. I had a case here where the man came and said, "My woman decided to get a tubal ligation without my consent." ... This was based on the consent not of the man, but of the patient, so we are not liable for that.

Women who seek resources offered by clinics and NGOs for contraception and reproductive health services may subvert male authority. But women who challenge tribal-colonial prescriptions and do not defer to male decision-making, may face violent consequences in their household.

At the same time that some women went against men's wishes to reduce their fertility, others chose not to use contraception because they were suspicious of hormonal methods or lacked accurate information about effective contraception. Evelyn, a 34-year-old mother of two who worked as WDF staff, said:

> Some women have not sat down to learn about family planning methods. Maybe because they don't even have time to go to the hospital for health problems. It is not at the top of the list or they don't have time for it. I don't know which. They don't seem to access these services. And with all of the family planning available, you really need to sit down with a medical professional and they explain stuff. So half the time, or all of the time, they just sit in their little circles and gossip about all the negative things. And then, maybe that's the thing that scares them to even think about it. But then, for religious reasons, especially for those who are Catholic, they want to go natural.

In Evelyn's view, women either did not prioritize family planning, lacked information, worried excessively about side effects, or followed religious prohibitions against artificial contraception. It did not help that Ugandans associated contraception with the imposition of Western values and used the English term "family planning" even when they spoke about it in Luganda.

In addition to challenges negotiating contraception in their families, gender-based violence was a significant source of reproductive injustice in Uganda. Even women who contributed economically to their families did not control sexual decision-making in the household, and denying a husband sex could lead to withdrawal of economic support, beatings, or rape (Kaye 2006; Nyanzi et al. 2005). Joyce, a 37-year-old mother of seven who earned her income from farming, said:

> For me and my family, in my home, I'm challenged with my husband. My husband takes alcohol. When he comes back he shouts around, and then he wants to beat me in front of the children. He abuses me in front of my children. Even at times we try to run away from the house and leave him to stay there alone.

Married, rural women between the ages of 30 and 39, like Joyce, are the most vulnerable to violence or abuse in their homes. In a national survey, nearly

30% of women in this age group reported that they experienced sexual violence (UBOS and ICF 2017).

While sexual violence in Uganda is most likely to occur within an intimate partnership, unmarried women also experienced epidemic levels of rape in the community, often when traveling to and from school or while doing chores (Jones 2008). Karen, a 35-year-old with four children who earned income from farming, said that teenage girls "are challenged by men, mostly when they go to waterholes or boreholes. They sometimes find them there. They chase them. Sometimes they are raped." Agatha, a 39-year-old teacher with two children, said that her community had restricted hours of access to the borehole to reduce the rampant sexual violence against young women when they fetched water.

Brenda, a 42-year-old mother of seven who earned income from farming, talked about how gender-based violence could impede girls' education: "There is also a problem of rape, especially when they are going to school. Especially those who go to schools that are far away. Because these are villages, the houses are far." According to the Ugandan Bureau of Statistics (UBOS), 10% of girls 15–19 reported experiencing sexual violence (UBOS and ICF 2017). This high level of violence and lack of sexual autonomy impeded Ugandan women's ability to determine their fertility. In this setting, many women get pregnant before they can complete their education, and few women have power within their families to negotiate limits on family size.

Thus, in rural Uganda, gender inequality, patriarchal customs, lack of complete information on contraception, and high levels of gender-based violence contribute to reproductive injustice. Our discussion of large and small ideal family size demonstrates how women use cultural repertoires to justify their preferences for a large or small family. They draw from available cultural repertoires that emphasize tribal/colonial ideals of high fertility or a development agenda that promotes low fertility. Both repertoires offer socially rational strategies under Uganda's conditions of reproductive injustice.

Ideal Family Size

In the interviews, the average ideal family size was four children, which is high by global standards but is lower than the actual fertility level in Uganda (5.4 children). We grouped women based on whether they said that their ideal family size was large (five or more children), small (zero to four children), or "it depends." Table 9.1 presents the sample characteristics for each group, in terms of the women's income source, role in WDF, age, rural location, and education. As Table 9.1 illustrates, 39.4% of the women interviewed had a large-family ideal. These women had low average education, and a tendency to rely on farming (including raising subsistence crops and animals) for income. They were also older, on average, had more children, and were less likely to live on a paved road, suggesting that they lived in more rural areas. In contrast, 48.5% of the women had a small-family ideal, and these women had more education, were younger, and were more likely to participate in the cash-economy and to live on a paved road. Women who worked as WDF staff tended to have a small-family ideal, as one would expect given the NGO's mission. The 12.1% who said that "it depends" were similar to those with large-family ideals in terms of education, age, number of children, WDF role, and income source.

We found that most women with a large-family ideal relied primarily on a tribal-colonial repertoire, while those with a small-family ideal tended to use a development repertoire to describe their ideal family size. However, many of the women that we interviewed also engaged in *code-switching*, drawing on both tribal-colonial and development repertoires to define an ideal that depends on material resources.

Women with a Large-Family Ideal (Five or More Children)
Women with a large-family ideal frequently drew on tribal-colonial cultural repertoires that defined marriage and high fertility as a source of social status for women (Kyomuhendo 2003). Regardless of women's ideal family size, they recognized marriage as an important status marker. Jane, a 34-year-old mother of six who earned income from agriculture, said, "Women get married to gain respect and to bear children. If you are married, you are respected, and nobody can con you again." Kissa, a 27-year-old mother of four who also farmed for income, was even more emphatic about the importance of marriage for status:

> When you don't marry, you aren't counted as a woman in your family here in Uganda. And when you marry, you gain respect. Women marry to bear children. And when you stay at home and you are not married, but you have reached the time of marriage, you become a problem to your parents ... The neighbors start talking. Why isn't she married? Maybe she has a problem.

Many women viewed marriage as economically essential for women, as well as a duty and a rite of passage. Women can become an economic burden to their parents if they do not marry and leave the household, especially once they have children of their own. As a result, the women that we interviewed described pressures to be married by a relatively early age, and 12 of these women (36%) were married before they turned 18. It is common for girls to leave school early and get married in Uganda, where only about 8% of girls continue education after secondary school (UBOS and ICF 2017).

The tribal-colonial repertoire rewards motherhood and women can gain status by using their fecundity to continue the tribal lineage. Patience, the

Table 9.1 Sample Characteristics of Interview Respondents by Ideal Family Size

	Large–Family Ideal (5+)	Small–Family Ideal (0–4)	"It Depends"	Total
	Mean			
Education (in years)	7.62	11.75	6.25	9.5
Age (in years)	42.62	37.38	45.25	40.4
# of children	5.82	3.21	5.25	4.5
Spacing between children (in years)	2.90	2.88	1.86	2.7
	N (Percent)			
Live on paved road	3 (23.1%)	8 (50.0%)	1 (25.0%)	12 (36.4%)
Married	9 (69.2%)	7 (43.8%)	2 (50.0%)	18 (54.5%)
WDF (NGO) Role				
Staff	1 (7.7%)	5 (23.1%)	0 (0.0%)	6 (18.2%)
Volunteer	8 (61.5%)	6 (46.2%)	3 (75.0%)	17 (51.5%)
New volunteer	1 (7.7%)	2 (15.4%)	0 (0.0%)	3 (9.1%)
Other	3 (2.3%)	3 (15.4%)	1 (25.0%)	7 (21.2%)

Income Source				
Agriculture (includes subsistence)	10 (76.9%)	4 (25.0%)	3 (75.0%)	17 (51.5%)
Unskilled[1]	0 (0.0%)	2 (12.5%)	1 (25.0%)	3 (9.1%)
Skilled[2]	2 (15.4%)	6 (37.5%)	0 (0.0%)	8 (24.2%)
Development worker[3]	1 (7.7%)	4 (25.0%)	0 (0.0%)	5 (15.2%)
Religion				
Catholic	5 (38.5%)	4 (15.4%)	1 (25.0%)	10 (30.3%)
Protestant	6 (46.2%)	10 (62.5%)	3 (75.0%)	19 (57.6%)
Muslim	2 (15.4%)	1 (7.7%)	0 (0.0%)	3 (9.1%)
None	0 (0.0%)	1 (7.7%)	0 (0.0%)	1 (3.0%)
RJ Issues				
Gender-based violence	2 (15.4%)	5 (38.5%)	0 (0.0%)	7 (21.2%)
Marital support for contraception	2 (15.4%)	2 (12.5%)	0 (0.0%)	4 (12.1%)
N	**13 (39.4%)**	**16 (48.5%)**	**4 (12.1%)**	**33**

Notes

[1] Includes hairdressers, small-shop owners, restaurant workers, and tailors.

[2] Includes accountants, secretaries, bankers, and translators.

[3] Those employed by a local NGO to facilitate programming in women's development.

55-year-old nun and hospital administrator, said, "Culturally speaking, they would say that the more children that you have, the better woman you are. 'This is a good woman who has produced many children.'" Although Patience had entered religious service and had no children, she acknowledged the cultural value of high fertility.

A large-family ideal was especially common among agricultural women (72.7%), which is unsurprising given a cross-cultural tendency for agricultural families to have higher fertility and to view children as a source of farm labor. Kamali, a 50-year-old woman with seven children who relied on farming for income described cultural norms that encouraged large families:

> According to Africans, until you have 12, you do not count yourself as being a parent! [Laughs] Six kids are enough. Africans take care of their children, and you take your biological ones and those born by your daughter and those of your son.

As Kamali notes, large families and extended kin involvement are common in Uganda, especially in agricultural families. Informal agricultural production accounts for 48% of the national GDP (UBOS 2015). Most families in rural Uganda rely on subsistence farming or small shops for income. It is not uncommon for grandmothers, aunts, or other relatives to take care of children whose parents cannot support them or who are no longer living (Jones 2008). In addition, we found that two skilled workers (accountants, secretaries, bankers, or translators) and one development worker described a large-family ideal.

The status associated with high fertility was an obstacle to development goals, as were negative attitudes toward contraception that were part of the tribal-colonial repertoire. Naomi, a 52-year-old mother of three who earned income from agriculture, said:

> For these girls aged forty and below, they have been told about family planning methods but, recently, they are starting to withdraw from these methods. ... [T]hey claim that they are making them sick, especially the injections and the pills. So they are telling [19 and 20-year-old women] to use condoms instead because at least there you can't have any side effects like with the other family planning methods.

Naomi suggests that some younger women avoid hormonal contraceptives, so family planning programs encouraged condoms instead. However, condoms require men's consent and cooperation to be effective, and this can be hard to obtain in patriarchal families where men have decision-making power (Cooper 2014; Kaye 2006).

Another aspect of the tribal-colonial repertoire was the claim that family size was "God's will" or a matter of fate. Women with a large-family ideal were the most likely to use fatalistic language to describe the number of children and the distribution of sons and daughters. When we asked about her ideal number of children, Naomi, the 53-year-old mother of three above, said, "I think that six, well-spaced, are enough. With boys and girls, but that depends on what God gives you."

Some women with a large-family ideal mentioned the scarcity of other resources, like food, as limits on the number of children, but not necessarily because of conscious family planning as much as broader environmental limitations. In their view, the maximum number of children is naturally limited by agricultural yields and a woman's physical ability to deliver more children, which are beyond the control of the individual. Jane, a 34-year-old with six children who relied on farming for income, said that her ideal was based on the number of children that she could care for:

> Six children, 3 boys and 3 girls is ideal, but you can find women who give birth to 20 or 12. But due to the situation, I am only capable of taking care of six ... Those who were ancient, they gave birth to twenty because the resources were enough. Right now, the situation is different.

Jane believed that resources were more plentiful in some earlier era, although this nostalgia may be misplaced—there is no period of abundance in Uganda's recorded history.

Women with a Small Family Ideal (Zero to Four Children)

Women with a small-family ideal tended to employ development repertoires, although they acknowledged the tribal-colonial status associated with high fertility. Given that the tribal-colonial repertoire encouraged high fertility, women with a small-family ideal were agents of social change. Prossy, a 25-year old lawyer without children said:

> Well, that's a difficult one. I do not want children. I sound really selfish because I grew up in a home with lots of children, and I really think that the ideal number of children would be one or two. Because it's manageable in terms of the financial, and then with two, they grow up and you can move on with your life.

While she grew up in a large family and had eight married siblings, Prossy had aspirations outside the sphere of domesticity and childrearing. She had invested a substantial amount in her education and viewed children as a barrier to her personal and career development. When she calculates the time and financial costs of children, Prossy views them as prohibitive. She drew on the development repertoire and its emphasis on individualism to prioritize her own well-being and fulfillment rather than subordinating herself to other family members. At the same time, she had to struggle to reconcile tribal-colonial beliefs that motherhood is the only honorable and virtuous role for women with her "selfish" desire for personal development, settling on an ideal of one or two children rather than none.

As Table 9.1 revealed, the women in this sample with a small-family ideal were the most elite in terms of education and income source, with very high average education compared to Ugandan women as a whole. They were younger than those with a large-family ideal, and they were more likely to work in skilled jobs and to be relatively urban. These are all factors that lead to lower levels of fertility in other settings (Ainsworth, Beegle, and Nyamete 1996; Garenne and Joseph 2002; Osili and Long 2008). One reason that development agendas focus on girls' education as a key to economic development is because it is associated with reductions in gender inequality, lower fertility, and higher rates of participation in the formal labor force (Paul Schultz 2002).

Drawing from the development repertoire, women with a small-family ideal argued that all girls should complete their education and be able to make a livable income. Agatha, a 39-year-old teacher with two children and a college education, viewed education as essential for women to be able to provide for their families.

> I think four children are enough. Because I think I can support that family if I am working and am innovative and can stand the challenges facing my family. But for a person who is not educated, you don't have a job and you can't support your children.

When Agatha talks about how educated women have a means to provide for their children and escape some of the suffering and hardship that uneducated women face, she uses the development repertoire to validate education and independence for women.

The development repertoire also emphasizes the importance of being able to afford children economically and to make material investments in each child. Agatha, the teacher above, said:

> I have two sons, and I am thinking that is enough. I want to be able to offer what is good for them. "Mami, I want yogurt." And will I be able to offer yogurt? "Here, I want an apple." An apple costs 1000 Ugandan Shillings, which is like 30 cents. So really, if I have 6

children, and they all want apples, how much am I going to spend per day? Before you think about having children, like how many, you have to decide how much you are going to work ... You have to pay for rent, you have to pay the bills. Children, yes, you've produced. Which type of school are you going to take them? How are you going to feed them? When I start thinking about that, I think, no, my two boys are enough.

For Agatha, it was important to invest in each child, and economic constraints like the cost of food, school supplies, and necessities meant that her ideal family was small. Agatha echoed neoliberal discourses of global capitalism, which emphasize investments in human capital and low fertility for the sake of economic development. At the same time, these discourses may conflict with some women's desires to have large families. Many international development agendas and efforts to control population growth have promoted low fertility without regard for women's preferences (Hartmann 2016). But without reproductive justice, poor women may be vulnerable to adopt whichever repertoire can provide the most economic security—which might include securing a man's financial contribution or resources from extended kin networks, NGOs, or government programs.

Uncertainty about men's financial contributions was an economic constraint that justified a small-family ideal. Evelyn, a 34-year-old development worker with two children described uncertainty about men's economic support as key considerations:

> I think that the woman should be the one to decide how many to have, because when you look at the economics, you don't always know. Like today you have money, tomorrow you don't. Unless the men want children, depending on how heavy their pockets are, but that could all disappear too. For women, I want them to look at their health and how many they can handle ... If they could try to assess what they can handle, without the fear of being rejected by the man, then I would say, two, because I am having only two.

Evelyn indicates that having fewer children makes it easier to manage financial uncertainty and material deprivation, which are endemic in rural Uganda. At the same time, she acknowledges that it requires cooperation from men because women with few children may fear "being rejected" by their husbands for going against tribal-colonial expectations.

Women with a small-family ideal also drew from the development repertoire to define others with high fertility as "irresponsible" rather than high-status if they could not afford all of their children. Evelyn, a 34-year-old development professional with two children, described her neighbors as neglecting their children because of their lack of economic resources:

> A [school] term should be very affordable, but surprisingly it doesn't seem affordable to the parents ... Like this family that I know, it's a household with five children, two girls and three boys ... The first meal of the day, you can see that already they are being denied food because they go directly to work in the garden until midday. There is no breakfast there ... And the way they dress, they are covered which is good, but you're not sure if they even have soap to wash. Why are the clothes so dirty? You don't know why the clothes are so dirty. Then the fact that they miss school a lot ... I know they never do examinations at the end of the term because they will let you into the school, but if you do not pay full tuition, they will not let you take the exams.

Evelyn thought that parents should only have as many children as they could afford, and viewed her neighbors as irresponsible. Drawing from the development repertoire, she said that parents should not have children that they cannot materially afford.

Women with a small-family ideal also emphasized controlling one's family size using modern contraceptives and avoiding unplanned births. Judy, a 30-year-old mother of two who worked as a WDF development professional, said:

> First of all, you have to be comfortable with your decision about the number of children that you want to have. That's the first step. Irrespective of the sex, you have to say the number. You have to say "I want two." Then if they are all boys and no girls, I will stick to my number ... So you first fix the number, and you can choose the method that you want to use ... If you say, "I want two. It's best every three years," you can use the injectable plans for three months or six months, four times. Or you can go for implants for three years or five years. It depends what age difference you want between your children. And for condoms, it depends on whether the husband is comfortable.

Judy was knowledgeable about contraception and even about how to obtain an illegal abortion in order to maintain control over one's family size. In her view, women's ability to decide their own fertility was critically important.

"It Depends": Ideal Family Size is Conditional

Finally, four women (12.1%) did not respond to the question about ideal family size with a concrete number, and instead switched between tribal-colonial and development repertoires by describing the conditions under which high fertility was socially acceptable. As Table 9.1 illustrates, these women resembled those with a large-family ideal in their education level, rural residence, number of children, and income source (agriculture or unskilled business). While the women in this group did not reject the tribal-colonial value placed on high fertility, they drew from WDF's emphasis on investing in human capital to define the conditions under which a large family was morally appropriate. In this respect, they highlight the shifting moral standards surrounding fertility in Uganda.

Women who said "it depends" thought that parents must be able to economically provide for their children, but that women should have as many as they could afford. Victoria, a 38-year-old mother of four who farmed, said:

> I don't know if there is an ideal number. I guess if it's what you want and if you can manage to take care of all those kids. The most important thing is are you going to take care of them financially, put them through school, give them the love and affection? If you can do that, then feel free.

Similarly, Maria, a 54-year-old long-term volunteer with WDF with 11 children who earned income from farming, said "About the ideal number, it depends on one's capabilities. You can have 20 kids as long as you are taking care of them." At the same time, she used WDF's development repertoire to define providing for children explicitly as a human right. She said:

> The volunteers should first inform parents about children's rights. The parents usually ignore their children's rights. Like the right to be educated, and the right to receive medical attention. I want support to help these girls to achieve their dreams.

Maria's use of the language of human rights and development of girls' human capital and self-expression all come from WDF's development repertoire.

The women who said "it depends" also used the development repertoire to emphasize controlling family size. Afia, a 31-year-old mother of one with a secondary school diploma who worked as an unskilled business owner, said:

> I am using family planning methods. Child spacing so I can get time off to rest my body and take care of the young kids as well. So, by the time I give birth, this one is at least of age. I'll give birth again when my child is in school, that's when I'll have the next one. I want that time in between so that I can work and prepare for the next one coming.

Like women with a small-family ideal, those who said "it depends" used the development repertoire to emphasize control over their fertility and having only had as many children as they could afford. Despite their demographic similarities with those who had a large-family ideal, these women viewed family planning through a development lens.

Conclusion

In this study, we analyze the way that contemporary Ugandan women draw on tribal-colonial and development repertoires to define their ideal family size. We argue that women in rural Uganda face tensions between the tribal-colonial status associated with high fertility and a desire to keep their families financially and physically manageable. Western-funded NGOs exposed rural women to a development repertoire that encouraged them to invest in their own and their children's human capital, to delay family formation and space their births, and to lower their fertility. At the same time, the women interviewed for this research recognized the traditional social status associated with high fertility and the limits to their own influence over family size. As a result, some respondents strategically defined the ideal family size as dependent on material resources. The infiltration of development values has changed what is socially acceptable, which is now "as many children as I can afford."

Development repertoires also encouraged Ugandan women in contact with WDF to stigmatize poor parents with large families as irresponsible and neglectful. Once they were fluent in the development repertoire, these women viewed high fertility as a source of status only when families had adequate resources to properly provide for the children. This suggests a conflation of modernity and morality in discussions of fertility: development repertoires have diffused globally to shape values about fertility. The resulting order stigmatizes traditional worldviews as immoral.

By describing how women use tribal/colonial repertoires to justify large families or development repertoires to justify small families, we see how the forces of globalization compete with local norms to shape women's fertility ideals. Under conditions of reproductive injustice, women must navigate the narrow pathways to social status and fulfillment that are open to them. For some, this means embracing traditional norms of high fertility, for others it means adopting neoliberal values that encourage low fertility, and some find themselves somewhere in-between. Changes in women's status, material changes, and increased educational and occupational opportunities for women and girls could shift these ideals further toward low-fertility goals.

References

Ainsworth, Martha, Kathleen Beegle, and Andrew Nyamete. 1996. "The Impact of Women's Schooling on Fertility and Contraceptive Use : A Study of Fourteen Sub-Saharan African Countries." *World Bank Economic Review* 10(1):85–122.

Becker, Gary S., Kevin M. Murphy, and Robert Tamura. 1994. "Human Capital, Fertility, and Economic Growth Chapter." Pp. 323–50 in *A Theoretical and Empirical Analysis with Special Reference to Education*, edited by Gary S. Becker. Chicago, IL: University of Chicago Press.

Bourdieu, Pierre. 1980. *The Logic of Practice*. Stanford, CA: Stanford University Press.

Chrisler, Joan C. 2012. *Reproductive Justice: A Global Concern*. Santa Barbara, CA: Praeger.

Chrisler, Joan C. 2014. "A Reproductive Justice Approach to Women's Health." *Analyses of Social Issues and Public Policy* 14(1):205–9.

Cooper, Melinda. 2014. "The Theology of Emergency: Welfare Reform, US Foreign Aid and the Faith-Based Initiative." *Theory, Culture & Society* 32(2):53–77.

DiMaggio, Paul. 1997. "Culture and Cognition." *Annual Review of Sociology* 23(1997): 263–87.

Garenne, Michel and Veronique Joseph. 2002. "The Timing of the Fertility Transition in Sub-Saharan Africa." *World Development* 30(10):1835–43.

Gurr, Barbara. 2011. "Complex Intersections: Reproductive Justice and Native American Women." *Sociology Compass* 5(8):721–35.

Hartmann, Betsy. 2016. *Reproductive Rights and Wrongs: The Global Politics of Population Control*. 3rd ed. Chicago, IL: Haymarket Books.

IWHRC (International Women's Human Rights Clinic). 2013. *The Stakes are High: The Tragic Impact of Unsafe Abortion and Inadequate Access to Contraception in Uganda*. Washington, DC: IWHRC.

Jones, S. K. 2008. *Secondary Schooling for Girls in Rural Uganda: Challenges, Opportunities and Emerging Identities* (Doctoral Dissertation). University of British Columbia. Retrieved from https://open.library.ubc.ca/cIRcle/collections/24/items/1.0066208.

Kaye, D. K. 2006. "Community Perceptions and Experiences of Domestic Violence and Induced Abortion in Wakiso District, Uganda." *Qualitative Health Research* 16(8): 1120–8.

Knudsen, Lara M. 2006. *Reproductive Rights in a Global Context*. Nashville, TN: Vanderbilt University Press.

Kyomuhendo, Grace Bantebya. 2003. "Low Use of Rural Maternity Services in Uganda: Impact of Women's Status, Traditional Beliefs and Limited Resources." *Reproductive Health Matters* 11(21):16–26.

Kyomuhendo, Grace Bantebya and Marjorie Keniston McIntosh. 2006. *Women, Work and Domestic Virtue in Uganda*. Athens, OH: Ohio University Press.

Luna, Zakiya. 2009. "From Rights to Justice: Women of Color Changing the Face of US Reproductive Rights Organizing." *Societies Without Borders* 4(3):343–65.

Luna, Zakiya and Kristin Luker. 2013. "Reproductive Justice." *Annual Review of Law and Social Science* 9:327–52.

Meyer, John W. 2010. "World Society, Institutional Theories, and the Actor." *Annual Review of Sociology* 36:1–20.

Montgomery, Mark R. and Cynthia B. Lloyd. 1999. "Excess Fertility, Unintended Births, and Children's Schooling." Pp. 216–66 in *Critical Perspectives on Schooling and Fertility in the Developing World*, edited by C. H. Bledsoe, J. B. Casterline, J. A. Johnson-Kuhn, and J. G. Haaga. Washington, DC: National Academy Press.

Muhoza, Dieudonné Ndaruhuye, Annelet Roekhuis, and Pieter Hooimeijer. 2014. "Variations in Desired Family Size and Excess Fertility in East Africa." *International Journal of Population Research* 1:1–11.

Norsworthy, Kathryn L., Margaret A. Mclaren, and Laura D. Waterfield. 2012. "Women's Power in Relationships : A Matter of Social Justice." Pp. 58–75 in *Reproductive Justice: A Global Concern*, edited by J. C. Chisler. Santa Barbara, CA: Praeger.

Nyanzi, Barbara, Stella Nyanzi, Brent Wolff, and James Whitworth. 2005. "Money, Men and Markets: Economic and Sexual Empowerment of Market Women in Southwestern Uganda." *Culture, Health and Sexuality* 7(1):13–26.

Obwona, M. B. 2001. "Determinants of FDI and Their Impact on Economic Growth in Uganda." *African Development Review-Revue Africaine De Developpement* 13(1):46–81.

Osili, Una Okonkwo and Bridget Terry Long. 2008. "Does Female Schooling Reduce Fertility? Evidence from Nigeria." *Journal of Development Economics* 87(1):57–75.

Paul Schultz, T. 2002. "Why Governments Should Invest More to Educate Girls." *World Development* 30(2):207–25.

Pillai, Vijayan K. and Guang-zhen Wang. 1999. *Women's Reproductive Rights in Developing Countries.* Brookfield, VT: Ashgate Publishing Company.

Ross, Loretta. 2006. "Understanding Reproductive Justice: Transforming the Pro-Choice Movement." *Off Our Backs* 36(4):14–19.

Sewell, William H. 1992. "A Theory of Structure: Duality, Agency, and Transformation." *American Journal of Sociology* 98(1):1–29.

Shaw, Jessica. 2013. "Full-Spectrum Reproductive Justice: The Affinity of Abortion Rights and Birth Activism." *Studies in Social Justice* 7(1):143–59.

Swidler, Ann. 1986. "Culture in Action: Symbols and Strategies." *American Sociological Review* 51(2):273–86.

Swidler, Ann. 2001. *Talk of Love: How Culture Matters.* Chicago, IL: University of Chicago Press.

UBOS (Ugandan Bureau of Statistics). 2015. *2015 Statistical Abstract.* Kampala, Uganda.

UBOS (Ugandan Bureau of Statistics) and ICF. 2017. *Uganda Demographic and Health Survey 2016: Key Indicators Report.* Rockville, MD.

UMOH and NADIC (Uganda Ministry of Health and Uganda AIDS Commission National Documentation and Information Center). 2015. *The HIV And AIDS Uganda Country Progress Report 2014.* Kampala, Uganda.

Zucker, Alyssa N. 2014. "Reproductive Justice: More than Choice." *Analyses of Social Issues and Public Policy* 14(1):210–13.

10

BOON AND BANE OF REPRODUCTIVE TECHNOLOGIES

THE IMPACT OF SON PREFERENCE AND PRENATAL SEX SELECTION IN A GLOBALIZED WORLD
JOHANNA KOSTENZER

Introduction

The emergence of reproductive technologies to support the achievement of pregnancy has raised hopes for childless individuals and couples to overcome fertility issues. The World Health Organization (WHO) defines infertility as the "failure to conceive following twelve months of unprotected intercourse" (2017a). The medical intervention of assisted reproduction does not only increase the chance of starting a family, however, it also provides opportunities to make use of additional "services" in this context, for example choosing the sex of a future child. Using medical techniques to select for the sex of the fetus may take place at various stages of the (assisted) reproductive process and encompasses a variety of practices; e.g., at pre- and post-implantation of an embryo as part of in vitro fertilization (IVF) or by selectively terminating the pregnancy (WHO, 2017b). Since the 1970s, sex selection has mainly taken place through determination during pregnancy, e.g., through ultrasound, amniocentesis, and chorionic villus sampling, followed by sex-selective abortion (Stump, 2011). In a global context, sex-selective abortion has been the most common form of prenatal sex selection up until today due to its accessibility and affordability.

The motives behind sex selection can be diverse, ranging from medical reasons (preventing X-linked diseases) and family balancing to gender preference—and very often male preference. Cultural norms, socioeconomic factors, politics, and legal regulations have influenced the preference for sons over daughters (Das Gupta et al., 2003; Hesketh and Xing, 2006). The strong wish for male offspring coupled with rapidly declining family size and access to technology has led to an increase in selective abortions and also to distorted sex ratios at birth (SRB) in many parts of the world (Guilmoto, 2015, p. 186). Gender-biased prenatal sex selection due to son preference, which is also referred to as femicide or gendercide (Eklund and Purewal, 2017, p. 36), is hence not an isolated phenomenon in one single region, it is prevalent in many countries across the globe including China, India, and Vietnam, and also Armenia, Azerbaijan, Georgia, and others (Stump, 2011). Excessive use of selective abortion has led to an imbalance of SRB with increasing distortions among higher order births (e.g., second, third, fourth child), as will be outlined later in this chapter (WHO, 2011). This imbalance is not solely a statistical peculiarity but also brings about further consequences. According to the United Nations Population Fund (UNFPA, 2017), more than 117 million women are missing as a result of son preference and selective abortion. The far-reaching dynamics of prenatal sex selection related to such a demographic imbalance is of concern to human rights advocates, policy makers, and the general public.

This chapter explores the issue of prenatal sex selection and son preference in a globalized world from a bioethical and modern reproductive biopolitics perspective. The chapter will first critically reflect on the practice of prenatal sex selection and the term son preference to explore the underlying reasons and consequences of the practice. The biopolitical and bioethical dimension of the issue will be further outlined. In accordance with the definitions of Beauchamp and Childress (2009), the principles of autonomy, beneficence, non-maleficence, and justice will be referred to in order to explore the issue from a bioethical perspective. Sex selection is a highly controversial topic in bioethics and has also become an important population and health issue, making this combined approach necessary.

In this chapter the term "sex selection" is used as opposed to "gender selection," which can also be found in both scientific and non-scientific literature. Prenatal sex selection, however, is practiced based on the biological sex of the fetus. In contrast to sex, gender is socially constructed and cannot be attributed to the fetus even though parents' expectations of the future child may refer to gender roles rather than to biological sex. It is understood that gender perceptions substantially shape the decision to abort a fetus, which is why the issue will also be referred to as "gender-biased prenatal sex selection." Furthermore, it is not the aim of this chapter to argue in favor or against abortion based on the issue of prenatal sex selection. Access to safe and legal abortion is essential to women's well-being. The aim of this chapter is to outline the consequences of prenatal sex selection within a wider context.

Selecting for Sons

The preference for sons over daughters is not a modern phenomenon; it has existed throughout history. Today, it is prevalent in various countries in Asia, the Middle East, and North Africa (Hesketh and Xing, 2006, p. 13272). What can be found in all countries where gender-biased prenatal sex selection is performed is a low value placed on girls and women, hence the so-called phenomenon of "son preference." In a variety of societies around the world, sons are preferred over daughters due to their higher status in society, whereas daughters are often considered a burden to the family (WHO, 2011, p. 12). Within this chapter, the term "son preference" is however not defined as a mere preference for males over females, but as a resulting phenomenon of complex circumstances discriminating against girls and women, thus leading to their lower social status and to a preference for male over female offspring. Guilmoto (2009, p. 540) defines three preconditions as follows: "(1) entrenched traditional preference for sons in patriarchal societies ('readiness'); (2) access to modern sex selection ('ability'); and (3) the pressure to have at least one son caused by small family size ('squeeze')."

The underlying reasons for son preference and sex-selective abortions are complex and differ according to the local context. The traditional superior role of males in society together with discriminating societal, cultural, religious, economic, and legal factors have in general increased the value of the boy child to a disproportionately high level as compared to the value of the girl child. In countries with strong patriarchal structures and where the family is the sole reliable security network, sons are preferred. Sons are responsible for the economic outcome of the family and hence act as a pension and social security system for their parents. In addition, there is an assumption that sons will bring in a daughter-in-law to care for the parents in old age. Discriminative inheritance rights, high dowry-payments (as for example in India), and the lower social status of women in general are only a few other examples of why boys may be preferred over girls (WHO, 2011, pp. 13–14). Also, the son's (and daughter-in-law's) duty to support the parents when they need care is an additional example that shows the complexity of driving factors. In general, however, the lower social status of girls and women in son preferring societies remains the main reason to undergo sex selection (Stump, 2011), and son preference leading to sex selection and skewed sex ratios is an indicator for gender inequality (Liisanantti and Beese, 2012; Guilmoto, 2012). The so-called "readiness" to select for sons (Guilmoto, 2009, p. 540) can of course have very diverse characteristics across countries and regions, and therefore always needs to be analyzed in a local context. This chapter focuses more on son preference in a global context and country specific examples are used to illustrate the issue.

In addition to the desire for male offspring, tremendous improvements in access to reproductive treatment and technologies in urban and rural areas across the globe have further contributed to the increase of sex-selective abortions. Sex determination during pregnancy has not only become available but also cheaper, providing the basis for the abortion of unwanted girls in regions where it had not been practiced previously (Guilmoto, 2009, pp. 528–529). An example of this correlation can be seen in India where access to portable ultrasound machines allows for sex determination even in rural areas lacking health care facilities. As a result, national guidelines on the use of technologies have been implemented and are applicable across the country, and even providers of the machines have published statements promoting the ethical use of ultrasound machines (General Electric, 2009; Mani, 2012).

The third precondition, the "family squeeze" as outlined by Guilmoto (2009, p. 540), certainly influences the demand for sex-selective services. Changing family structures, with reduced fertility rates and smaller sized families strengthens the desire for at least one son in son preferring societies. If the family size is reduced to only one or two children, the need for male offspring is apparently stronger than in larger families with a higher number of children. Family balancing, wanting to have an "even" number of children of a particular sex (Bongaarts, 2013, p. 201), plays a further role with regard to sex selection in general, but in the context of this chapter only a minor one.

Sex selection in general is not a completely new occurrence. Prior to the emergence of modern technologies, selecting the sex of the child has been done in the form of postnatal discrimination through infanticide—the killing of new-born female infants, neglect of the girl child, and violence (UNFPA, 2017). Excess female mortality was the consequence of such strong discrimination against girls (Sen, 1990). Postnatal sex selection is still practiced but it is less common as emerging reproductive tools like ultrasound machines and others have facilitated sex determination during pregnancy and enabled discrimination at an even earlier stage—during the prenatal phase (Stump, 2011). The question has been raised whether the shift from postnatal to prenatal discrimination reduces harm (Goodkind, 1999) and is therefore the better option or the lesser evil.

Implications of Prenatal Sex Selection

The consequences of son preference and prenatal sex selection are multifold: discrimination against girls and women, reproductive health issues, increasing violence and trafficking, and the so-called "marriage squeeze" are areas of concern. However, one of the main consequences of prenatal sex selection that has raised interest not only among demographers and researchers, but also policy makers, non-governmental organizations (NGOs), and the media, is the imbalance of sex ratios in the population. Demographic imbalance is one of the most visible consequences of prenatal sex selection and has been one factor in why the issue of excessive use of sex-selective abortions has been noticed at all.

The natural SRB ranges from 102 to 106 males per 100 females (UNFPA, 2012). This small surplus is considered biologically normal as male infants have a higher risk of child mortality and this slight disparity evens out over time (Barot, 2012, p. 19). Levels exceeding 106 males per 100 females, however, suggest that human intervention has occurred, most likely in the form of prenatal sex selection and through sex-selective abortions (WHO, 2011, p. 1). SRB is therefore used as an indicator for prenatal sex selection. Table 10.1 provides an overview of registered skewed SRB in selected countries; China, Vietnam, Azerbaijan, and Armenia show the highest distortions. Except for India and Kosovo, fertility rates are below replacement levels in all countries. It must be noted here that the table displays national

Table 10.1 SRBs in Selected Countries 2008–2014

Country	SRB	Period	Source[a]	Population[b]	Fertility[c]
ASIA					
China	115.9	2014	National Bureau of Statistics	1,401.6	1.7
South Korea	105.3	2013	Birth registration	49.7	1.3
Hong Kong	109.3	2013	Birth registration (residents)	7.3	1.1
India	110.0	2011–2013	Sample system registration	1,282.4	2.5
Singapore	107.0	2013	Birth registration	5.6	1.3
Taiwan	107.4	2012	Birth registration	23.4	1.2
Vietnam	112.2	2013–2014	Intercensal survey 2014	93.4	1.8
SOUTHERN CAUCASUS					
Azerbaijan	115.6	2013	Birth registration	9.6	1.9
Armenia	114.0	2012–2013	Birth registration	3.0	1.7
Georgia	108.0	2012–2015	Birth registration	4.3	1.8
SOUTHEAST EUROPE					
Albania	109.0	2012–2013	Birth registration	3.2	1.8
Kosovo	110.4	2011–2013	Birth registration	1.8	2.3
Northwest Macedonia[d]	110.4	2009–2013	Birth registration	0.3	1.5
Montenegro	109.0	2009–2013	Birth registration	0.6	1.7

Source: Adapted from Guilmoto, 2015, p. 186.

Notes
a Population and fertility figures are based on UN Population Division and the World Bank data (see Guilmoto, 2015, p. 186).
b Estimated total population in millions in 2015.
c Average number of children per woman in 2010–2015.
d Northwest Macedonia corresponds to the region of Polog, the fertility rate has been estimated.

data; variations may exist at the regional and local level. It is further important to mention that the table includes data on countries where SRB is distorted on the national level. This does not mean, however, that prenatal sex selection does not occur elsewhere. Bongaarts (2013, p. 204) states that the phenomenon of son preference is even more widespread than has been known until now and, as outlined by Irshad and Werner-Felmayer (2016, pp. 499–500), demand for assisted reproduction could increase in other countries such as Pakistan. As explained in their study analyzing websites of providers of assisted reproduction in Pakistan, preconception and preimplantation sex selection is already being offered for nonmedical reasons. The availability of the service is increasing without any legal regulations in place. In the context of a patriarchal and son preferring society, sex-selective abortion of girls and distorted SRB could have future consequences in the country (Irshad and Werner-Felmayer, 2016, p. 501). Prenatal sex selection is becoming an issue even in countries with no previous history of the phenomenon.

As can be seen in Table 10.2 prenatal sex selection is also influenced by the sex of the preceding child. It can be assumed that when the first child is a girl, the felt need for a son increases even more and intervention through selective abortion occurs in son preferring societies. This is particularly true for China, Armenia, and Georgia. Due to a lack of data, figures for India are not presented in the table. It is assumed, however, that distortions of SRB of higher order births are increasing to a similar extent.

The consequences of sex selection in the context of son preference are multifold. Continuing discrimination, violence, and health issues are main concerns. Girls who are born into son preferring societies are at risk of suffering violence and discrimination in many areas of their lives. Limited access to nutrition, education, and health care are further examples of potential consequences. Sex selection not only discriminates against girls and women but also further deepens gender inequality in society at large (Liisanantti and Beese, 2012, p. 10). Prenatal sex selection violates women's rights and has

Table 10.2 Sex Ratio at Birth by Parity in Different Countries

Country	1st Birth	2nd Birth	3rd And Higher Birth
Armenia (2008–2012)	106.5	110.5	162.4
China (2010)	113.7	130.3	158.4
South Korea (2012)	105.3	104.9	109.2
Georgia (2006–2012)	108.3	108.9	130.5
Taiwan (2012)	106.8	107.1	112.4
Vietnam (2009)	110.2	109.0	115.5

Source: See Guilmoto, 2015, p. 202.

threatened the achievement of the Millennium Development Goals (MDGs), in particular goal 3 ("Promote Gender Equality and Empower Women") and goal 4 ("Reduce Child Mortality"). It continues to negatively affect the striving for the Sustainable Development Goals (SDGs) that were adopted in September 2015 and should be achieved by 2030 (United Nations General Assembly, 2015). In general, one might assume that in societies with a lack of females, the status of women increases. However, this has not been observed so far. Quite to the contrary, as the prevalence of prenatal sex selection increases, the status of men, and particularly of those who are considered to have control over women (e.g., father, brother, husband) also increases. Furthermore, due to the rise in dowry payments, the risk for kidnapping and trafficking increases (Hesketh and Xing, 2006, p. 13274).

The negative health consequences of prenatal sex selection must not be underestimated. The lower status of women and the procedure of sex selection have negative health effects on women in general due to repeated abortions and the placement of psychological pressure on women to "produce" sons (Stump, 2011), impeding women's rights to reproductive freedom (WHO, 2002, pp. 160–162). Men, on the other hand, may also face health and psychological problems living in son preferring societies. Boys who were born because of their male sex may suffer from psychological disorders as the selection involves "inappropriate control over nonessential characteristics" (WHO, 2017b). This can impinge on the identity of male children and puts them under pressure later in life as they face high expectations by their family.

Whereas more than a decade ago the potential consequences of a surplus of men was still somewhat speculative (Hesketh and Xing, 2006, p. 13273), China for example is now experiencing a surplus of 32 million men below the age of 20 (Hesketh, Lu, and Xing, 2011). It is apparent that regions with a surplus of 12–15% young men, who will most likely be unable to marry even though marriage is considered necessary for social acceptance, will result in challenges for the overall society. The lack of women therefore leaves a considerable number of men in singlehood contrary to their potential desire or the social expectation to get married. Men with lower social status and those living in rural areas are especially affected. The so-called "marriage squeeze" is estimated to increase further in the near future (Hudson and Den Boer, 2007, p. 20). It needs to be mentioned at this point, however, that the "lack of brides" cannot solely be attributed to son preference and sex selection. Decreasing fertility rates and a shift in the marriage culture in Asian countries (e.g., women migrating to urban areas, and women—often those with high levels of education—consciously deciding against marriage) are also contributing toward the marriage squeeze (Westley and Choe, 2007, p. 8).

However, especially in societies with strong patriarchal structures, increases in commercial sex and violent practices involving coercion can be consequences if sexual needs cannot be met through more conventional avenues (Hesketh and Xing, 2006, p. 13273). Further, the risk of violence and trafficking, particularly with regard to bride trafficking and bride sharing, increases (Liisanantti and Beese, 2012; Stump, 2011). Cross-border marriage arrangements have increased in the affected regions in the last three decades (Kim, Yun, Park, and Williams, 2009, pp. 162–166; Le Bach, Bélanger, and Khuat, 2007, p. 394). Scientific evidence is lacking regarding trafficking in girls and women, and little is known about its real dimension, as only a few studies have been conducted so far. Vietnam, for example, has been found to be one of the transit and source countries for bride trafficking, with China as one of the main destination countries (Le Bach et al., 2007, p. 397). Also North Korean women have been bride trafficking victims to China as was found in a case study conducted by Kim et al. (2009). This extreme form of coercion and exploitation also shows the international dimension of the consequences of prenatal sex selection and makes clear that the issue cannot be understood as an isolated issue of nation states. Trafficking related to sex selection and demographic imbalance cannot be underestimated.

Migration in general is shaping the landscape of son preference and prenatal sex selection in the globalized world. Few studies have been conducted so far analyzing sex selecting behavior among migrant communities with son preferring backgrounds. An analysis of birth statistics in England and Wales has identified a slight increase in SRB of children whose mothers were born in India, especially among higher order births (Dubuc and Coleman, 2007). Ambrosetti, Ortensi, Castagnaro, and Attili (2015) found that SRB is skewed for children of migrants from China, India, and Albania who are now living in Italy and SRB of higher-order births shows even greater disparities. Comparable results were also found in Canada, where the sex ratio for third births to Vietnamese, Chinese, and Korean immigrants who already had two daughters was almost 1.4, and for migrants of Indian origin, this ratio was 1.9 (Vogel, 2012). Furthermore, a study by Almond and Sun (2017) analyzing US census data found elevated SRB for second and higher order births in the absence of a previous male child among families of Asian offspring. For the years of 2011 until 2013, the first two live births to Chinese, Asian Indian, and Korean parents had sex ratios ranging between 1.06 and 1.08, increasing to 1.14 and 1.16 for the third and fourth child (Almond and Sun, 2017, p. 22). However, this sex composition pattern might be attenuated, since isolated data for Korean-Americans shows an absence of sex selection in favor of boys. The data further does not provide insights as to how sex selection has taken place. However, 1.4% of Asian births between 2011 and 2013 were a result of assisted reproductive technology (ART) with sex ratios of 1.13 among Asian Indians, Koreans, and Chinese (Almond and Sun, 2017, p. 22). This suggests that pre-implantation sex-selection technologies are used in the context of assisted reproduction and it further raises the assumption that if technology is available, accessible, and used, prenatal sex selection may be performed through pre-implantation rather than through selective abortion. In general, however, the data shows that son preference is a deeply entrenched pattern and that sex-selective practices cross borders through migration.

Medical and reproductive tourism as well as access to technology add another dimension to the son preference and sex selection dilemma. Medical travel for the purpose of assisted reproduction offers new opportunities for individuals and couples to access sex selection services irrespective of the legal regulations in the home country. Chinese individuals traveling to Hong Kong in order to access sex selection services is just one example (Eklund and Purewal, 2017, p. 42). But also the absence of regulation of prenatal genetic diagnosis (PGD) in the United States for example, could be an incentive for couples undergoing assisted reproduction to seek sex selection services in the country and of course also allows the local population to access the service (Bayefsky, 2017). Affordability, however, may still be a hindering factor. But, prices to undergo PGD are decreasing at the same time that access to other technologies is improving.

Migration and medical travel may also bring about positive change. Even though globalization offers opportunities to undergo sex selection as described before, it also enables an exchange of ideas across cultures and provides insights to different viewpoints which can be beneficial toward the achievement of gender equality and increase women's social status in society. In her article "Integrating Equality: Globalization, Women's Rights, and Human Trafficking", Cho (2013) evaluates whether globalization can improve the rights of women. She argues that economic globalization alone does not improve women's status in society, however, social globalization, which can be defined as cultural sharing, personal contacts, and flow of information across borders, is an important indicator for women's rights and it helps to empower women.

Due to the complex set of driving factors and implications mentioned earlier, and the potential of expanding to other countries, bioethical consequences of prenatal sex selection exist. The following may not be understood as a complete bioethical analysis but should rather provide insights to the complexity of the issue to initiate further discussions. The Human Genome and Human Rights Declaration (1997), the Declaration on Human Genetic Data (2003), the Convention on Human Rights and Biomedicine (Oviedo Convention), and the Universal Declaration on Bioethics and Human Rights (UNESCO, 2005) (adopted by UNESCO in 2005) provide international frameworks for the handling of (bio)ethically sensitive issues. Beauchamp and Childress (2009) have considerably shaped the definition and framework of bioethics. In their standard work *Principles of Biomedical Ethics*

(2009) they outline several equally important principles: respect for autonomy, non-maleficence, beneficence, and justice.

Autonomy refers to conscious, informed and independent decision making
without manipulation or control of external parties (Beauchamp and Childress, 2009, pp. 99–100). Both liberty and agency are important criteria to
achieve autonomy. As Blyth, Frith, and Crawshaw (2008, p. 41) outline in
their ethical analysis of sex selection for non-medical reasons, supporters of
the practice often employ the argument of "reproductive autonomy." Parents
should be allowed to choose the sex of their future child to the same extent as
they are allowed if or when to have children and how many. As long as no
serious harm has been caused, this autonomy may not be restricted by policies. However, a more nuanced definition of harm is missing in this context.
Does harm solely affect the child who will (not) be born based on its sex? In
the context of this chapter, the definition of harm must be seen in a broader,
societal context. "Autonomy" refers to the freedom of choice. A study conducted by UNFPA (2012) on "the prevalence of and reasons for sex-selective
abortions in Armenia" found that more than 80% of the pregnant women
made the decision themselves to have a sex-selective abortion. These women
had the capacity to act, but in how far these decisions were made on a completely voluntary basis remains up for discussion. Societal and familial pressure to "produce sons" may impact autonomous choices. The same applies to
women and couples in other son preferring cultures. Whether women make
autonomous choices when undergoing sex-selective abortions would require
further intervention and studies. It can be assumed, however, that even
though these decisions may be made consciously and in an informed way, the
women choosing sex-selective abortion may still not be fully free regarding
the potential negative social, economic, and other consequences when having
a girl child. The question of whether reproductive autonomy applies in
complex son preferring contexts needs further discussion.

Avoiding damage and harm and contributing toward people's health and
wellbeing are the very basic notions of the principles of non-maleficence and
beneficence (Beauchamp and Childress, 2009, pp. 149–152). The potential
damage that son preference and sex selection can cause has been addressed
earlier in this chapter, with negative implications for girls and women, men,
 and the overall society. Yet it also needs to be highlighted that women are the
ones who must bear the immediate health and emotional consequences of sex
selection by undergoing (potentially numerous) abortions to give birth to a
son, and women's responsibility to take care of family planning and to control
family size puts them under immense pressure (Harutyunyan, 2013, p. 148).
To address the principles of benefit and harm from another perspective, it
would be valuable to examine whether the potential intention to protect
daughters from future violence in male dominated societies, by not giving

No further endangers other women

birth to them, can be used as an argument for the prevention of harm by undergoing sex selection. And, finally, considering the principle of justice, which deals with fair allocation of rights and duties (Beauchamp and Childress, 2009, pp. 241–244), issues related to gender equality arise. Discrimination against girls and women, and the manifested violation of their human rights is at the core of the discussion around justice and prenatal sex selection in son preferring societies (WHO, 2011).

Addressing Prenatal Sex Selection

Influencing people's reproductive choices inevitably leads to the intersectional concepts of biopower and biopolitics, as shaped by Foucault (2008), and which relate to nation states and the techniques they use to manage populations and to administer and govern life. The French philosopher, social theorist, and historian was the first to introduce the concepts in his lecture series at Collège de France and defined them as "power over bodies" and "power over life" respectively; reproduction being a crucial aspect. The structural circumstances driving son preference suggest intervention in a field that has been considered a private issue in the past. As Sándor (2013, p. 3) argues "there is a widespread tendency in the world to regulate the most private sphere of our individual lives: reproduction." When it comes to son preference and sex selection, biopower and biopolitics have not only played a role in providing conditions for the development of the phenomenon through population control and family planning policies but have also been used as instruments to reverse the trend of distorted sex ratios through the regulation of access to health care and technology (e.g., prohibition of sex determination and/or abortion). A few country specific examples will be outlined in the following.

Policy regulations can have strong impacts on reproductive choices and demography as can be seen from the example of the One Child Policy in China. The policy, which was introduced in 1979—and which was replaced by a universal two-child policy in 2015—has contributed to a large extent to decreasing fertility rates in the country and to increasing rates of sex-selective abortions (Eklund and Purewal, 2017, p. 38; Zeng and Hesketh, 2016). As strictly only one child was allowed in urban areas, selecting for sex with the first pregnancy was more common. In rural areas, however, a second child was allowed if the first one was a girl. Hesketh and Xing (2006, p. 13272) argue that "when fertility rates are low, by choice or coercion, female births must be prevented to allow for the desired number of sons within the family size norm." The policy was certainly not the sole driver for gender-biased sex-selective abortions in China, but the compulsory small family size together with a strong preference for sons and the availability of the technology contributed to prevalence of the procedure. However, the potential future problem of sex selection and distorted sex ratios led to the prohibition of pre-natal diagnosis—with the exception of diagnosing hereditary diseases—in the mid 1980s. The criminalization of sex determination and selective abortion took place in 1994 (Eklund and Purewal, 2017, p. 40). A variety of measures including awareness raising campaigns, introducing health and support ser-vices, improved reporting systems, and better management of sex determina-tion and selection, were implemented to reverse the trend of demographic imbalance. However, these actions were not successful in sustainably strengthening gender equality (Eklund and Purewal, 2017, p. 41; see Kosten-zer, 2016). As Eklund and Purewal (2017, p. 42) outline, the "bio-politicization" of sex-selective abortion is deepening as the Chinese government has recently introduced several new measures, as for example a reward system for informants and fines for couples and organizations under-going or performing sex determination or selection which is considered medi-cally unnecessary.

India, as well, has a long history of family planning initiatives, including birth control and forced sterilization and small family size was promoted in similar ways as in China. While population growth dropped overall, some families still decided to have a higher number of children to ensure survival of sons. Increasing access to technology also offered parents in rural areas the option to undergo sex selection, reducing the number of children and trans-forming postnatal sex selection, termed "female infanticide," into prenatal sex selection or "female feticide." In India, sex determination and selection was banned in the 1990s. Further measures included awareness raising campaigns, incentives like conditional-cash transfer programs to raise girl children, and the criminalization of sex selection (Eklund and Purewal, 2017, pp. 44–45).

To provide a further example, in Armenia abortion has been legal since 1955 and has been used as a tool for population control. Abortion always played a role in terms of controlling fertility due to the absence of or refusal to use contraceptives. Particularly, married women have used abortions to control family size and sex-selective abortion has been used primarily on higher order births, as for example in case of the third or fourth child. However, the number of abortions and fertility rates have declined rapidly in the last couple of years; the abortion rate per woman has dropped from 2.6 in the year 2000 to 0.8 in 2010 with a fertility rate of 1.7 in the same year (Harutyunyan, 2013, pp. 145–146). Meanwhile, the Armenian government has started to take action against son preference and sex selection in the country and has cooperated with the UNFPA on a variety of measures includ-ing data collection (UNFPA, 2012).

Many other countries have started to act to prevent prenatal sex selection in the future; Albania, Georgia, and Vietnam amongst them. South Korea has been mentioned in literature as a best practice example in terms of reversing the trend of distorted SRB (Chung and Das Gupta, 2007; Ganatra, 2008; WHO, 2011). However, holistic monitoring and evaluation of the implemented measures have not taken place so far, which makes an evidence-based judgement of the actual success of the programs difficult.

In terms of addressing son preference and prenatal sex selection on an international level, the UNFPA has been a driving force for the past 20 years and has developed a variety of measures together with governments of affected states. In 2011, the UNFPA in cooperation with the Office of the United Nations High Commissioner for Human Rights (OHCHR), the United Nations Children's Fund (UNICEF), UN Women, and the WHO released the first Interagency Statement "Preventing Gender-biased Sex Selection" (WHO, 2011). In addition, the Council of Europe declared sex selection as a practice "which finds its roots in culture of gender inequality and reinforces a climate of violence against women" and condemns the practice in its Resolution 1829: Prenatal Sex Selection (Parliamentary Assembly Council of Europe, 2011). Many other organizations and policy makers have joined this approach and numerous studies have been published. Quite recently, in March 2017, the first Global Program to Prevent Son Preference and Gender-Biased Sex Selection was launched by the UNFPA and financially supported by the European Union (UNFPA, 2017). In cooperation with governments of Armenia, Azerbaijan, Bangladesh, Georgia, Nepal, and Vietnam, this program aims at gathering evidence and addressing the root causes of prenatal sex selection to raise the value and status of girls and women in society.

What becomes clear from outlining the various causes and consequences of sex selection, and from taking an interdisciplinary perspective, is that rather than solely addressing symptoms of gender-biased prenatal sex selection, it is important to address the root cause—gender inequality and the lower status of women in society. As Goodkind (1999, p. 59) argues, measures to address the issue should be used and implemented wisely, so that the agendas which have been agreed upon at the International Conference on Population and Development (ICPD) in Cairo in 1994, enabling gender equality and reproductive freedom at the same time, are not harmed. Having in mind the policies on the national and international level to address the issue of son preference and prenatal sex selection, this seems to be the biggest challenge. Reproductive technologies offer great opportunities, but isolated regulatory approaches and perspectives may cause unintended effects. The future will show if and to what extent trends of distorted SRB can be reversed and how far the status of girls and women can be raised allowing for equal rights and equal opportunities. Societal change in terms of cultural practices remains a challenging yet crucial factor to prevent gender-biased prenatal sex selection in the future.

References

Almond, D., and Sun, Y. (2017). Son-biased sex ratios in 2010 US Census and 2011–2013 US natality data. *Social Science and Medicine, 176*, pp. 21–24. Available at: https://doi.org/10.1016/j.socscimed.2016.12.038.

Ambrosetti, E., Ortensi, L. E., Castagnaro, C., and Attili, M. (2015). Sex imbalances at birth in migratory context: Evidence from Italy. *GENUS Journal of Population Sciences, 71*(2–3), pp. 29–51. Available at: https://doi.org/10.4402/genus-677.

Barot, S. (2012). A problem-and-solution mismatch: Son preference and sex-selective abortion bans. *Guttmacher Policy Review, 15*(2), pp. 18–22.

Bayefsky, M. J. (2017). Comparative preimplantation genetic diagnosis policy in Europe and the USA and its implications for reproductive tourism. *Reproductive Biomedicine and Society Online*, pp. 1–7. Available at: https://doi.org/10.1016/j.rbms.2017.01.001.

Beauchamp, T. L., and Childress, J. F. (2009). *Principles of Biomedical Ethics* (6th ed.). New York: Oxford University Press.

Blyth, E., Frith, L., and Crawshaw, M. (2008). Ethical objections to sex selection for non-medical reasons. *Reproductive BioMedicine Online, 16*, pp. 41–45. Available at: https://doi.org/10.1016/S1472-6483(10)60398-7.

Bongaarts, J. (2013). The implementation of preferences for male offspring. *Population and Development Review, 39*(2), pp. 185–208. Available at: https://doi.org/10.1111/j.1728-4457.2013.00588.x.

Cho, S.-Y. (2013). Integrating equality: Globalization, women's rights, and human trafficking. *International Studies Quarterly, 57*(4), pp. 683–697. Available at: https://doi.org/10.1111/isqu.12056.

Chung, W., and Das Gupta, M. (2007). *Why is Son Preference Declining in South Korea? The Role of Development and Public Policy, and the Implications for China and India.* Washington: The World Bank.

Das Gupta, M., Zhenghua, J., Bohua, L., Zhenming, X., Chung, W., and Hwa-Ok, B. (2003). Why is son preference so persistent in East and South Asia? A cross-country study of China, India and the Republic of Korea. *Journal of Development Studies, 40*(2), pp. 153–187. Available at: https://doi.org/10.1080/00220380412331293807.

Dubuc, S., and Coleman, D. (2007). An increase in the sex ratio of births to India-born mothers in England and Wales: Evidence for sex-selective abortion. *Population and Development Review, 33*(2), pp. 383–400. Available at: https://doi.org/10.1111/j.1728-4457.2007.00173.x.

Eklund, L., and Purewal, N. (2017). The bio-politics of population control and sex-selective abortion in China and India. *Feminism and Psychology, 27*(1), pp. 34–55. Available at: https://doi.org/10.1177/0959353516682262.

Foucault, M. (2008). *The Birth of Biopolitics: Lectures at the Collège de France 1978–1979.* New York: Palgrave Macmillan.

Ganatra, B. (2008). Maintaining access to safe abortion and reducing sex ratio imbalances in Asia. *Reproductive Health Matters, 16*(supp.31), pp. 90–98. Available at: https://doi.org/10.1016/S0968-8080(08)31394-9.

General Electric. (2009). *Promoting ethical ultrasound use in India* [pdf]. Available at: http://files.gecompany.com/gecom/citizenship/pdfs/ge_ethical_ultrasound_use_india_case study.pdf.

Goodkind, D. (1999). Should prenatal sex selection be restricted? Ethical questions and their implications for research and policy. *Population Studies, 53*(1), pp. 49–61. Available at: https://doi.org/10.1080/00324720308069.

Guilmoto, C. Z. (2009). The sex ratio transition in Asia. *Population and Development Review, 35*(3), pp. 519–549. Available at: https://doi.org/10.1111/j.1728-4457.2009.00295.x.

Guilmoto, C. Z. (2012). Skewed sex ratios at birth and future marriage squeeze in China and India, 2005–2100. *Demography, 49*(1), pp. 77–100. Available at: https://doi.org/10.1007/s13524-011-0083-7.

Guilmoto, C. Z. (2015). The masculinization of births: Overview and current knowledge. *Population, 70*(2), pp. 185–243. Available at: https://doi.org/10.3917/popu.1502.0201.

Harutyunyan, S. (2013). Sex selective abortions in Armenia: Between gender issues, economic crises, and body politics. In J. Sándor (Ed.), *Studies in Biopolitics*, pp. 141–148. Budapest: Center for Ethics and Law in Biomedicine.

Hesketh, T., and Xing, Z. W. (2006). Abnormal sex ratios in human populations: Causes and consequences. *Proceedings of the National Academy of Sciences of the United States of America, 103*(36), pp. 13271–13275. Available at: https://doi.org/10.1073/pnas.0602203103.

Hesketh, T., Lu, L., and Xing, Z. W. (2011). The consequences of son preference and sex-selective abortion in China and other Asian countries. *Canadian Medical Association Journal, 183*(12), pp. 1374–1377. Available at: https://doi.org/10.1503/cmaj.101368.

Hudson, V. M., and Den Boer, A. M. (2007). Bare branches and security in Asia. *Harvard Asia Pacific Review*, pp. 18–20.

Irshad, A., and Werner-Felmayer, G. (2016). An ethical analysis of assisted reproduction providers' websites in Pakistan. *Cambridge Quarterly of Healthcare Ethics, 25*(3), pp. 497–504. Available at: https://doi.org/10.1017/S0963180116000141.

Kim, E., Yun, M., Park, M., and Williams, H. (2009). Cross border North Korean women trafficking and victimization between North Korea and China: An ethnographic case study. *International Journal of Law, Crime and Justice, 37*(4), pp. 154–169. Available at: https://doi.org/10.1016/j.ijlcj.2009.10.001.

Kostenzer, J. (2016). Eliminating prenatal sex selection? *Global Studies Journal, 9*(2), pp. 41–52. Available at: https://doi.org/10.18848/1835-4432/CGP/v09i02/41-52.

Le Bach, D., Bélanger, D., and Khuat, T. H. (2007). Transnational migration, marriage and trafficking at the China-Vietnam Border. In I. Attané and C. Z. Guilmoto (Eds.), *Watering the Neighbour's Garden. The Growing Demographic Female Deficit in Asia*, pp. 393–425. Paris: CICRED.

Liisanantti, A., and Beese, K. (2012). *Gendercide: The Missing Women?* Brussels: European Union.

Mani, S. (2012). Guidelines for ultrasound owners and owners of clinics, diagnostic centres, nursing homes and hospitals. *Indian Journal of Radiology and Imaging, 22*(2), pp. 125–128. Available at: https://doi.org/10.4103/0971-3026.101102.

Parliamentary Assembly Council of Europe. (2011). Resolution 1829: Prenatal sex selection.

Sándor, J. (Ed.). (2013). *Studies in Biopolitics*. Budapest: Center for Ethics and Law in Biomedicine.

Sen, A. (1990). *More than 100 million women are missing* [online]. Available at: www.nybooks.com/articles/1990/12/20/more-than-100-million-women-are-missing.

Stump, D. (2011). Doc. 12715: Prenatal sex selection. Parliamentary Assembly, Strasbourg.

UNESCO (United Nations Educational, Scientific, and Cultural Organization). (2005). Universal Declaration on Bioethics and Human Rights.

UNFPA (United Nations Population Fund). (2012). *Report: Prevalence of and reasons for sex-selective abortions in Armenia* [pdf]. Available at: http://eeca.unfpa.org/sites/default/files/pub-pdf/Sex-selective_abortions_report_Eng.pdf.

UNFPA (United Nations Population Fund). (2017). *Gender-biased sex selection* [online]. Available at: www.unfpa.org/gender-biased-sex-selection.

United Nations General Assembly. (2015). Transforming our world: The 2030 Agenda for Sustainable Development. A/RES/70/1.

Vogel, L. (2012). Sex selection migrates to Canada. *CMAJ: Canadian Medical Association Journal/journal de l'Association medicale canadienne*, *184*(3), pp. 163–164. Available at: https://doi.org/10.1503/cmaj.109-4091.

Westley, S. B., and Choe, M. K. (2007). How does son preference affect populations in Asia? *Asia Pacific*, *84*, pp. 1–12.

WHO (World Health Organization). (2002). *Genomics and world health: Report of the advisory committee on health research*. Geneva.

WHO (World Health Organization). (2011). *Preventing gender-biased sex selection: An interagency statement OHCHR, UNFPA, UNICEF, UN Women and WHO*. Geneva.

WHO (World Health Organization). (2017a). *Gender and genetics: Assisted reproductive technologies (ARTs)* [online]. Available at: www.who.int/genomics/gender/en/index6. html.

WHO (World Health Organization). (2017b). *Gender and genetics: Sex selection and discrimination* [online]. Available at: www.who.int/genomics/gender/en/index4.html.

Zeng, Y., and Hesketh, T. (2016). The effects of China's universal two-child policy. *Lancet*, *388*(10054), pp. 1930–1938. Available at: https://doi.org/10.1016/S0140-6736(16) 31405-2.

11

PROVINCIALIZING INTERSEX

U.S. INTERSEX ACTIVISM, HUMAN RIGHTS, AND TRANSNATIONAL BODY POLITICS
DAVID A. RUBIN

> Do we really need to change some children to make them human
> enough to get human rights?
>
> (Alice Dreger, 2006, p. 79)

How are debates about intersex—an umbrella term for individuals born with "atypical" sex characteristics[1]—shaped by the politics of difference and struggles for sexual and gender justice in a multicultural, transnational world? How do activist and academic critiques of the medicalization of "bodies in doubt" rearticulate the meaning and materiality of human rights in a neoliberal landscape (Reis, 2012)? How do geopolitics, colonial legacies, consumer citizenship, and biopower inform and mitigate contemporary intersex politics? And how might transnational feminist perspectives contribute to a critical rethinking of the local and global travels and trajectories of the intersex movement?

In the space opened up by these questions, this chapter explores how U.S. debates about intersex are shaped, challenged, and interrupted by global activism and transnational feminist perspectives.[2] Acknowledging that the term "transnational feminism" is contested (Fernandes, 2013), I employ it here as "an intersectional set of understandings, tools, and practices" that can attend "to racialized, classed, masculinized, and heteronormative logics and practices of globalization and capitalist patriarchies, and the multiple ways in which they (re)structure colonial and neocolonial relations of domination and subordination" (Nagar and Swarr, 2010, p. 5). Transnational feminisms both draw from and are aligned with other traditions of feminist praxis (including postcolonial, women of color, indigenous, materialist, queer, and poststructuralist feminisms). Challenging "monological and monocausal approaches to subjectivity and power" (Soto, 2011, p. 1) and refusing "colonial logics of similitude" (Barlow, 1998, p. 119), they do not presume that all sexed/ gendered subjects around the globe are essentially the same, or that sex/ gender is separable from other axes of difference (Fausto-Sterling, 2012).[3] Transnational feminist perspectives are therefore distinct from, and adopt a critical stance toward, cosmopolitan and internationalist celebrations of "global sisterhood." Furthermore, they do not view capitalist globalization's cross-border flows (of people, goods, capital, and information) as either inherently liberatory or exclusively exploitative. Instead, transnational feminist analytics focalize the shifting, unstable, but vital interdependencies between nation-states, political economies, social formations, and subjects—revealing these entities to be fundamentally contested, non-natural, non-identical across space and time, and laced with contradictions (Briggs et al., 2008). Recognizing that "there is no such thing as a feminism free of asymmetrical power relations," transnational feminisms "involve forms of alliance, subversion and complicity within which asymmetries and inequalities can be critiqued" (Kaplan and Grewal, 2002, p. 73).

I utilize transnational feminist perspectives to argue that U.S.-based intersex advocacy risks reiterating structures of U.S. and global northern dominance when it does not self-reflexively interrogate its own politics of location in relation to transnational histories of imperialism, neoliberalism, and biopower. In her reading of Adrienne Rich's influential concept of the "politics of location," Caren Kaplan argues that practicing ethical accountability in transnational contexts requires acknowledging "the historical roles of mediation, betrayal, and alliance in the relationships between" various subjects in diverse locations (1996, p. 169). Drawing on Kaplan's intervention, I investigate how human rights discourse, colonial legacies, biopolitics, and neoliberal ideologies contour the locational politics of U.S. intersex activism. I do so by examining a crucial event in the history of the Intersex Society of North America (ISNA), an advocacy group that became, during the tenure of its existence (1993–2008), the most highly visible and influential intersex activist organization in the world: ISNA's failed attempt to lobby for the inclusion of intersex surgery in the U.S. Congress's 1997 federal ban on "female genital mutilation" (FGM).

I contend that transnational feminist perspectives provide indispensable tools for analyzing the politics of location of U.S. intersex activism and, ultimately, for provincializing and decolonizing the intersex imaginary. I use the term "intersex imaginary" to refer to shared yet situated ways of imagining intersex bodies (Perez, 1999). The intersex imaginary is a site of political struggle and contestation. U.S. and Western understandings of intersex are historically and geopolitically particular, not universal. In the English language, for instance, the term *intersex* assumes an analytic separation between sex, gender, and sexual orientation that is not indigenous to many cultures around the globe (Stryker and Currah, 2014, pp. 303–304). For this reason, articulations of the intersex imaginary can falsely universalize Western narratives of intersex consciousness, personhood, and political organizing as paradigmatic, misrecognizing different configurations of embodiment and subjectivity as nascent reflections of a universal intersex identity. The potential imperialism of constructing the intersex imaginary in U.S./Euro-centric ways can be countered by provincializing that imaginary, a project with de-colonial motivations (Chakrabarty, 2008). This project begins with the recognition that colonialism lives on in the history of the present in myriad ways: in the processes of white settler colonialism that established the U.S. government's territorial control of native lands and resources; in the uneven and unequal distribution of life chances under globalization; and in ongoing practices of U.S. and Western political and economic intervention in international affairs. Provincializing the intersex imaginary involves connecting ways of thinking about intersex bodies to these histories—in short, to specific times and places. It entails critiquing the geopolitical over-determination of U.S. and Western understandings of intersex as they circulate globally and are transformed and sometimes called into question in the process. The project of provincializing intersex reveals that the imprinting of place upon conceptions of intersex embodiment has crucial but under-interrogated implications for transnational struggles for corporeal freedom.

The first section of this chapter tracks the global rise of the concept of intersex human rights. The second section synthesizes transnational feminist perspectives on human rights. And the third section analyzes ISNA's lobbying efforts around intersex surgery and FGM. Through these analyses, I show that transnational feminist perspectives offer new ways of understanding the local and global effects and implications of intersex activism. Concurrently, I argue that the transnational regulation of sexed bodies occurs not only through the globalization of Western biomedical conceptions of sex/gender normativity, but also through global circulations of human rights discourse and impositions of U.S. neoliberal democratic frames of subjectivity.

Recently, these frames have been rearticulated anew in two interrelated developments: the hegemonic Western biomedical shift to replace *intersex* with the term Disorders of Sex Development (DSD) and the rise of the paradigm of patient-centered care. Some American and European intersex/DSD advocates flag these developments as particularly progressive strategies for prompting medical reform in ways that protect patients' human rights.

I therefore conclude by suggesting that provincializing intersex requires rethinking the imbrication of these strategies in Western imperial formations and neoliberal logics.

Intersex Human Rights

Over the past two decades, intersex became a "human rights issue," as one ISNA press release put it in 2005 (ISNA, 2005). The press release asserts "that the standard medical approach to intersex conditions leads pediatric specialists to violate their patients' human rights." Cheryl Chase, the longtime Executive Director of ISNA, is quoted in the press release as saying that intersex people

> deserve the same basic human rights as others ... No longer should we be lied to, displayed, be injected with hormones for questionable purposes, and have our genitals cut to alleviate the anxieties of parents and doctors. Doctors' good intentions are not enough. Practices must now change.
>
> (ISNA, 2005)

Chase's impassioned remarks foreground the high stakes of contestations over the medical treatment of intersex people. They also prefigure a handful of contemporary events from around the globe that highlight the growing transnational circulation of the notion of intersex human rights.

According to Julie A. Greenberg (2012), who draws on insights from feminist and LGBT jurisprudence, legal institutions have the potential to play a significant role in protecting the rights of intersex people. As I discuss elsewhere (Rubin, 2017), in 1999 Colombia became the first country in the world to use human rights as a ground for imposing legal regulations on intersex genital surgery. In 2000, in recognition of ISNA's influence (on the Constitutional Court of Colombia's decisions and in other arenas), the International Lesbian and Gay Human Rights Commission awarded ISNA the Felipa de Souza Award for making "significant contributions toward securing the human rights and freedoms of sexual minorities anywhere in the world" (ISNA, 2000). In the years following, international awareness about and media interest in intersex continued to increase, thanks in large part to the work of ISNA and other intersex alliances.

In 2005 and 2011 respectively, the San Francisco Human Rights Commission and the European Network of Legal Experts published critical reports on the stigmatization and medical normalization of intersex people (Arana, 2005; European Network of Legal Experts, 2011). In 2013 highly visible international figures and associations including the UN Special Rapporteur on Torture, the Inter-American Commission on Human Rights, the

Australian Senate, and the 3rd International Intersex Forum all issued statements opposing nonconsensual genital normalization surgery and other human rights abuses faced by intersex people (Dreger, 2013; Organization of American States, 2013). That same year, Australia passed an amendment that prohibits discrimination on the basis of intersex status, and Germany became the first country in Europe to allow parents of newborns without "clear gender-determining physical characteristics" not to register them as either male or female, but to choose a third blank box instead (Australian Parliament, 2013; Nandl, 2013; Agius et al., 2013).[4] Also in 2013, the Heinrich Boll Foundation published a groundbreaking report by Dan Christian Ghattas, a representative of Organisation Intersex International (OII) (Ghattas, 2013). Based on a survey of intersex individuals from 12 selected countries in the global south and east as well as Europe, Ghattas's report provides indisputable evidence of discrimination against intersex people and describes the needs of intersex activist organizations in these countries. Additionally, in 2013 a lawsuit was filed in South Carolina that sought to challenge medically unnecessary sex-assignment surgery done on a 16-month-old child with an intersex condition (Bennett-Smith, 2013). This case—the first of its kind in the United States—was rejected by the Court of Appeals for the Fourth Circuit, but a state lawsuit filed by the child's family against the Greenville Medical System and the Medical University of South Carolina was settled out of court in 2017. The settlement came the same week as the publication of a report by Human Rights Watch, in partnership with InterACT, condemning unnecessary intersex genital surgeries (Ghorayshi, 2017).

In what follows I do not explore these specific developments, but I cite them here to call attention to the uneven and escalating transnational momentum of intersex human rights activism. Instead, I analyze events that took place in an earlier phase of the intersex movement, the late 1990s, a period when the local and global trajectories of intersex activism were initially being charted. I focus on ISNA not only because it was the first intersex activist association in the world, but also because this organization was the first to realize the strategic potential of the discourse of human rights as a medium of political articulation for addressing intersex issues. My analysis does not imply that other intersex activist organizations have not been influential, or that the examination of the strategies of those organizations, which both converge and diverge with those of ISNA, is any less important. Rather, analyzing ISNA's early activism through a transnational feminist lens offers valuable historical insight into the contemporary possibilities and limitations of grounding intersex advocacy in a human rights framework.

Transnational Feminist Perspectives on Human Rights

Celebratory accounts of human rights proliferate in the current era. However, framing human rights solely as a positive political achievement—as a protective shield from the intrusion of unjust exercises of power—risks obscuring the ways in which human rights also materialize unequal juridical, political, and socioeconomic relationships. Transnational feminist critiques thus draw attention to human rights as double edged. Recourse to human rights has undoubtedly enabled many oppressed groups (including women, sexual, racial, ethnic, and religious minorities, stateless peoples, and people with disabilities) to challenge exclusionary and unjust institutions and practices. Yet, although human rights instruments have empowered multiple marginalized constituencies around the globe, the moral universalism and U.S.-/Euro-centrism of human rights tends to erase important differences among and between various political subjects (Grewal, 2005, p. 121). By reducing power relations to a stark narrative of "us" versus "them," victims versus victimizers, human-rights narratives are intrinsically exclusionary: they forget that different subjects arise through different histories and forms of power, and that they may have different political desires and different conceptions of justice (Abu-Lughod, 2002, pp. 783–790). Moreover, such narratives oversimplify socioeconomic and political realities, conceal the complexities and enabling violations of subject formation, and obscure the interdependency of local and global flows.

From a transnational feminist perspective three additional, interrelated issues need to be addressed to analyze the politics of contemporary deployments of human rights: (1) rights-based regulation; (2) neoliberalism; and (3) gender and sexual exceptionalism. I will briefly consider each issue in turn.

1   *Rights-based regulation.* As legal and political technologies that guide the actions of individuals, institutions, and populaces, human rights are not merely empowering, but also regulatory. Wendy Brown explains this paradox in the context of feminist debates over women's rights as human rights as follows:

> To have a right as a woman is not to be free of being designated and subordinated by gender. Rather, though it may entail some protection from the most immobilizing features of that designation, it reinscribes the designation as it protects us, and thus enables our further regulation through that designation.
>
> (2002, p. 422)

Rights interpellate subjects within discursive and regulatory relations of power, knowledge, and normalization. Human rights must therefore be understood as not just offering positive juridical protection to otherwise vulnerable subjects, but as simultaneously producing and intensifying individuals' distribution across the "dispositif" of modern disciplinary subjectivity and biopower (Foucault, 1990). That is, to be a subject of human rights is to be subjectified *by* but also subjected *to* a range of distinct but often overlapping systems of governance. Many scholars have analyzed the ways in which communities and institutions have used sex/gender, race, class, religion, sexuality, ability, and other categories of difference to police the formal and informal parameters of citizenship and belonging (Berlant, 1997; Cruikshank, 1999; Spade, 2011; Thangaraj, 2015). These analyses demonstrate that national inclusion alone does not guarantee equal rights or fair treatment. As Brown (2002) puts it, "rights almost always serve as a mitigation—but not a resolution—of subordinating powers" (p. 422).

2   *Neoliberalism.* The mitigating function of rights is evident in a variety of global and local dynamics, especially neoliberal processes that fortify disparities between populations (Cheah, 2007). While its meaning is contested, for the purposes of this chapter I define neoliberalism in terms of the political economic principles that the international state system adopted during the last forty years. These principles include market deregulation, privatization, flexible accumulation, financialization, and personal responsibilization. The institution of these principles significantly restricts the social welfare function of the state while simultaneously promoting the interests of the "free market" and its attendant international division of labor in ways that reinforce racialized, gendered, and classed hierarchies (Harvey, 2005; Ong, 2006; Joseph and Rubin, 2007). Understood as such, neoliberalism has major implications for cultural politics. Some critics argue that neoliberalism undermines the promise of democratic freedom (Duggan, 2004). Others suggest that neoliberal projects of global restructuring both extend and rewrite older colonial legacies (Kyungwon Hong, 2006; Reddy, 2011). In these ways, economic globalization increases disparities between populations through the upward redistribution of wealth, by precaritizing lower- and middle-class communities, and by marking certain populations as disposable.

3   *Gender and sexual exceptionalism.* Human rights discourse not only is implicated in ongoing neoliberal transformations and the reordering of contemporary U.S. and Western empires, but also is linked with gender and sexual exceptionalism. U.S. interests frequently position themselves as the authority on and exemplar of human rights, condemning human rights abuses in other countries while ignoring such abuses domestically. Iris Marion Young and other scholars and activists argue that the

U.S. government's use of Afghani and Iraqi women's human rights to justify the U.S.-led "war on terror" fostered forms of gender exceptionalism that reified ideologies of American superiority and Western universalism (Young, 2006). Jasbir K. Puar (2007) identifies sexual exceptionalism or "homonationalism" as an abiding feature of contemporary Western LGBT rights movements. Homonationalism is a form of LGBT patriotism that works with heteronormative citizenship by promoting marriage equality, compulsory monogamy, the nuclear family, consumerism, and militarism as the idealized expressions of national reproduction. Crucially, homonationalism also operates outside the nation-state to elevate certain nations as more humane and liberal than others. In other words, gender and sexual exceptionalism not only naturalize and normalize but also attempt to globalize and falsely universalize contemporary U.S. and Western epistemologies and ontologies of sex/gender, sexuality, and citizenship. In so doing, these forms of exceptionalism marginalize non-Western concepts and practices of embodiment, subjectivity, and community.

By highlighting the issues of rights-based regulation, neoliberalism, and the imperial politics of U.S. gender and sexual exceptionalism, transnational feminist perspectives reveal that human rights are not exterior to power, but are one of the mechanisms by which power—in its myriad forms—enables *and* constrains different subjects in dissimilar ways. Thus, deployments of human rights do not automatically manifest radical change. Rather, recourse to rights can challenge and disrupt, but can also reinforce dominant ideological, political, and economic formations. This point is worth emphasizing because it focalizes the contextual nature of human rights; human rights advocacy is always shaped by a biopolitics and geopolitics of location. In the remainder of this chapter I explore this thesis in relation to U.S. intersex activism and its transnational travels.

The FGM Analogy

Though in its inaugural years ISNA often defined intersexuality through the language of queer (anti-identitarian) identity politics and sought to de-medicalize intersex altogether, toward the turn of the millennium the organization undertook an effort to reach a broader audience, especially medical providers and parents of intersex children.[5] ISNA began to reframe intersex as a discrete set of embodied conditions, less an identity than an etiology. In embracing this view ISNA implicitly reaffirmed the biomedical understanding of intersex as anatomically based even as it explicitly challenged the medical pathologization of people born with atypical sex characteristics (Ben-Asher, 2006, p. 62). It was during this period that ISNA discovered that the framework of human rights harbored useful resources for encouraging medical providers and the public at large to rethink the medical management of intersexuality. This adoption of human rights discourse by ISNA and other intersex activist groups reflected how various disenfranchised groups in social movements of the mid-twentieth century called for state-sanctioned legal and civil protections by appealing to internationally recognized instruments of human rights (including the Geneva Convention, the Nuremburg Code, the Universal Declaration of Human Rights, the Convention on the Elimination of All Forms of Discrimination Against Women, and the United Nations Convention on the Rights of the Child). This human rights framework, however, simultaneously generated important opportunities and created unique problems for intersex activists.

Framing intersex as a human rights issue, members of ISNA in the late 1990s began to compare nonconsensual intersex genital normalization surgeries with a fraught and contested practice of some African traditions referred to in mainstream Western discourse as "female genital mutilation." "To emphasize the likeness of intersex surgeries and female genital mutilation, ISNA's press releases in 1997 started referring to intersex surgeries as Intersex Genital Mutilation" or IGM (Ben-Asher, 2006, p. 73). Inserting their critique of Western intersex surgery into highly charged debates about women's autonomy, cultural rights, and body politics within and across postcolonial and transnational contexts, ISNA activists narrativized intersex surgery as a violation of human rights similar to the violation that FGM is said to embody. This analogy thus sought to conjure and popularize a sense of moral outrage about intersex surgery that would mirror dominant global northern feminist and liberal humanist reactions to FGM.

Members of ISNA lobbied the U.S. Congress in 1997 to include intersex as a protected category in a proposed federal statutory ban on "female genital mutilation." ISNA's argument was that American intersex surgery like FGM constitutes a violation of individual citizens' human rights to bodily integrity, informed consent, and personal autonomy. According to Chase some anti-excision African migrant women in the U.S. were sympathetic to ISNA's argument, but white Western feminists were reluctant to include intersex in their anti-FGM campaigns (Chase, 1998, p. 204). Noting the relative lack of Western feminist and mainstream media attention to intersex surgeries in the context of high-profile debates about FGM and women's rights, Chase argues that the "othering" of African cultural practices by "first-world feminists" deflects attention away from genital cutting in the United States. That is, Chase critiques the complicity of American feminist gender essentialism with Western imperialism, while also figuring intersex as a challenge to heteronormative and sexually dimorphic epistemologies (including feminist ones).

Chase extends this argument in a 2002 essay by arguing that the Western understanding of clitoridectomy as "culturally remote"—always located "elsewhere," in distant geographic and temporal zones—"allows feminist outrage to be diverted into potentially colonialist meddling in the social affairs of others while hampering work for social justice at home" (pp. 144–145). Seemingly affirming postcolonial feminist critiques of Western universalism, Chase argues that genital normalization surgery in the United States must be understood as a cultural—and not purely biomedical—practice. Chase's argument is based on analogies: likening Western intersex surgery to FGM, Chase reads intersex surgery as a culturally specific manifestation of heteropatriarchal domination (Joseph, 2002, pp. 267–292). However, as this quote indicates, Chase also presumes that the organic unity of the nation-state prescribes or predetermines the appropriate contours and needs of "local" social justice agendas. The underlying implication of her critique of first-world feminist discourses on FGM is that "social justice at home" (in the United States), while connected with social justice struggles abroad, is nevertheless politically more important than, and ought to be privileged above, feminist concerns that arise in foreign affairs. Yet the very presumption that FGM is a "social affair of others," a "foreign" matter in the American context, is called into question by both the long history of the migration of African cultural practices to the United States and by Congress's and U.S. feminist activists' stated interest in banning a set of practices they uncritically deem "other" to the American way of life. From a transnational feminist perspective, neither "FGM" nor "IGM" can be said to discretely belong to a single nation-state or cultural tradition. One might even say that the intersex surgery/FGM analogy foregrounds the former to some degree at the expense of the latter. It is therefore deeply ironic that Chase critiques the "colonialist meddling in the social affairs of others" in this essay, as Chase was directing ISNA when the organization campaigned for the inclusion of "intersex" in the U.S. federal ban on FGM.

By analogizing intersex surgery with FGM, Chase at once erases these complexities and reiterates rather than interrupts the "othering" of African cultural practices that she highlights. The intersex surgery/FGM analogy is especially problematic insofar as it consolidates the Western/non-Western and global north/global south binaries (Ben-Asher, 2006, p. 73). As is well known, during the 1980s and 1990s Eurocentric discourses of so-called "global" or Western liberal feminism denounced practices of FGM (Morgan and Steinem, 1980, pp. 65–67; Daly, 1978; Walker, 1992). FGM was sensationalized in the Western media, resulting in a sweeping criminalization of FGM in the United States and in many parts of the global north. Numerous Western feminists who used FGM as a lever to call for the liberation of their "third-world sisters" relied upon highly stereotypical, inaccurate, and frankly racist representations of "African" female genital cutting (Obiora, 2000, pp. 260–274; Abusharaf, 1998, pp. 23–27). Such representations construct a monolithic account of FGM and African culture, and subtend a series of troubling binaries which pit the "first world" against the "third world," the "West" against the "non-West," the global "north" against the global "south," and "enlightened" liberal feminism against "primitive" patriarchal societies.

These binaries obscure the fraught and complex histories of European empire, U.S. settler colonialism, transnational capitalism, and modernity more broadly. They also re-inscribe a patently neocolonial narrative that simultaneously secures and dissimulates the hegemony of American and European epistemic, cultural, and political economic formations. As Leslye Obiora (2000) argues, Western anti-FGM campaigns cannot be adequately understood without critically attending to the roles that race and racism play in Western feminist portrayals of African culture and African women as static and one-dimensional. Countering these stereotypes, Obiora points out that African practices of genital cutting are heterogeneous, as are the cultural milieus in which they occur. For this reason, she contends that mainstream Western feminist discussions of FGM homogenize African culture and eclipse the diversity of African perspectives on genital cutting, extending and deepening troubling colonial legacies.

Wairimu Ngaruiya Njambi similarly critiques Western anti-FGM discourse, noting that it erases the complex ways in which regionally specific cultural norms both enable and constrain the bodily agency of differently situated African women and girls (2004, pp. 281–303). She writes:

> In presuming that bodies can be separated from their cultural contexts, the anti-FGM discourse, not only replicates a nature/culture dualism that has been roundly questioned by feminists in science studies and cultural studies, but has also perpetuated a colonialist assumption by universalizing a particular Western image of a "normal" body and sexuality in its quest to liberate women and girls.
>
> (p. 281)

In an autoethnographic analysis of her own experience as a circumcised Gikuyu woman, Njambi argues that female circumcision does not have a uni-valent, monolithic, or self-evident meaning, and cannot be adequately understood outside the cultural contexts in which it is practiced. Njambi observes that within the gender order of Gikuyu culture, young women of her social group largely viewed circumcision as a "rite of passage," and that the surgery earned them a newfound sense of adulthood, confidence, and respect from others. "By completing my irua, I became a Gikuyu woman ... I entered a category whose pleasures and benefits had previously been denied to me"

(p. 295). Acknowledging that some African feminists disagree with her interpretation of the enabling possibilities of circumcision, Njambi writes:

> Hopefully, what my story conveys is that there are ways of looking at
> the female circumcision issue which go beyond colonialist stories of
> barbarity and primitivity; stories that surely leave the represented
> without a sense of agency. Practices of female circumcision involve
> negotiations, ambiguities, complexities, and contradictions that must be
> addressed and not dismissed, even as we problematize them.
>
> (p. 299)

By addressing the complex forms of agency and power exercised through
African forms of genital cutting, Njambi's analysis offers an alternative to the
reductionism of Western feminist anti-FGM discourse. Her work reveals that
creating more effective cross-border dialogues about body politics requires a
heightened sensitivity to the ways different subjects arise through different
histories and forms of power, and therefore may have different conceptions of
the ethics of embodiment, agency, and justice (Abu-Lughod, 2002;
Mahmood, 2005; Spivak, 1999). As Claire Hemmings explains her reading
of the debates surrounding Njambi's intervention:

> what cannot be contemplated in ... Western feminist accounts ... is
> that the practice of FGC [female genital cutting] may be experienced
> neither as an oppression to be left behind nor an unspeakable horror or
> even unpleasant necessity. What is inconceivable is that any FGC prac-
> tice may be actively embraced, pleasurably anticipated, and experienced
> as a marker of becoming an adult or becoming a member of a desired
> community.
>
> (2004, p. 224)

The moralism of Western feminist debates on FGM not only silences the
wide range of African interpretations of genital cutting, but also prevents
Western feminists from addressing African activists as legitimate political
agents. Deflecting attention from questions of African women's general well-
being, it forecloses opportunities to construct more genuinely transnational
feminist alliances (Robertson, 2002, pp. 54–86). From this perspective, one
might say that the intersex surgery/FGM analogy instantaneously discloses
and effaces the asymmetries of contemporary transnational power relations.
Put differently, ISNA's deployment of the analogy exposes the organization's
failure to reflexively account for its own location of power in the global north
in relation to African women specifically and the global south more generally
(Sullivan, 2007, pp. 395–409).

The intersex surgery/FGM analogy also obscures crucial differences between these disparate practices and their regulation in Western societies (Ben-Asher, 2006, p. 73). Intersex surgeries seek to reduce any sexual "ambiguity" at infancy in order to promote sexual dimorphism and heteronormative gender development and are sanctioned and performed by Western-trained biomedical experts. Genital cutting in Africa, by contrast, tends to occur in developing, postcolonial rural communities that lack access to potable water and other resources, and are performed by local cultural experts whose primary concern is not the regulation of sexual ambiguity but rather the maximization of a certain cultural ideal of feminine corporeality frequently tied to the chastity, modesty, and marriageability of young women (Abusharaf, 1998, pp. 26–27). While such examples raise important questions about the hetero-patriarchal regulation of African women's bodies in some tribal contexts, as Njambi argues, circumcision may also be understood as a bodily transition into a new form of subjectivity affording its own distinct pleasures, agentive capacities, and ethical responsibilities (2004, p. 299).

Consequently, the intersex surgery/FGM analogy raises both strategic and ethical questions about intersex politics. According to Ben-Asher,

> These two types of genital surgeries are exceptionally different, in time, place, and ideology, and their merger in legal strategy erases these crucial differences. Furthermore, there is an ethical concern when group projects of de-subjugation undercut each other. Thus, intersex politics that is insensitive to the Western normalization of non-Western African traditions exchanges one social harm for another.
>
> (2006, p. 75)

Underscoring the regulatory operations of different forms of power, Ben Asher recognizes that the politics of FGC and intersex surgery are qualitatively and quantitatively different "in time, place, and ideology." By piggybacking onto anti-FGM campaigns, ISNA activists oversimplified these differences, a gesture which in turn obscures the "Western normalization of non-Western African traditions." In effect, the analogy presumes that the appropriate response to intersex surgery and FGM must be one and the same: the imposition of U.S. neoliberal democratic frames of subjectivity. The analogy posits the neoliberal "autonomous" individual as the telos of both intersex and anti-FGM activisms. In this way, it perpetuates a U.S. exceptionalist and Western-centric understanding of human rights.

ISNA's lobbying effort to include intersex surgery within the legislative ban on FGM ultimately failed. Specifically, activists were unable to convince the U.S. Congress that intersex surgeries fall under the category of "cultural practices" and are therefore not "medically necessary." The legislative ban explicitly makes an exception for cases of "medical necessity," stating in the pertinent section that "a surgical operation is not a violation ... if the operation is ... necessary to the health of the person on whom it is performed and is performed by a person licensed in the place of its performance as a medical practitioner" (18 U.S.C. § 116 (Supp. III 1997) cited in Ben-Asher, 2006, p. 73). Using biomedical authority to legislate the boundaries of health, the ban presumes that the "health of the person" is objectively measurable, when in fact historians of medicine have shown that "health" is a variable cultural construction (Mattingly and Garro, 2000). As Njambi points out, many legal and fashionable forms of body modification in the global north—such as tattooing, piercing, penis/clitoris slicing, tongue slicing, and cosmetic procedures, including botox injections, liposuction, breast and posterior implants and augmentation, and vaginal rejuvenation—might be viewed as potentially unhealthy, especially if we recognize that their performances are sometimes compelled by powerful regulatory ideals (Bordo, 2004). The factors that determine whether a procedure, bodily regimen, or corporeal way of life is considered healthy are themselves culturally, politically, and economically overdetermined.

Instituting a binary opposition between health and culture, the statute bans genital surgeries that are performed for cultural purposes (such as the transmission of traditions, rituals, or values), which it views as inherently unhealthy. That is, the statute maintains a more general distinction between culture and science that places intersex under the jurisdiction of biomedical expertise. The ban thus criminalizes FGM on cultural grounds while it legitimates intersex surgery on medical grounds. Crucially, the ban simultaneously others African bodies and American intersex bodies, but it does so in distinct ways. Taken together these othering practices underwrite the ban's U.S.-centric, neoimperial understanding of what constitutes a normal and healthy body.

Beyond the ban's specific ideological contours, the point I wish to emphasize is that the twentieth century medicalization of people with unusual sex anatomies in the global north and some parts of the global south can be read as a manifestation of what Anibal Quijano (2000) calls the coloniality of power: the ways in which colonial epistemologies and ideologies of sex/gender, sexuality, race, and class have outlived formal territorial colonialism and persist in contemporary societies. In other words, intersex politics—both in the United States and globally—cannot be disaggregated from genealogies of imperialism, settler colonialism, and racial formation that have fundamentally shaped longstanding Euro-American eugenic, Malthusian, and sexological ideas about the relative degree of sexual development of Anglophone versus non-Anglophone racial groups (Gilman, 1985; Gould, 1996). While Quijano's thesis remains underexplored in the field of intersex studies, a few scholars have pursued notable work in this direction. Hilary Malatino (2009) observes that colonization was central (both literally and metaphorically) to the consolidation of scientific disciplines—including teratology, eugenics, and sexology—that study of the appearance and development of monstrous bodies. The medicalization of intersexuality can be seen as an effect of Western scientific efforts to rationalize fleshly bodies into the normative constraints of the colonial-modern social order. Zine Magubane (2014) suggests that race, imperial history, and national context have played vital but underanalyzed roles in the production and reproduction of the concept of intersex. And María Lugones (2007) argues that the

> sexual fears of colonizers led them to imagine the indigenous people of the Americas as hermaphrodites or intersexed, with large penises and breasts with flowing milk. But as Paula Gunn Allen and others have made clear, intersexed individuals were recognized in many tribal societies prior to colonization without assimilation to the sexual binary.
>
> (p. 195)

Lugones contends that colonialism established a new sex/gender system that created very different arrangements for colonized subjects than for white bourgeois colonizers. "Not all different traditions," Lugones writes, "correct and normalize intersex people. So, as with other assumptions, it is important to ask how sexual dimorphism served and continues to serve global, Eurocentered, capitalist domination/exploitation" (pp. 195–196).

These authors reframe the global history and politics of intersex in important ways. They reveal that the medical normalization of intersexuality cannot be reduced to narratives that focus solely on the "stigma and trauma" caused by human rights violations, as ISNA argued (ISNA, 2008). Nor is medicalization only about the regulatory production of sexual dimorphism and binary gender. Rather, debates about whether and how to respond to bodies in doubt are also overdetermined by national context and classed and racialized logics. From a transnational feminist perspective, then, the Western medicalization of people with nonstandard sex anatomies can be interpreted as a key element of biopolitics: "an explosion of numerous and diverse techniques for achieving the subjugations of bodies and the control of populations" (Foucault, 1990, p. 140; Stoler, 1995; Mbembe, 2001).

Conclusion

The biopolitics of racialized, nationalized, and classed sex/gender establish the terms by which individuals and institutions respond to nonnormative bodies. For this reason, it is notable that the U.S. legislative FGM ban relies heavily on Western biomedicine as a source of knowledge about the proper way to respond to and treat intersex bodies. In a gesture that strikingly reiterates this reliance, some contemporary activists have affirmed the global northern biomedical establishment's recent adoption of the term *Disorders of Sex Development*, in favor of *intersex* (Hughes et al., 2005). Moreover, proponents claim that the DSD rubric will enable a shift toward a patient-centered model of care, a model that mitigates but does not rule out infant genital surgery in the treatment of said disorders.

The project of provincializing the intersex imaginary—of linking ways of thinking about intersex bodies to specific places and histories—reveals that these strategies depend on particular assumptions about embodiment, medical beneficence, and subjectivity that deserve interrogation and critique. The DSD rubric, which emerged out of conversations between American and European clinicians and patient advocates, extends the medicalization of intersexual difference: it figures variations of anatomical sex as pathological, and reifies the ideology of sexual dimorphism by framing non-intersex anatomies as both normal and natural (Reis, 2007). Notably, OII, the largest intersex activist alliance in the world with affiliates in twenty countries on six continents, "strongly opposes current scientific terminology such as 'disorders of sexual development,' arguing that it is reductionist and imperialist" (Caudwell, 2012, p. 157). Members of OII have created posters, t-shirts, and broadsides that polemically challenge the assumptions underlying the DSD nomenclature. One declares, "Sorry, We're Not Disordered," while another contains a "Warning" sign and skull and crossbones placed next to text that reads: "DSD: Death to Sex Differences. DSD = Eugenics, DSD = Heterosexism, DSD = Transphobia, DSD = Homophobia" (OII, n.d.). OII's intersectional critique of the DSD nomenclature positions the medicalization of intersex as fundamentally linked with multiple, overlapping systems of power-knowledge (Rubin, 2012; Rubin, 2017). Their critique implicates Western DSD *and* intersex advocacy within a larger web of historical, ideological, and political economic relationships—none of which is transparent or unmediated. This is why the politics of location of such activism, like all forms of world making, warrants critical examination. OII's question, in essence, is: what worlds are advocates of the DSD nomenclature *for*?

The project of provincializing intersex also allows us to extend OII's question to patient-centered medicine (Frampton and Charmel, 2009). In contemporary intersex/DSD rights activism, the patient-centered model is often hailed as a lynchpin for moving toward progressive medical reform. Patient-centered care prioritizes "the person's right to make informed choices about their own bodies, and delaying treatment until the patient can make informed consent" (Arana, 2005, p. 25). Using the language of "rights," "choice," and "consent," advocates frame the patient-centered approach as an extension of U.S. neoliberal democratic frames of subjectivity. According to Emily

Grabham, the patient-centered model "uses the rhetoric of the patient as consumer: a service-user who expects a certain standard of care, and who should
expect a range of treatment options and the opportunity to exercise their personal choice in making treatment decisions" (2007, p. 40). Grabham contends
that this rhetoric problematically conflates consumerism with citizenship in
ways that have the potential to "re-embed material inequalities" (p. 38).
Grabham writes,

> The rhetoric on which [the patient-centered model] is based is, argu-
> ably, the neoliberal rhetoric of an autonomous intersex individual who,
> given the current socio-medical context, simply does not exist ...
> Gaining consumer citizenship on the back of postponing "consent" to
> intersex surgeries or other forms of non-medically necessary intersex
> treatments to later in the child's life, as advocated by the patient-
> centered model, does not fundamentally challenge the disciplinary func-
> tion of medical constructions of sex. It does not contest the idea that
> the medical sphere is in fact the correct sphere for intersex issues to be
> negotiated. At some future point, a more radical non-interventionist
> strategy might work to contest the privileging of medical discourses in
> responding to intersex issues in the first place. Thinking through these
> issues illuminates the significance of a critical approach to rights in the
> intersex context.
>
> (p. 40)

For Grabham, the central question is whether and how advocates of intersex
human rights might evade "the disciplinary effects of their strategic claims for
consumer citizenship" (p. 40). Crucially, the patient-centered model treats
medical care as apolitical, and thereby obfuscates the role that medicine has
played in upholding colonial, capitalist, heteropatriarchal, and other types of
hierarchies (Briggs et al., 2008). With its emphasis on neoliberal modes of
self-fashioning, the patient-centered model not only reifies the fiction of the
sovereign subject, but also fails to recognize that patients' autonomy is always
already regulated by "the disciplinary function of medical constructions of
sex," as well as raced, classed, gendered and other forms of health care disparities (Grabham, 2007, p. 40).

   Although patient-centered care appears to be a clear improvement over the
"concealment model" of intersex management, centering the patient without
critically attending to the ideological, political, and economic forces that
shape the unequal institutional distribution and quality of care risks promoting an excessive individualism (Karkazis, 2008, p. 242). It targets patients and
their bodies, rather than the social worlds they inhabit, as the site in need of
transformation. Like the DSD rubric, then, patient-centered care does not

disrupt the pathologization of bodies that exceed normalized Western classificatory schemas. It does not contest the medicalization of intersexuality as such. Instead, patient-centered care reformats medicalization in neoliberal terms as a seemingly sensible "choice" for individuals born with bodies that do not conform to the mythical norm (Lorde, 1984, p. 116). In this regard, another reason why patient-centered care and the DSD rubric warrant critique is because they dissimulate the colonial legacies of biopolitics. That is, they assign unequal gradations of social value to different embodied states, and presume to know in advance what kind of body one must have in order to qualify as intelligibly human.

The rapid global dissemination of the DSD nomenclature and the patient-centered model, much like ISNA's FGM analogy, raises the problem of "intersex imperialism"—namely, the imposition of Western conceptions of atypically sexed bodies and of how best to treat and respond to such bodies (Kerry, 2011). Decolonizing intersex requires thinking about atypically sexed bodies otherwise, in a different language so to speak. As the Argentinean philosopher and intersex and trans activist Mauro Cabral (2015) puts it, the problem of intersex imperialism raises

> three considerations about language: (1) for those who, like me, speak, write, breathe, love and fight in a language other than English, decolonizing the way in which we are named multiplies to include not only medical speech but also the terms imposed by the Anglophone hegemony within international conversations on intersex; (2) the construction of an international intersex movement not only has depended—and still depends—on that hegemony, but has also considerably restricted the possibilities of other ways of communicating, including those of poetry, fiction, erotic, and other manifestations of "inefficient" speech; (3) even against this double suture, the word "intersex" still designates a persistent question, a scarred question that lies from tongue to language, a scar never fully healed, constantly reopened.

As Cabral emphasizes, decolonizing intersex requires taking seriously the ethical imperative to learn from and form solidarities with indigenous and emergent traditions that offer alternative languages, cartographies, and valuations of bodily difference, while also guarding against the dangers of cultural appropriation. It requires animating oppositional and differential modes of consciousness that deconstruct the presumed superiority of Western knowledges of the body and frames of subjectivity (Sandoval, 2000). In other words, decolonizing intersex necessitates a broader recognition that "the word 'intersex' still designates a persistent question, a scarred question that lies from tongue to language, a scar never fully healed, constantly reopened." Coming to terms with that constantly reopened, never fully healed scar/question entails learning to bear witness to a trauma that ceaselessly reproduces itself, marking intersex bodies with the scalpel and the suture, rendering them as the exceptions that give the lie to the normalizing corporeal rule. Decolonizing intersex, then, also entails fostering an emphatically unnatural tolerance for a pain at once individual and collective, which also paradoxically unfolds as a holistic capacity for epistemological disobedience and an ethical willingness to be undone and remade by our relationships with others.

As preparatory work for that decolonial project, this chapter has attempted to provincialize U.S. debates about intersex—that is, to explore how U.S. ideas about human sex variation, human rights, and personhood that appear universal are "also, at one and the same time, drawn from very particular intellectual and historical traditions that [cannot] claim any universal validity" (Chakrabarty, 2008, p. xiii). Movements for intersex human rights in the global north and west that do not self-reflexively question their overdetermination by colonial legacies, biopolitics, and geopolitical power disparities not only risk erasing and othering the distinct histories, epistemologies, subjectivities, sex/gender systems, and bodies of peoples in the global south and east; they also undercut the formation of cross-border alliances to advance struggles for sexual and gender justice. The challenge is to create multilingual and multicultural dialogues about body politics that can acknowledge the messy, precarious, and asymmetrical relationships between differently sexed and gendered subjects in diverse locations. Transnational feminist perspectives can help to challenge intersex imperialism by emphasizing that critical scrutiny of the politics of location of *all* intersex activist projects is essential for building more ethically accountable transnational movements for corporeal freedom.

Notes

1 Intersex is an umbrella term for individuals born with sexual anatomies that various societies deem to be nonstandard. Formerly called "hermaphroditism" (a word now often regarded as offensive), intersex encompasses a heterogeneous array of somatic differences. Since the mid-twentieth century, Western medicine has viewed the birth of a child with an intersex "condition" as a psychosocial emergency that requires immediate surgical and hormonal "correction." However, the majority of intersex states actually pose few if any physiological health risks. In this regard, intersex bodies are pathologized and medicalized not because of genuine health concerns, but rather because intersexuality threatens the cultural ideals of sexual dimorphism and binary gender (see, among many others, Kessler, 1998; Fausto-Sterling, 2000). Intersex is distinct from "transgender," which is an umbrella term for a wide range of gender non-conforming behaviors and identifications. Although activism and scholarship on intersex and transgender sometimes address overlapping and interconnected issues (such as medicalization, corporeal self-determination, and bioethics), it is important to recognize that intersex and transgender have distinct genealogies, meanings, and social movements associated with them.

2 In pursuing this line of argument, I build on Iain Morland's insight that intersex activism deserves just as careful critical scrutiny as does medical dogma around intersex (Morland, 2009, p. 191).

3 I use the term "sex/gender" in this chapter to emphasize the dynamic co-constitutive relationship between social and biological systems in the formation of human embodiment and subjectivity (see Fausto-Sterling, 2012).

4 German intersex activists have critiqued the legislation on gender classification, arguing that the new law does not de-medicalize intersex and consequently does not address the human rights violations intersex people are subject to (see Agius et al., 2013).

5 De-medicalization remains a central goal of a number of contemporary intersex alliances, including Intersex South Africa (founded in 2000 by the late Sally Gross), Bodies Like Ours (founded in 2002 by Peter Trinkle), and OII (founded in 2003 by Curtis Hinkle).

Bibliography

Abu-Lughod, Lila, 2002, "Do Muslim Women Really Need Saving? Anthropological Reflections on Cultural Relativism and Its Others," *American Anthropologist* 104.3: 783–790.

Abusharaf, Rogaia, 1998, "Unmasking Tradition," *Sciences* (March/April): 23–27.

Agius, Silvan, Carpenter, Morgan, and Ghattas, Dan Christian, 2013, "Third Gender: A Step Toward Ending Intersex Discrimination," *Spiegel Online International* (August 22), from www.spiegel.de/international/europe/third-gender-option-in-germany-a-small-step-for-intersex-recognition-a-917650.html (last accessed December 1, 2014).

Arana, Marcus de Maria, 2005, "A Human Rights Investigation into the Medical 'Normalization' of Intersex People," from www.isna.org/files/SFHRC_Intersex_Report.pdf (last accessed March 9, 2014).

Australian Parliament, 2013, "Sex Discrimination Amendment (Sexual Orientation, Gender Identity and Intersex Status) Bill," from www.aph.gov.au/Parliamentary_Business/Bills_Legislation/Bills_Search_Results/Result?bId=r5026 (last accessed March 9, 2014).

Barlow, Tani E., 1998, "'Green Blade in the Act of Being Grazed': Late Capital, Flexible Bodies, Critical Intelligibility," *Differences: A Journal of Feminist Cultural Studies* 10.3: 119.

Ben-Asher, Noah, 2006, "The Necessity of Sex Change: A Struggle for Transsex and Intersex Liberties," *Harvard Journal of Law and Gender* 29.1: 62.

Bennett-Smith, Meredith, 2013, "Mark and Pam Crawford, Parents of Intersex Child, Sue South Carolina for Sex Assignment Surgery," *Huffington Post* (May 5), from www.huffingtonpost.com/2013/05/15/mark-pam-crawford-intersex-child_n_3280353.html (last accessed March 9, 2014).

Berlant, Lauren, 1997, *The Queen of America Goes to Washington City: Essays on Sex and Citizenship*, Duke University Press, Durham, NC.

Bordo, Susan, 2004, *Unbearable Weight: Feminism, Western Culture, and the Body*, University of California Press, Berkeley.

Briggs, Laura, 2002. *Reproducing Empire: Race, Sex, Science, and U.S. Imperialism in Puerto Rico*, University of California Press, Berkeley.

Briggs, Laura, McKormick, Gladys, and Way, J. T., 2008, "Transnationalism: A Category of Analysis," *American Quarterly* 60.3: 625–648.

Brown, Wendy, 2002, "Suffering the Paradoxes of Rights," in *Left Legalism/Left Critique*, Wendy Brown and Janet Halley (eds.), Duke University Press, Durham, NC, p. 422.

Cabral, Mauro, 2015, "The Marks on Our Bodies," *Intersex Day* (October 25), from http://intersexday.org/en/mauro-cabral-marks-bodies/ (last accessed March 9, 2014).

Caudwell, Jayne, 2012, "Sex Watch: Surveying Women's Sexed and Gendered Bodies at the Olympics," in *Watching the Olympics: Politics, Power, and Representation*, John Peter Sugden and Alan Tomlinson (eds.), Routledge, New York, p. 157.

Chakrabarty, Dipesh, 2008, *Provincializing Europe: Postcolonial Thought and Historical Difference*, Princeton University Press, Princeton, NJ.

Chase, Cheryl, 1998, "Hermaphrodites with Attitude: Mapping the Emergence of Intersex Political Activism" *GLQ* 4.2: 204.

Chase, Cheryl, 2002, "'Cultural Practice' or 'Reconstructive Surgery'? US Genital Cutting, the Intersex Movement, and Medical Double Standards," in *Genital Cutting and Transnational Sisterhood: Disputing U.S. Polemics*, Stanlie M. James and Claire C. Robertson (eds.), University of Illinois Press, Urbana, pp. 144–145.

Cheah, Pheng, 2007, *Inhuman Conditions: On Cosmopolitanism and Human Rights*, Harvard University Press, Cambridge, MA.

Cruikshank, Barbara, 1999, *The Will to Empower: Democratic Citizens and Other Subjects*, Cornell University Press, Ithaca, NY.

Daly, Mary, 1978, *Gyn/Ecology: The Metaethics of Radical Feminism*, Beacon Press, Boston, MA.

Dreger, Alice, 2006, "Intersex and Human Rights: The Long View," in *Ethics and Intersex*, Sharon E. Sytsma (ed.), Springer, Netherlands, p. 79.

Dreger, Alice, 2013, "Ending Forced 'Genital-Normalizing' Surgeries," *Atlantic* (February 25), from www.theatlantic.com/health/archive/2013/02/ending-forced-genital-normalizing-surgeries/273300/ (last accessed March 9, 2014).

Duggan, Lisa, 2004, *The Twilight of Equality? Neoliberalism, Cultural Politics, and the Attack on Democracy*, Beacon Press, Boston, MA.

European Network of Legal Experts, 2011, "Trans and Intersex People: Discrimination on the Grounds of Sex, Gender Identity and Gender Expression," European Union, Luxembourg, from www.coe.int/t/dg4/lgbt/Source/trans_and_intersex_people_EC_EN.pdf (last accessed December 1, 2014).

Fausto-Sterling, Anne, 2000, *Sexing the Body: Gender Politics and the Construction of Sexuality*, Basic Books, New York.

Fausto-Sterling, Anne, 2012, *Sex/Gender: Biology in a Social World*, Routledge, New York.

Fernandes, Leela, 2013, *Transnational Feminism in the United States: Knowledge, Ethics, Power*, New York University Press, New York.

Foucault, Michel, 1990, *The History of Sexuality, Vol. 1: An Introduction*, Vintage, New York.

Frampton, Susan B., and Charmel, Patrick (eds.), 2009, *Putting Patients First: Best Practices in Patient-Centered Care*, Jossey-Bass, San Francisco, CA.

Ghattas, Dan Christian, 2013, *Human Rights Between the Sexes: A Preliminary Study on the Life Situations of Inter* Individuals*, Heinrich-Boll-Stiftung, Berlin.

Ghorayshi, Azeen, 2017, "A Landmark Lawsuit About an Intersex Baby's Genital Surgery Just Settled for $440,000,' *Buzzfeed News* (July 26), from www.buzzfeed.com/azeenghorayshi/intersex-surgery-lawsuit-settles?utm_term=.vw6oOLrqD#.hcPoaWPJv (last accessed March 9, 2014).

Gilman, Sander L., 1985, *Difference and Pathology: Stereotypes of Sexuality, Race, and Madness*, Cornell University Press, Ithaca, NY.

Gould, Stephen Jay, 1996, *The Mismeasure of Man*, W.W. Norton, New York.

Grabham, Emily, 2007, "Citizen Bodies, Intersex Citizenship," *Sexualities* 10.1: 40.

Greenberg, Julie A., 2012, *Intersexuality and the Law: Why Sex Matters*, New York University Press, New York.

Grewal, Inderpal, 2005, *Transnational America: Feminisms, Diasporas, Neoliberalisms*, Duke University Press, Durham, NC, p. 121.

Harvey, David, 2005, *A Brief History of Neoliberalism*, Oxford University Press, Oxford.

Hemmings, Claire, 2011, *Why Stories Matter: The Political Grammar of Feminist Theory*, Duke University Press, Durham, NC, p. 224.

Hughes, I. A., Houk, C., Ahmed, S. F., Lee, P. A., LWPES Consensus Group, ESPE Consensus Group, 2005, "Consensus Statement on Management of Intersex Disorders," *Archives of Diseases in Childhood* 91: 554–563.

ISNA (Intersex Society of North America), 2000, "ISNA Honored with Human Rights Award," Press Release, from www.isna.org/node/15 (last accessed March 9, 2014).

ISNA (Intersex Society of North America), 2005, "Intersex Declared a Human Rights Issue," Press Release, from www.isna.org/node/841 (last accessed March 2, 2014).

ISNA (Intersex Society of North America), 2008, "Our Mission," from www.isna.org/ (last accessed July 31, 2015).

Joseph, Miranda, 2002, "Analogy and Complicity: Women's Studies, Lesbian/Gay Studies, and Capitalism," in *Women's Studies on Its Own*, Robyn Wiegman (ed.), Duke University Press, Durham, NC, pp. 267–292.

Joseph, Miranda, and Rubin, David, 2007, "Promising Complicities: On the Sex, Race, and Globalization Project," in *A Companion to Lesbian, Gay, Bisexual, Transgender, and Queer Studies*, George E. Haggerty and Molly McGarry (eds.), Blackwell, London, pp. 430–451.

Kaplan, Caren, 1996, *Questions of Travel: Postmodern Discourses of Displacement*, Duke University Press, Durham, NC, p. 169.

Kaplan, Caren, and Grewal, Inderpal, 2002, "Transnational Practices and Interdisciplinary Feminist Scholarship: Refiguring Women's and Gender Studies," in *Women's Studies on Its Own*, Robyn Wiegman (ed.), Duke University Press, Durham, NC, p. 73.

Karkazis, Katrina, 2008, *Fixing Sex*, Duke University Press, Durham, NC, p. 242.

Kerry, Stephen, 2011, "'Intersex Imperialism' and the Case of Caster Semenya: The Unacceptable Woman's Body," *Scan: Journal of Media, Arts, Culture* 8.1, from http://scan.net. au/scan/journal/display.php?journal_id=158 (last accessed July 1, 2014).

Kessler, Suzanne J., 1998, *Lessons from the Intersexed*, Rutgers University Press, New Brunswick.

Kyungwon Hong, Grace, 2006, *The Ruptures of American Capital: Women of Color Feminism and the Culture of Immigrant Labor*, University of Minnesota Press, Minneapolis.

Lorde, Audre, 1984, *Sister Outsider: Essays and Speeches*, Crossing Press, New York, p. 116.

Lugones, María, 2007, "Heterosexualism and the Colonial/Modern Gender System," *Hypatia* 22.1: 195.

Magubane, Zine, 2014, "Spectacles and Scholarship: Caster Semenya, Intersex Studies, and the Problem of Race in Feminist Theory," *Signs* 39.3: 761–785.

Mahmood, Saba, 2005, *Politics of Piety: The Islamic Revival and the Feminist Subject*, Princeton University Press, Princeton, NJ.

Malatino, Hilary, 2009, "Situating Bio-Logic, Refiguring Sex: Intersexuality and Coloniality,' in *Critical Intersex*, Morgan Holmes (ed.), Ashgate, Farnham, UK, pp. 73–96.

Mattingly, Cheryl, and Garro, Linda C. (eds.), 2000, *Narrative and the Cultural Construction of Illness and Healing*, University of California Press, Berkeley.

Mbembe, Achille, 2001, *On the Postcolony*, University of California Press, Berkeley.

Morgan, Robin, and Steinem, Gloria, 1980, "The International Crime of Genital Mutilation," *Ms.* (March): 65–67.

Morland, Iain, 2009, "Between Critique and Reform: Ways of Reading the Intersex Controversy," in *Critical Intersex*, Morgan Holmes (ed.), Ashgate, Farnham, UK, p. 191.

Morland, Iain, 2015, "Gender, Genitals, and the Meaning of Being Human," in *Fuckology: Critical Essays on John Money's Diagnostic Concepts*, Lisa Downing, Iain Morland, and Nikki Sullivan (eds.), University of Chicago Press, Chicago, pp. 69–98.

Nagar, Richa, and Swarr, Amanda Lock, 2010, "Introduction," in *Critical Transnational Feminist Praxis*, Amanda Lock Swarr and Richa Nagar (eds.), SUNY Press, New York, p. 5.

Nandl, Jacinta, 2013, "Germany Got It Right by Offering a Third Gender Option on Birth Certificates," *Guardian* (November 10), from www.theguardian.com/commentis free/2013/nov/10/germany-third-gender-birth-certificate (last accessed March 9, 2014).

Njambi, Wairimu Ngaruiya, 2004, "Dualisms and Female Bodies in Representations of African Female Circumcision: A Feminist Critique," *Feminist Theory* 5.3: 281–303.

Obiora, Leslye, 2000, "Bridges and Barricades: Rethinking Polemics and Intransigence in the Campaign Against Female Circumcision," in *Global Critical Race Feminism: An International Reader*, Adrien Katherine Wing (ed.), New York University Press, New York, pp. 260–274.

Ong, Aihwa, 2006, *Neoliberalism as Exception: Mutations in Citizenship and Sovereignty*, Duke University Press, Durham, NC.

Organisation Intersex International (OII), n.d., "DSD Warning," from www.intersexualite. org/DSD_warnings.html (last accessed March 10, 2010) (this resource is no longer available online).

Organization of American States, 2013, "Rights of Lesbian, Gay, Bisexual, Trans, and Intersex Persons," from www.oas.org/en/iachr/lgtbi/ (last accessed July 14, 2014).

Perez, Emma, 1999, *The Decolonial Imaginary: Writing Chicanas into History*, Indiana University Press, Bloomington.

Puar, Jasbir K., 2007, *Terrorist Assemblages: Homonationalism in Queer Times*, Duke University Press, Durham, NC.

Quijano, Anibal, 2000, "Coloniality of Power, Eurocentrism, and Latin America," *Nepantla: Views from South*, 1.3: 533–580.

Reddy, Chandan, 2011, *Freedom with Violence: Race, Sexuality, and the US State*, Duke University Press, Durham, NC.

Reis, Elizabeth, 2007, "Divergence or Disorder? The Politics of Naming Intersex," *Perspectives in Biology and Medicine*, 50.4: 535–543.

Reis, Elizabeth, 2012, *Bodies in Doubt: An American History of Intersex*, Johns Hopkins University Press, Baltimore, MD.

Robertson, Claire C., 2002, "Getting Beyond the Ew! Factor: Rethinking US Approaches to African Genital Cutting," in *Genital Cutting and Transnational Sisterhood: Disputing US Polemics*, Stanlie M. James and Clair C. Robertson (eds.),University of Illinois Press, Urbana, pp. 54–86.

Rubin, David A., 2012, "'An Unnamed Blank that Craved a Name': A Geneology of Intersex as Gender," *Signs* 37.4: 883–908.

Rubin, David A., 2017, *Intersex Matters: Biomedical Embodiment, Gender Regulation, and Transnational Activism*, SUNY Press, Albany, NY.

Sandoval, Chela, 2000, *Methodology of the Oppressed*, University of Minnesota Press, Minneapolis.

Soto, Sandra K., 2011, *Reading Chican@ Like a Queer: The Demastery of Desire*, University of Texas Press, Austin, p. 1.

Spade, Dean, 2011, *Normal Life: Administrative Violence, Critical Trans Politics, and the Limits of the Law*, South End Press, Boston, MA.

Spivak, Gayatri Chakravorty, 1999, *A Critique of Postcolonial Reason: Toward a History of the Vanishing Present*, Harvard University Press, Cambridge, MA.

Stoler, Ann Laura, 1995, *Race and the Education of Desire: Foucault's History of Sexuality and the Colonial Order of Things*, Duke University Press, Durham, NC.

Stryker, Susan, and Currah, Paisley, 2014, "General Editors Introduction," *Transgender Studies Quarterly* 1.3: 303–304.

Sullivan, Nikki, 2007, "'The Price to Pay for our Common Good': Genital Modification and the Somatechnologies of Cultural (In)Difference," *Social Semiotics* 17.3: 395–409.

Tamar-Mattis, Anne, and Diamond, Milton, 2007, "Managing Variations in Sex Development," *Journal of Pediatric Endocrinology and Metabolism*, 20.4: 552–553.

Thangaraj, Stanley I., 2015, *Desi Hoop Dreams: Pickup Basketball and the Making of Asian-American Masculinity*, New York University Press, New York.

Walker, Alice, 1992, *Possessing the Secret of Joy*, Pocket Books, New York.

Young, Iris Marion, 2006, *Global Challenges: War, Self-Determination, and Responsibility for Justice*, Polity, New York.

INDEX

Note: page numbers in **bold** denote tables.